# THE
# NEW YORK ETHNIC FOOD MARKET
# GUIDE & COOKBOOK

To Bob and Pug — Caroline's
talented uncle and aunt,

May this book add
jazz and pizazz to your shopping
and cooking!

Warm wishes,

Vilma Chantiles

# THE
# New York
# Ethnic Food Market
# GUIDE & COOKBOOK

VILMA LIACOURAS CHANTILES

*illustrations by Tom LaPadula*

DODD, MEAD & COMPANY

NEW YORK

LIBRARY OF CONGRESS CATALOGING IN PUBLICATION DATA

Chantiles, Vilma Liacouras.
The New York ethnic food market guide and cookbook.

Includes index.
1. Marketing (Home economics)—New York Metropolitan
Area—Directories.   2. Grocery trade—New York
Metropolitan Area—Directories.   3. Cookery, International.
I. Title.
TX356.C47   1984      380.1'456413'0097471      83-25314
ISBN 0-396-08282-3 (pbk.)

IN LOVING MEMORY OF MY FATHER

*James Peter Liacouras*

AND WITH GRATITUDE TO UNCLE TOM

*Thomas George Manos*

FOR THEIR CONTAGIOUS LOVE OF LIFE AND FOOD

*He who eats until he is ill must
fast until he is well.*
ENGLISH PROVERB

# CONTENTS

## PART 1: THE FIVE BOROUGHS
*Neighborhoods, Food Markets, Shops, Stalls*

# ACKNOWLEDGMENTS

I WOULD HAPPILY bring the earth's finest fruits to the hundreds of considerate people who have helped and encouraged me while I researched this book. Some I have known for years; others stopped working the first time I walked into their shop or stall to talk about their lives, foods, recipes and menus, neighborhood changes, and ideas. Customers, too, shared their expertise and personal recollections. And two authors offered such illuminating insights, I regret that I cannot thank them personally. The first is Thomas F. DeVoe, who wrote *The Market Book: A History of Public Markets of the City of New York* (1862). He traced not only the origins of many public markets from early in New York's history to the mid-nineteenth century when he was a butcher and remarkable historian in the old Jefferson Market, but also provided valuable social, business, and economic background. The second is Selwyn Gurney Champion whose extensive compilation *Racial Proverbs* (1938) used many examples, including foods, to reflect the attitudes of numerous ethnic groups which seem pertinent today.

I am grateful to many New York City officials who answered my questions—especially Frank Vardy, of the City Planning Commission, an expert demographer who unrolled his neighborhood and borough maps and described past and current demographics; and Anthony Mattone, of the Department of Ports and Terminals. I am grateful also to Professor Helen Epstein, Department of Journalism, Graduate School of Arts and Sciences, New York University, in whose journalism class I wrote an article, with her guidance, from which this book evolved. Special thanks go to my colleague-"editors" in that unforgettable magazine-writing workshop. I appreciate the suggestions of my editor, Jerry Gross and Evan Marshall, another Dodd, Mead editor. I thank my husband, Nicholas, for his always unfailing support, my daughter, Maria Nicole, and my sons, Dean and Jamie, for the insights they constantly offer me. Most of all, I thank my extraordinary mother, Stella Lagakos Liacouras, who instilled in us a deep respect for delicious home-cooked food. After my marriage, when I returned to our family home in Pennsylvania with my husband and children, she overwhelmed us with warmth, wonderful meals, and hospitality. Long after she became a naturalized citizen, Mother gradually learned to cook and serve "new" dishes from other cuisines. But, always, as the highest tribute to guests, she re-created her own Hellenic dishes, which is the essence—the spirit—of ethnic foodways, pride in one's native foods.

# INTRODUCTION

*I love to see you eat but not overeat.*
GREEK PROVERB

NEW YORK food markets ride high on an ethnic food wave expected to reach $7.8 billion by the late 1980s and certain to create
more staple ethnic specialties in the American diet. The American palate continually craves more exotic, more sophisticated
flavors. Oriental, Italian, and Mexican foods have zoomed in popularity. In-home consumption of foreign dishes rose 47 percent in
the last twelve years. Americans consumed 500 million pounds of
spices, herbs, and seasonings in 1980, more than a third increase
over the previous decade. Advertising features ethnic foods for
nationwide audiences that formerly were enjoyed by very small
groups.

In New York City, the ethnic wave has been building quietly
throughout this century, and earlier. Shops and stalls offer a
cultural mosaic of foreign aromas, seafoods, meats, sensuous
barky roots, lustrous tropical fruits, kaleidoscopic varieties of
cheese and breads, grains, and pulses (legumes including beans,
peas, lentils). New York shopping tours arouse the senses and
stimulate thoughts of distant, unseen lands, while the air is peppered with the sounds of Chinese or Spanish, Italian and Hindi,
Yiddish, French, and Greek counterpointed by Tibetan and
Korean, Japanese, Romanian, Tagalog, and English of the New
York and West Indian variety.

## New York's Ethnic Population and Food History

New York has always been a pluralistic society with a hetero-
geneous population. *Encyclopedia Americana* states that eigh-

teen languages were spoken in New Amsterdam (Manhattan) in 1644. That was eighteen years after the Dutch bought the island for $24—twenty-one years after the first of a 300-year succession of public food markets was opened (where not only native American Indian and Dutch foods, but also European wines, were stocked!). The ethnic waves kept coming through the seventeenth and eighteenth centuries and on—Dutch, French, English, Swedes, Quakers, Jews, Germans, Irish, African black slaves, and Poles. Then came the Chinese in the 1870s.

European stock predominated, influenced by the 1880 passage of the Chinese Exclusion Act, until immigration was thwarted by the First World War. Puerto Ricans began emigrating in 1952. Then the 1968 immigration laws expanded Asian, South American, Mexican, Cuban, Puerto Rican, and African populations. Within the last decade alone, the oriental population in New York has doubled.

The 1970 census* includes New Yorkers of "foreign stock" who hail from twelve northwestern European, six central, six eastern, four southern, and four other European countries as well as from the USSR. From Asia, people from twelve countries are represented. Sixteen countries from North and Central, ten from South America are represented and eleven from other countries— a total of eighty-one countries, including, no doubt, many more regional, religious, and cultural distinctions.

A breakdown of the dominant ethnic groups of the 7,071,030 population in the five New York boroughs (1980)** indicates the quantity within the variety (counted by country of ancestry [can include immigrants or their children]): Italians, 802,700; Irish, 317,600; Russian, 215,700; Polish, 195,500; German, 181,700; English, 138,000; Hellenes, 82,300; Hungarians, 63,800; French, 31,600; Ukrainians, 25,000; Norwegians, 14,900; Scottish, 13,600; Portuguese, 10,400; Swedish, 9,600; Dutch, 7,600). Counted by

* U.S. *Bureau of the Census. 1970 Census of Population. Characteristics of the Population*, Part 34, *New York*, Section 2, Table 141: Country of Origin of the Foreign Stock by Nativity and Race. (The 1980 Census table has not been completed, but for breakdown of New York ethnic groups, see page 000).
** 1980 Population by Race and Ethnicity, New York City by Borough, Population Research Section/Division of Human Resources, NYC Department of City Planning (rounded off to nearest hundred).

race: Black populations (excluding those of Spanish/Hispanic origin or descent) number 1,695,000; people of Spanish/Hispanic origin, 1,406,000; Chinese, 124,370; Asian-Indian, 46,700; Philippine, 25,390; Korean, 22,000; Japanese, 13,690; Native American Indian, 13,140; Vietnamese number less than 3,000, Hawaiians less than 1,400, and Guamian less than 1,000. Jewish populations in New York were counted at 1,100,000 with the largest number—411,000—living in Brooklyn.* Jewish populations are included among the Russian, Polish, and other countries, depending on ancestry, according to Frank Vardy, New York City demographer.

Like Americans elsewhere, New York's new arrivals needed to learn, to adjust, to survive, and the assimilation patterns varied as much in food habits as in cultural traits. Early immigrants quickly assimilated each others' favorites—the settlers drawing heavily from indigenous Indian ideas and foods. The Dutch brought and sold grains (wheat, rye, barley), their fresh dairy butter, milk, cheeses, roots (carrots, turnips, beets, parsnips, radishes) and seeds for cabbages, leeks, and onions—foods of the Old World. Beef from Utrecht became a mainstay. Dutch favorites included doughnuts and pancakes, waffles, and spicy cinnamon cakes with coffee and tea. Fruit lovers, they planted the first quinces in America, more Spanish cherry, peach, apple, and pear seedlings.

From the New World, a fantastic variety, absorbed from Iroquois and Algonquin Indians, permanently influenced New York cuisine and availability in the stores: maize (corn) and pumpkins ("Spanish or mammoth pumpkin is considered best," the records state), sweet potatoes, beans, squash, sunflower seeds and, among the berries, cranberries. New York woodlands, rich in domestic and wild species, delighted the new settlers with capon and turkey, duck and geese, buffalo meat, deer and elk dishes, plus many small animals—from minks and groundhogs to squirrels. Bear (an herbivorous type) from which native Indians ate the forequarters, became an early favorite among New Yorkers. From these foods emerged specialties—succulent roast turkey, lusty meat and fra-

*Jewish Population Study, Federation of Jewish Philanthropies of New York, May, 1982.

grant game dishes, glazed sweet potatoes, pumpkin soup, and a spicy array of quick corn breads, berry muffins, and fruit pies.

As the English arrived and began to dominate locally (at the time of the Revolution the New York population was half English), they spread the popularity of their beloved roast beef, thick steaks, hearty Yorkshire puddings, biscuits, mutton chops, mincemeat, and plum puddings. Even George Washington encouraged local butchers to fatten cattle for soldiers, "To treat us with roast beef and savory steaks."

New waves of immigrants brought their own favorites. New York's nationality mix has made it the world's quintessential cupboard spilling over with fascinating foods and dishes. The Irish brought their love of cabbage and potatoes, tripe and stews. The Scots have always loved oatmeal and barley broth. German frankfurters (hot dogs), hams, smoked meats, dill pickles, rye, pumpernickel, cottage cheese became lasting favorites along with other specialties from zwieback and pretzels to hot strudels.

Today, *Souvlaki* and *Falafel*, *Tempura* and egg rolls are sold alongside frankfurters, nuts, and ice cream on the streets of New York (see *Street Snacks*, page 341). In the 1970s when I asked my college food classes to compile a list of the ten most significant foods that would typify current U.S. tastes (to be locked into a time capsule and opened in 100 years), the unanimous choices included frankfurters, hamburgers, pizza, milk, apple pie, corn on the cob, fried chicken, white bread, french fries, and steaks. Each specialty, introduced by an ethnic group, was gradually absorbed into the mainstream of American tastes. Will the 1980s list include bagels, egg rolls, tofu and bean sprouts, yogurt, *Tacos*, bean and rice dishes, whole wheat bread?

## Personal Experiences

I have responded to these ethnic foods and markets since moving to New York in 1967. Shops and neighborhoods evoke deep unexplained feelings that seek expression. Are they reminiscent of the charming food shops I first saw in Europe during the 1950s and farmers' markets throughout Europe and the Far East, the colorful street markets in Greece where villagers cart their homegrown herbs and vegetables and fruits shine brightly in the sun and flavor the air with sweetness?

Or are they just old-fashioned like my father's meat market/ produce specialty store near Independence Hall in Philadelphia where I loved to help him after school, counting out change from the glass-topped cashier's box, cooling off in summer in the oak walk-in icebox (our instant air conditioner) and pinching cherries?

Or do they invoke the spell of the tiny Armenian spice shop, a journey to enchanted lands, near our West Philadelphia home? Fascinating scents hovered over the bulging sacks and baskets containing strange berries, powders, seeds, and leaves. Many years passed before I unraveled the mysteries of the intriguing cumin, coriander, cardamom, turmeric, fenugreek, aniseed, mahlepi colliding furiously with the familiar cinnamon, nutmeg, cloves, sage, marjoram, thyme, savory, basil, and laurel.

Or, is it simply that the shops where sellers know the foods they sell offer to shoppers the intimacy of asking for food from someone who enjoys cutting, weighing, and wrapping the order with a greeting and, usually, a smile?

Whatever the magic attraction, it soon expanded into academia and a gradual awareness that other New Yorkers also enjoyed new food shops. I chose Chinatown for a graduate paper in the course, "Cultural Understanding Through Foods," when working on my master's degree in the Department of Home Economics and Nutrition at New York University. I sketched many new foods, bought my wok and cleaver, Chinese bowls and tea cups and the love affair bloomed.

*Essex Street Market* (page 16) on the Lower East Side stimulated another study the following year, this time for a graduate nutrition class. In Spanish Harlem, *La Marqueta* (page 106) startled me with its exuberance and freshness, displaying tropical foods, *bodega* style. I taught "Cultural Perspectives of Food and Nutrition" at Herbert Lehman College. Following a field trip, a student echoed my deepest thoughts. "I have lived in New York all my life," she wrote in her report, "and until today had never seen any of these foods."

In turn, an Italian-American student in the class introduced me to Arthur Avenue and its "Little Italy in the Bronx" atmosphere, especially the sky-lighted *Arthur Avenue Market* (page 114) with many stalls, like *Essex Street Market* and *La Marqueta*, run as individually owned shops. Closest to home, Arthur Avenue became my one-stop neighborhood for fresh food varieties.

As I became increasingly absorbed in the anthropology of ethnic foods, these neighborhood ethnic markets were important resource centers for me. Studying, teaching, and traveling during the next ten years, I filled thirty-three food files (appetizers to wines) and fifty-four files (ethnic groups and countries) with notes about people, their foods and cultures. During the interim, I wrote *The Food of Greece* (Atheneum, 1975; reprinted by Avenel/ Crown, 1979, 1981), a cultural food history and cookbook with 350 recipes. Since 1975, as food editor of *The Athenian*, an English-language monthly magazine published in Athens, and as a contributor to other publications, I wrote articles with recipes about various groups. These experiences helped me understand one universal principle: no matter how little I know about people and their lives, they are always quickly absorbed into talk about their food habits! This created an approach when I met new people in China, Japan, and Brazil where I knew little of the languages as in Greece, Germany, France, and England where language was no barrier.

### New York Public Markets and Demographics

A local focus for all the foodways studies emerged from an article, "New York Ethnic Markets: Public Markets as a Hub of Ethnicity," that I wrote in 1981 in graduate journalism class in the Graduate School of Arts and Sciences, New York University. Because my research was voluminous for an article, the class "editors" suggested I concentrate on New York's public markets; that is, markets functioning on city property. It was a great suggestion. I soon realized that when you say "public markets," New Yorkers think you mean farmers' markets or outdoor stands. And I discovered that these markets to which I had been attracted for their ethnic orientation—*Essex Street Market, Arthur Avenue Market,* and *La Marqueta (Park Avenue Market)*—actually were *public* markets—"community" markets. Functioning on city property, these had been administered by the city until the early 1970s. Two Brooklyn city markets were also part of the study: *Moore Street Retail Market* in Williamsburg (page 143) and Borough Park's *Thirteenth Avenue Farmers' Market* (page 139).

Built during the 1930s and 1940s to house the pushcart markets cluttering New York streets and pavements, these public markets provided livelihoods for hundreds of retailers. At the same time these markets became centers or hubs for local ethnic groups seeking their foods and meeting their neighbors. I was amazed to find that their founders still operated these markets and stalls. My conversations with stallkeepers (which I deeply appreciate for their knowledge and insights) reflect the ethnic changes in the communities around them as well as their own personal lives. I learned that when discussing food and food shops, particularly in New York, demographics and neighborhood influences invariably are meshed with the overall picture. Like butter and flour in a cake, you can't separate one from the other when the batter is mixed.

"The public markets have served a good purpose for the community," states Anthony Mattone, Director of Market Properties, Department of Ports and Terminals, which administers all city markets, retail and wholesale. "Public markets were planned to provide shelter for the sellers who brought their produce to the streets in inclement weather where it was impossible to stay, and they served the ethnic groups of the area," he added. Unfortunately, many of the old-timers moved away from their older neighborhoods after the influx of new groups. Of particular effect, the city official points out, has been the influx of Chinese people in Lower Manhattan. "They take away sales from *Essex Street Market*. For every Jew gone away to other areas, instead of buying from the market, Chinese people have built up around Division and East Broadway. As a result, *Essex Street Market* suffers. "There's no question about *Arthur Avenue Market*," he says, "it's marvelous," indicating success in its self-management since the merchants formed a corporation. Obviously, teamwork of stall owners has been more effective in some markets than in others since the city stopped managing them. Particularly, however, the community changes have impacted crucially.

Analyzing these ethnic changes and demographics in New York and their influences on food patterns, Frank Vardy, a demographer with the Population Research and Analysis Division, Department of City Planning, categorizes ethnic groups by their historic settlements. "Italians, blacks, and Chinese historically stayed where they settled. Arthur Avenue is a strong indication of this, providing a homogeneous atmosphere for the Italian-American community. Italians settled in Little Italy, the Lower East Side and, to a lesser degree, in Harlem and the Bronx." Standing at his draftsman's table covered with charts and graphs, the blue-eyed, white-haired demographer pulls out enormous maps from a nearby bin, unrolls them to expose New York City neighborhoods charted by ethnic group. Heavily populated areas are indicated by deepest tones and less populated areas by the lightest tones. "The Italians have shown remarkable stability of tenure," he says, pointing to a North Bronx map where Arthur Avenue shopping and residential areas are completely surrounded by black populations.

Traditional black concentrations at the turn of the century clustered on Manhattan's West Side in the Chelsea "Tenderloin" section until Pennsylvania Station and the hotel (currently called the New York Penta) were built in 1912, Frank Vardy explains. "Displaced from its original settlement, St. Phillips Episcopal Church moved to the north side of 135th Street, in a speculative area, and also bought some housing. Gradually, black people followed the church to Harlem and established the largest settlement. Other historic black concentrations were in Central Brooklyn (five sections), South Jamaica (Far Rockaway), and South Bronx, near Katonah Park, stated the demographer. "But blacks have lost their central area concentration."

"Jewish populations, on the other hand, have relocated from their original areas," he continues. "In 1900 German-Jews heavily populated West Harlem; they gradually moved out to the Bronx and upper Manhattan on the West Side." But Russian Jews settled on the Lower East Side. "The comedians and mayors all came out of there," Frank Vardy recalls, "and concentrations peaked between 1890 and 1905. Condemnation of tenements forced an exodus, so that by 1900 the Jewish population of Harlem had reached 17,000.

"Irish, in much larger numbers than Jews, also settled on the Lower East Side. Germans settled in Yorkville and the East 50th Turtle Bay area. Although Germans moved away from Yorkville, the name remained," he observes. "By 1879, Chinese had begun to settle in New York. Chinese built the Central Pacific Railroad (Irish built the Union Pacific) and as they worked westward, many stayed in New York and settled on Doyers Street. This settlement spread to Pell, Bayard, and Chatham Square." By 1939 there were 10,000 Chinese living in Manhattan. Groceries, restaurants, and specialty shops flourished in Chinatown.

Meanwhile, other ethnics increased their numbers, settling into various neighborhoods. Among the burgeoning groups, Hispanic populations have grown, with tides of Puerto Ricans, Mexicans, South Americans, Cubans, Caribbean Islanders settling in the Bronx, Brooklyn, Manhattan, Queens, and on Staten Island.

Regarding influences on food patterns, Frank Vardy indicates that Scandinavians, Irish, and Germans assimilated quickly. Italians, who maintain stability in their neighborhoods, also support their local stores. Hellenes have formed communities in Astoria, South Brooklyn, Sunset Park, Jamaica Hills, and Bayside. "The flourishing stores and cultural attractions of Astoria are examples," he continues. "But the Greeks and Koreans are merchants," he emphasizes, "who market to the existing trade. They do not market themselves as such" [meaning they do not concentrate on their *own* foods]. More recent waves have included Jamaicans, beginning in the 1920s, and immigrants from Haiti, Trinidad, Tobago, and Barbados—the last three groups since 1965, part of the West Indian Afro-Caribbean community.

## Ethnicity and Ethnic Food Markets

In New York, many ethnic shops create the variety that characterizes the city's spectacular food picture. Shops and food stalls listed in this book are counted by the Analysis and Research

Division, New York City Consumer Affairs, among the 3,700 small stores of the almost 15,000 food stores in five boroughs. On the one hand, the traditional and new ethnic groups seeking their own familiar foods spur the demand for and supply of ethnic foods and shops. These are typified in many neighborhoods by newer retailers and stalls as well as established ones continuing second- and third-generation businesses.

More recent are the "international" and "gourmet" food shops and departments. Impelled by consumers' travel and affluence, and their exposure to foreign foods, this trend is fueled, in addition, by the "health and nutrition" movements among the young and socially upscale. "Healthful" foods—those enjoyed by traditional ethnic groups since time immemorial—are suddenly "in" foods. Many people, too, have developed a desire for expressiveness—creativity—in foods. Further, the recent economic recession has probably intensified the craze to treat oneself to an exotic food now and then to compensate, possibly, for the general slump. As a result, the ethnic food interest—whether of the inherited, assimilated, or vicarious variety—is highly visible, flavorful, and contagious in New York.

These food trends influence an awareness of ethnicity—our own and others'. And our buying habits are stimulated by the proliferation of ethnic food markets. Individual retailers' ethnic customs affect their store hours; their ethnic holidays affect the foods found on their shelves and in our cupboards. Should you wish to learn more about an ethnic group, for example, plan to visit that group's food displays coinciding with a religious or cultural festival. In New York neighborhoods, festivals, bazaars, and street fairs are so extensive that the New York Cultural Affairs Council, which provides street activity permits, cannot make available the entire listing. (Only the mayor's office receives a weekly account.) Some of the most widely publicized that color the scene at various times of the year are: Indigenous Native American Indian festivals; Chinese New Year, first day of the Lunar Year in late January, celebrated in Chinatown; Irish St. Patrick's Day parade on Fifth Avenue on March 17; Hellenic Greek Independence Day parade on Fifth Avenue on March 25 and various festivals such as the spring festival in Astoria,

Queens; Ninth Avenue multiethnic festival from 37th to 52nd streets in May; Puerto Rican Day parade on Fifth Avenue the first Sunday in June; Lower East Side Jewish Spring Festival on East Broadway in mid-June; Japanese Obon Festival at the Japanese Buddhist Church in July; Festival of San Gennaro on Mulberry Street in Little Italy in September and Feast of St. Anthony on Sullivan Street in Soho in June; Arab Bazaar on Atlantic Avenue, Brooklyn in September or October; Divali Hindu Festival of Lights in Flushing in November.

Many, many more fairs and festivals contribute to the city's culinary distinctiveness because specialty dishes are always a very prominent feature of the events. Streets are festooned with flags and lights, and festivities abound, but the food arrays are among the most fascinating aspects. The Ninth Avenue Festival, especially, with its spectacular ethnic variety, is a must to visit for an instant view of the New York cornucopia (if you can manage to walk through).

What makes "ethnicity" in people so intense and what makes groups "ethnic"? Ethnic groups perceive themselves and others perceive them as intangibly linked by country of origin, as the census lists us, by ancestry, by race, by blood ties. Like culture, ethnicity is inherited, dynamic, and persists throughout life. Educators and nutritionists refer to "cultural foods" when they mean "ethnic foods."

Feeling is an integral part of "cultural foods" and "ethnicity." It matters enormously *with whom* and *how* foods were eaten as a child—with one's mother, with the family, in a cultural group or ethnic setting, in a village, town, or city. Flavors, scents, textures, temperatures are part of the "ethnic" habits or foodways. From one generation to the next, foodways transmit specific but usually unspoken values and attitudes about foods and the seasonings that go into them, cooking styles, even the way food is served and the utensils used. In later years, separated from home and family surroundings, one can suddenly eat a food from childhood and feel comforted, secure. Many people of differing ethnic groups have expressed this universal phenomenon. As Dr. Henrietta Fleck believes, "The food roots of an individual—be they geographical, religious, national, racial, regional, or cult-oriented—

have an influence on choice of foods. Each person is born into a culture or group matrix that is usually reflected in food patterns. With the current interest in heritage, there is a surge of attention to cultural foods."* More than ever before in the United States, and particularly in New York City, neighboring groups are becoming more familiar with other groups' foods—getting a look into ethnic cupboards. Until recently, most ethnic people bought their own ingredients and went home to cook them in their own mysterious ways. Now cupboards are opening.

Surveying the richness provided by ethnicity merging among the many groups living in New York, one is reminded of Oscar Handlin's observation in his classic *The Uprooted* (which has been a magnificent help to me in understanding my own and others' ethnic backgrounds): "Once I thought to write a history of the immigrants in America. Then I discovered that the immigrants *were* American history."**

Immigrants' foods are becoming *our* foods, to understand and to appreciate their zestful and spiritual meanings. Anthropologists' pleas for understanding are being heard. As Frederick J. Simoons wrote in 1967, "It is odd that few social scientists have been seriously concerned with the nature and distribution of man's foodways—the modes of feeling, thinking, and behaving about food that are common to a cultural group."*** Not only anthropologists and nutritionists, but also marketers now stress this need for understanding.

For this book I revisited familiar New York markets and neighborhoods and found new ones totaling 279 shops in twenty-nine neighborhoods of the five boroughs. This has been a time of walking, talking, buying, learning, observing, taping, writing, sketching, rewriting, trying new dishes. I wore out heels as soon as they were replaced. My favorite shoes fell off from wear. I wondered every afternoon about the shooting pains in my ankles. Why did

* Fleck, Henrietta. *Introduction to Nutrition,* 4th Ed., New York: Macmillan, 1981, Chapter 20: "Geography, Culture and Nutrition," pp 251-266.
** Handlin, Oscar. *The Uprooted.* New York: Grosset & Dunlap, 1951, p. 3.
*** Simoons, Frederick J. *Eat Not This Flesh: Food Avoidances of the Old World.* Madison, Milwaukee and London: The University of Wisconsin Press. 1967, p. 3.

my feet ache? Five, six hours of walking the shops did it! But I saw so many people in the various neighborhoods and am grateful for the experiences. And from so many people I learned to say "thank you" in their language. These "thank yous" are included here and there throughout the book to add more fun and color for you when you shop.

As I accumulated recipes and notes from shopkeepers and customers, found new ingredients, tried out the dishes—continuing my long passion for sketching and identifying unfamiliar foods, the recipes soon classified themselves. These are the obvious divisions: *Appetizers, Soups* (many hearty enough to make a one-bowl dinner), *Fish and Seafoods, Meats, Desserts, Beverages.* And many wonderful ethnic grain dishes (rice, wheat, corn [maize], oats, barley), pasta (a wheat product) and legumes or pulses (peas, beans, lentils) demanded their own distinct chapter *Grains (including Pasta) and Legumes (Pulses).* Centered on rice, for instance, Indonesian *Rames* (page 230) recipes are included in the grain chapter, even though they may contain meats and condiments. *Combination dishes* (meat/vegetable, fruit/meat, etc.) evolved into a fascinating collection from both the Oriental and Western cuisines. *Fresh fruits* certainly reflect the colors and flavors of many delightful city stalls, stands, and markets, as well as a resurgent interest in fresh fruits and vegetables for their nutritional values.

Another group, *Street Snacks* (pages 341-358), is a very special part of our food heritage and increasingly popular. Street snacks, which can be eaten anytime, anywhere, to make an instant rib-sticking picnic meal, probably evolved during the early nineteenth century. Arthur M. Schlesinger writes about the "gobble, gulp, and go" trends of fast cooking and fast eating from 1827 to 1880.* Despite the plentiful varieties available, the everyday diet developed into heavy breads and pies, with few fruits and vegetables. Street snacks seemed to appease the appetites. Today we can enjoy them within more balanced diets, with special thanks to the friendly street vendors who make them for us.

---

* Schlesinger, Arthur M. *Paths to the Present.* New York: Macmillan, 1949. Chapter XII, "Food in the Making of America," p. 235.

Limited by the number of recipes that could be included in each chapter without becoming encyclopedic, I aimed for a useful, helpful collection for young and inexperienced cooks as well as long-time adventuresome experts.

Creating a balance representing all New York ethnic groups was not quite as simple. I used many approaches to search out people in various boroughs, asking them where they shopped and what they bought. Hunting and seeking is totally satisfying, the elation of success overwhelming. I suppose it is the primitive "food gathering and hunting" instinct that combines both a sense of discovery with the joy of finally eating. I hope you feel this sense of exploration and discovery and shower your life and home with new flavors.

Among the recipes, the notes reflect the contributors' mood, choices, variations, and helpful clues about their dishes. Contributors to Part II include many shoppers and New Yorkers I have met in my classes (where I taught or was a student), various offices and organizations when I needed to find specific ethnic foods and could not easily locate them through shops. These helpful men and women are named, unless they preferred to remain anonymous.

No shopkeeper paid to be included in this guide and, in fact, I reassured a few newer shopkeepers (who may have mistaken me for a space salesperson) that they would not be billed. In turn, they wished me luck and asked to hear news about the book.

As you read and use *The New York Ethnic Food Market Guide & Cookbook*, you will glimpse the cupboards and culinary wonders of many ethnic groups representing many continents. Above all, this is a book about *people and their foods*—selling food, shopping for ingredients, absorbing, adjusting to, and assimilating new ideas—while continuing to value their own distinctive cuisines. As you explore the shops, taste new foods, and try new recipes, I truly hope your food adventures enhance your understanding of the people who introduced them just as you continue to express fondness for your own food heritage. Especially, I hope these experiences enrich your life and the lives of people near you.                                                         *Vilma Liacouras Chantiles*
*New York, 1984*

# HOW TO USE THIS BOOK

USE THIS BOOK, which is organized in two related sections—
Part 1: *The Five Boroughs: Neighborhoods, Food Markets, Shops,
Stalls,* and Part 2: *Recipes*—as you would approach shopping and
cooking with a friend. Use your senses. React to the signals from
your eyes, ears, taste, touch, feeling, and intelligence. I am the
"friend" through whom you meet shop owners and shoppers in
279 stores and market stalls—people representing more than
sixty ethnic groups. You will read many shopping and cooking
notes offered to you warmly and carefully. In a reciprocal friend-
ship, you may respond and use Part I and Part II of this book as
guides for many food adventures. By responding to the rich resources of ethnic groups—New York's greatest untapped food
thesaurus—you will be making good use of this book.

Part 1, a guide to the neighborhood shops of the five boroughs,
begins in the Whitehall/Wall Street neighborhood where New
York food-shop history really began. Moving northward, it takes
you into shops in the City Hall/Civic Center and Lower East Side,
Chinatown and Little Italy through Soho and the Villages (Green-
wich Village and East Village) to Union Square. On through the
east and west side of Manhattan, you move through Gramercy/
Little India/Murray Hill into Midtown passing through the Gar-
ment District and Theater District. Up through Ninth Avenue
(Paddy's Market/Clinton/Hell's Kitchen) to the Upper West Side.
Then across to the Upper East Side/Yorkville/Little Hungary to
Spanish Harlem, move into the Bronx, and eventually visit
Brooklyn, Queens, and Staten Island.

In most shops or stalls of the larger public markets or small independently owned ones, you will meet the owner or manager and I have noted the essences and character of each shop. Address, phone number, hours and days open, and mail order information, when available, are listed following my comments on each shop.

So that you would know which ethnic foods are available in which neighborhoods and shops, I included the following: I often asked the shop owners which ethnic *foods* were bought by which *groups* (this information tells you about food stocks and the ethnic groups who shop there to find their ingredients); at the top of each neighborhood section, ethnic groups are listed (Chinese, Hungarian, Jewish, etc.) indicating foods available for these specific groups. These are guides to assist you when you plan to "neighborhood" shop for certain foods, and although they may not be the *only* types of ethnic foods available, these are significant.

As you would rub dried oregano or basil in your palms to release their essences into the food you're cooking, I want to give you a sense of the shop's specialty and ambiance.

Since store hours and mail-order businesses sometimes vary seasonally (some shops provide the mail-order service and specially prepared foods only at holiday time; others close certain days or for a few weeks' vacation during the summer), it is wise to call in advance if you plan to travel some distance to the shop.

Readers must keep in mind the individuality of each shopkeeper, shown in merchandising styles, displays, and food stocks, as much as in the owner's personality and the store's hours. Certainly the personality of the owners and shops spurred me on through the city and I hope will excite you as well. With only a few exceptions, shops are owner-operated. Owners reflect high and long-range interest in the business, not as an investment, but as a life's work. Their dedication, concern, and hard, hard work are clear. Enthusiasm is contagious. When you ask about the food origins, you get responsive answers. Willing to share their food habits and recipes, shop owners vividly related anecdotes about their past and future plans as well.

Remember, you may feel mystified when the shop owner

speaks no English and when foods may be identified only in a foreign language you cannot read. I guarantee, these qualities will *never* spoil your trip; rather, they will enhance the experience when you have found a way to communicate.

Many shops are so simple you will be amazed to see them seemingly unchanged during this century—old shelves, sawdust on the floor, a wooden bench to rest for a minute. The other type of shop—international, prestigious, and affluent—may dazzle you with its spankingly new fixtures. Here, ingredients very likely are identified in two languages—English and usually French, Italian, Japanese, Chinese, or Spanish. Baby zucchini, for example, though grown in Florida, may also be called by the French name, *Courgette*, in the "prestigious" shops. In the older, "ethnic" shops, geared primarily for the owner's own ethnic group (such as Thai, Chinese, etc.), there is a growing trend to identify foods in English as well.

One of my favorite questions was: "When you go home tired, what is your favorite dinner or dish, especially from your childhood?" This stimulated much of the recipe section, Part 2 of this book. Shopkeepers enjoyed describing this fantasy dinner, and offered recipes and cooking tips. With their permission, I included their names with the recipe.

Recipes are styled simply: Ingredients are listed in order of their use in the recipe. The only ingredients I *assume* you have (although one should never assume anything) are water and a little oil, butter, or margarine to rub on baking pans and steamers when needed. I believe you know how much salt and pepper you like to add along with soy sauce, ginger, and the other fabulous herbs and spices we have at our fingertips. With so many kinds of rice, wheat (whole and cracked), and other grains, I hope you ask shop owners how some new foods you buy should be cooked; you will be rewarded by their food knowledge. I also assume you wash fruits and vegetables scrupulously before cooking and eating them and are familiar with trimming, scraping, and preparing the many varieties suggested in this book.

Following the ingredients, the method of preparation is written in conversational style to make cooking easy and as creative as possible. Be creative—there is an infinity of variety. The number of people served is sometimes difficult to estimate in some recipes, depending on appetites and whether the food is only part of the meal or the entire meal (I am always amazed by the quantities people eat compared to my calculations; for example, Chinese people suggested a pound of fresh noodles *plus* wontons for four guests!). Adjust these numbers to your own needs.

I enjoy enormously insights about food and culture, so I included this information at the top of the recipes for you to read when you have time (an editor once told me that many people read cookbooks in bed!).

I hope this book will be a handy guide and practical aid for you and an incentive to venture into the shops after reading about them, curious to explore, eager to see, smell, and taste new foods.

Involve yourself fully when shopping and cooking. Increase your awareness by looking closely for freshness, size, and ripeness; feel the fruits and vegetables and watch as they are weighed to judge weights. As you cook the colors, sounds, aromas, and tastes will tell you much, much more than I can. My words really only introduce and guide your adventures. You are the adventurer.

# PART 1
# THE FIVE BOROUGHS
## Neighborhoods, Food Markets, Shops, Stalls

The eye is harder to please
than the stomach.
JAPANESE PROVERB

# MANHATTAN

# WHITEHALL, WALL STREET
## International

In the beginning God gave to every
people a cup of clay, and from this
cup they drank their life.

DIGGER INDIAN PROVERB

## The Earliest New York Markets

The Whitehall, Wall Street neighborhood hooks you immediately into Manhattan's food history. Early markets (not yet stocks and bonds) flourished on these shores long before roads and bridges or the horse and buggy, or even the little boats that were rowed from Brooklyn "with kail [kale] and cabbage." When the hungry Dutch arrived in New York, marketing strategies and futures meant only getting enough to eat.

Expanding the meaning of the Digger Indian proverb quoted above, in New York the "cup" became the cooking pot. Borrowing, lending, and blending became an investment in survival. Indigenous (Algonquin and Iroquois) Indian tribes shared their abundance of fish and game, vegetables and seeds of maize (corn). The food of the Dutch emigrés—turnips and cabbages, Old World wheat and oats, barley, dairy butter, milk and cheese—blended with the already established Spanish foods and the New York kettle heated up. Succulent roast turkey, lusty meats (Utrecht cattle and Spanish pork), fragrant local ducks and capons, glazed sweet potatoes and pumpkin soup, a galaxy of luscious berry muffins and pancakes, corn breads and fruit pies emerged from early kitchens to become American staples.

As different ethnic groups emigrated to Manhattan Island and sprinkled their flavors into the New York pot, the world's most diverse cuisine flourished. Nowhere is the ethnic flavor of the people and their foods more evident than in the food markets where newly arrived immigrants seek their cherished foods, their eyes shining with ethnic and cultural fervor, their tongues yearning for a taste of the familiar, the secure childhood foods. The New York pattern began even before the island was acquired for $24. In 1623, the Dutch settlers built the earliest market on record—the West India Company—five stone buildings on Whitehall Street (when Water, Front, and South streets had not yet been reclaimed and Whitehall and Pearl streets were on the shoreline). Diverse, even then, not only Dutch, but native American and Spanish foods were stocked alongside European wines. Records indicate that New Yorkers even in those days complained about high prices!

Here on Manhattan's tip where the walk across town is short and the Hudson and East rivers never very far from sight, there are more than memories of the past.

For example, Pearl Street still winds gracefully in "a crooked line," as early writers put it, changing mood from block to block. Sometimes quaint restaurants melt into office buildings. Where Pearl crosses Hanover Square, on a midsummer day, some thirty long benches fill with people munching apples and popsicles, resting under the gracious plane trees. In the seventeenth century, an old meat market sprang up the same way—under the trees—when country people paddled across from Brooklyn with their meats and paused under the trees to escape the sun's heat. They were met by burghers. Soon it became a market, The Old Slip Market. The street name, Old Slip, remains—a reminder— on the same spot.

As canoes came in from Brooklyn, Manhattanites ran hungrily to meet the boats all along the eastern shoreline (as we flock today around street vendors selling hot dogs and ice cream). Demand forced the supply and the Market Place at the Strand was built and a rapid flurry of markets—Coenties Slip Market, Peck Slip Market, Catherine Slip Market, Broadway Shambles, Broad Street Market—echoes of the past in street names we use today. Those were the days when from Brooklyn:

> The country maids with sauce to market come,
> And carry loads of tatter'd money home.*

On the wharf at Fulton Street, where the air is heavy with fish scents, the Fulton Fish Market survives. Built in 1821 with 88 butcher stands, poultry, vegetable and fruit stalls (that were each sold at auction), the fish stalls were gradually introduced in a small wing separated by South Street. Today the Fulton Fish Market reigns as the world's largest fish wholesaler and New York's

---

* *The Market Book* (see page 6).

oldest remaining early market. By mid-morning, when stalls have been washed down, intrigues have subsided, and doors have been closed, the scene is much like the life of an earlier era of the city fish market.

> The wholesale fish trade, for many years, has been constantly increasing, and now, hours before daylight every morning of the week, may be found here fish wagons, carts, and other vehicles, from the various public markets, meat shops and street peddlers from this and the neighboring cities, towns and villages for their daily supplies; which part of the business is generally over by seven o'clock A.M.
>
> Thomas F. DeVoe, *The Market Book*, p. 515

Today, across the street from this wholesale market, reflecting the typical New York spirit that clings to old markets, another "Fulton Market" has been built, the focal point of the exciting cobblestoned South Street Seaport complex, opened July 28, 1983. Unlike the old Bear, Fly, Essex, Washington, and Jefferson markets which had been rebuilt from the originals with many similar, competitive stalls, the *new* Fulton Market offers primarily one-of-a-kind food specialty boutiques in very contemporary settings—many of them branches of businesses in other neighborhoods. And there are enough fast food bars, cafés, bakeries, and restaurants to feed thousands. But, nevertheless, fish and seafoods are the highlights of the Fulton Market, quite a switch from the 1821 opening! Around the new Fulton Market, activities in the eleven-block seaport development keep the visitor amused and constantly nibbling. The 1797 seaport museum has been expanded to include shops and restaurants. Twelve nineteenth-century buildings have been restored at Schermerhorn Row that include more specialty shops and restaurants. Old ships, docked at the East River, graciously await shoppers. Wherever you turn on the seaport, vendors sell snacks and mimes entertain bemused audiences in the salty atmosphere filled with upscale merchandising that has revived this wonderful old New York market district.

Fraunces Tavern, another reminder of early market history,

restored as a fine restaurant, was the 1719 Georgian mansion of Samuel Fraunces. Innkeeper Fraunces became George Washington's steward and shopped at the famous Fly Market (where live slaves and slaughtered meats were sold) at the west end of Maiden Lane. In those days a meadow covered Pearl Street up to the slope at Beekman Street. In fact, the Dutch named the area Smidt's Vley (meaning "valley"), but the English, who had a penchant for renaming Dutch names, called the area Smith's Fly and the name clung to this famous market where "people go almost daily to Fly Market" for their meats.

The other famous neighborhood center was the Bear Market, built in 1771 on the present site of the World Trade Center, and named when an enterprising butcher captured a bear he saw swimming from the Jersey shore and hung it for sale in the market! Established in 1699 and expanded every so often, it also included a Buttermilk Stand, where Jersey Dutch women sold buttermilk. Buttermilk Channel between Brooklyn and Governor's (formerly Nut) Island, where the little boats traversed, was named in 1678.

Full of assorted food stalls and snack counters, the Bear Market so overflowed its capacity that sellers hawked their wares all the way onto sidewalks (ancestors of today's street merchants). To fill the need, another market opened across the street in 1812—the great Washington Market, beloved for decades and surviving until the late 1960s. When Washington Market opened, however, twenty-two acres around Union Square were planted with vegetables growing produce for the Fly and Bear markets; and farther north, wildflowers bloomed.

Booming and expanding with New York's population (60,000 in 1800 to 3,434,000 in 1900), the Washington Market only gradually supplanted the Bear Market and, in fact, for forty years was called the Bear Market. More than any other, this trait symbolized the neighborhood feeling. Because butchers who were given new stalls in the Washington Market could not give up the old association, they clung to the name.

Butchers were, in fact, among the most famous attractions of the early markets. Shoppers were known to come to the Washington Market to "goggle at the fancy butchers—healthy and robust characters, aristocrats of their day." These "gogglers" could have been any of the thousands of Irish, German, English, or Scots flooding New York during the 1840s and 1850s.

Walk around the Whitehall, Wall Street area (part of Tribeca) and you will find these links to the past.

VINCENT PETROSINO RESTAURANT AND SEAFOOD SHOP sings a salty tune echoing from the great Washington Market stalls where Vincent Petrosino with a nephew ran a stall called Petrosino Brothers. Now his widow, son Vincent, Jr., and daughter carry on with the shrimps, sea scallops, squid, rainbow trout, and other fresh fish. The shop/restaurant has operated here since the Washington Market closed. The family stuffs bluefish with crabmeat (Alaskan snow crab) and creates specialties for their adjoining restaurant and will share recipes, if coaxed—especially Italian favorites.

*100 Greenwich Street. 227-5398. 8-6, Monday to Friday; closed Saturday and Sunday. Phone orders. Delivers.*

THE EPICURE GIFT BASKET sweetens shoppers in the heart of Wall Street's financial district, no doubt the contemporary cousin of early settlers' stalls. Owned by the same family for fifty years (they moved here from Liberty Street in the early 1950s), the shop specializes in European and domestic chocolates, candies, cookies, jams, and fresh fruit. Wall Street workers stop in at lunchtime for nonpareils and gumdrops. Nestled among gray stone office buildings, the little square shop, vibrant with colors and displays, headed by Joan Apostol and friendly assistants, keeps food history alive. Create your own delightful *Pan Dan* (page 327) from this assortment.

*80 Broad Street. 269-3976. 8-6, Monday to Friday; closed Saturday and Sunday. Phone orders. Delivers.*

THE WORLD TRADE CENTER concourse (where half the New York population seems to walk), tempts you with all kinds of snacks:

THE BIG KITCHEN offers baked goods and cheeses in the twenty-three units run by Inhilco, Inc., a subsidiary of Hilton

International, in conjunction with the New York Port Authority.

THE LITTLE CHEESE SHOP bursts with cheeses—nine French types, four English, and many Scandinavian varieties. But Swiss and Jarlsberg cheeses are the most popular sellers, says Craig Cavaluzzi, salesman here since 1979.

THE BAKERY specializes in breads and fifteen kinds of rolls, but they may be sold out by 2:30 in the afternoon, so come early. Pina Colada, Indian Squaw, and Potato breads (listed on the black-board) are available "once in a blue moon." Around the con-course, a hive of restaurants, take-out counters, seafood and snack bars, emulate the stalls of the Bear Market and Washington Market that once stood here—but in a very different way.

*One World Trade Center. 938-1153 (The Kitchen number for all shops). 7-7, Monday to Friday; 9-5, Saturday; closed Sunday. Phone orders. Delivers only within the building.*

The new **FULTON MARKET,** with sedate brick and mortar exterior and waving flags, sparkles indoors with three floors of food offerings guaranteed to weaken even the sternest dieter.

At the main entrance, on ground level, R.M. CURTIS PRODUCE *(608-7766)* greets you with a shining display of bright fruits and vegetables. As you roam back and forth among the food displays, your eyes are dazzled and your sense of smell continuously delighted by the variety and quality of the foods.

In the unbroken flow of small shops, walk into MERCHANTS COFFEE, TEA AND SPICE COMPANY *(608-6767)* where coffee beans in baskets vie for attention near exotic seasonings.

The adjacent PAXTON & WHITFIELD *(608-1344)* display of 300 cheeses, patés, and crackers will tempt you until GUSS PICKLES, in huge barrels, lures you with pickle scents (main branch, *35 Essex Street, 254-4477).* The Fulton Market, arranged like specialty shop boutiques with highly individualized display styles, is more like an uptown specialty store than the city's other public markets.

Brightened by an enormous skylight, incredible activity, food colors and expansiveness, the effect is high-keyed vivacity.

Also on the ground level, PROVISIONS, owned by Ricardo Diaz, carries gourmet foods from chocolates to smoked meats

*(608-6531)*. Nearby, you'll find nuts and dried fruits, a branch of ZARO'S BREAD BASKET (page 67), and plenty of fish.

Not only is there a FULTON MARKET RETAIL FISH STORE *(483-8391)* in a central location, but also the FULTON STREET CAFÉ, a seafood restaurant.

The second level is an ethnic snack paradise. There are shops featuring Soul Food, Chinese *dim sum*, Japanese sushi and soup, Argentinian *empanadas*, Greek barbecue, French croissants, and Asian Indian tandoor food. In the non-stop array, you can choose from stands devoted entirely to sausages, cookies, yogurt, French fries, and ice cream.

There's also a BEEKMAN STREET BAKERY *(608-7088)* and a branch of PASTA & CHEESE (page 94). The FULTON MARKET RAW BAR is a treat for shellfish lovers. A sea of little tables with chairs awaits the hungry shoppers, eager to devour their selections. On the third level, STEINHANDLER'S GRILL, a steakhouse, and THE COHO, a seafood restaurant and sushi bar, serve more hungry visitors.

*FULTON MARKET. South Street Seaport. Fulton, South, Beekman, and Front Streets. Some shops have no phone. For information call 608-0642. Monday to Saturday 10-10; Sunday 10-5.*

# CITY HALL, CIVIC CENTER
## International, Oriental, Italian

*The poor man must walk to get meat for his stomach,*
*the rich man to get a stomach for his meat.*

POOR RICHARD'S ALMANAC

BRIDGES DOMINATE food markets wherever they were built, and Brooklyn Bridge looks like a giant hand stretching from City Hall Park. Municipal buildings and Pace University surround a handsome square lined with trees and dotted with shrubs, while shops—mostly chains and fast-food shops—bustle among the office buildings. Crossing into Chambers Street, at last, you'll discover a cove-in-the-wall fruit shop where the polite vendor will sell you bananas to munch in the park.

Fruit and nut shops, especially, evoke memories of the historic flow of food sellers into the neighborhood. As New York's population mushroomed during the nineteenth century, a new type of public "market" emerged—the New York street vendor. Hawking wares on the sidewalks, screeching and tooting horns, pulling hand-drawn carts, the vendors multiplied like rabbits.

A favorite selling place for vendors was at the Old Five Points, "a colony of considerable exclusiveness" behind the State and County Court buildings at Baxter, Worth, and Park streets. *Leslie's Illustrated Newspaper* reported on May 8, 1867:

Musty carts, fractured wheelbarrows and large dirty baskets dot the sidewalks and expose for sale the various delicacies of the season. . . . Fishes slipped off wagons, onions and other vegetables rolled about as indolent residents speedily surrounded their favorite merchants and indulged in all the wranglings and arguments known to the bargaining public.

Today, however, street hawking has been absorbed into several specialized shops:

SWEET SATISFACTION, a mixed ethnic nut, candy, and coffee shop—since 1977 run by Taisoon Kim—stocks eight kinds of coffee ground to order. In winter, thirty varieties of nuts are the big business; in summer, family members sell fresh fruits from a sidewalk stand, including mixed fruit cups, sliced by Taisoon into fragrant medleys or to make a tropical beverage (page 337) or Guatemalan Fruit Parfait (page 323).
*149 Church Street. 233-1545. 9:30-6, Monday to Friday; 10:30-6, Saturday; closed Sunday. Phone orders. No deliveries.*

TRANS-ASIA "NOAH'S GOURMET" intrigues you with its large SPICES sign outside and its 200 herbs and spices, packaged under the Spice Market label, inside. Catering to "gourmets," according to owner B.T. Lee and his wife, fifteen kinds of coffees, many teas, imported cheeses and crackers, canned and jar foods are stocked. The Lees also sell kitchen utensils.

*94 Reade Street. 406-0185, 0186. 8-6:30, Monday to Friday; 8-5, Saturday; closed Sunday.*

YAT GAW MIN CO., importers and noodle manufacturers since 1905, sells fresh and fried noodles, wonton and egg roll wrappers, almond cakes, fortune cakes, and peanut candy—wholesale and retail. When I visited at 10 A.M., everyone sat at his desk enjoying a noodle-break—Yat Gaw Min noodles, of course. (One of the men remarked, "There are about ten noodle factories in China-town.")

*100 Reade Street. 233-7200. 8:30-4, Monday to Friday; 8:30-2, Saturday; closed Sunday. Phone orders. Delivery depends on size of order.*

CHEESE OF ALL NATIONS, a small shop plastered with signs, has a small side case and tall case in back where you can just about see the heads of two salesmen. It stocks and sells moun-tains of cheeses. In business for decades, the shop carries soft and semi-soft, part skim cheese, unsalted cheddar, muenster, gouda, lorraine, and Swiss, hard, semi-hard, from grating cheese to the softest creams. There must be sixty-five types of cheese spreads available in addition to the goat's and sheep's milk favorites and classics. Manny, the expert cheeseman, will probably offer you a taste, especially if you say *"Parakalo"* ("please" in Greek).

*153 Chambers Street. 732-0752. 7:30-5:30, Monday to Satur-day; closed Sunday. Phone, mail, and airmail orders.*

PETROSINO FISH MARKET is run by Vincent and Ralph Petro-sino who were nourished on fish from their father's and great uncle's stall, Petrosino Brothers, in the great Washington Market. "I cried the day the market closed," Vincent recalls, standing by his ample fish case full of snappers, Norwegian salmon, lobsters,

and other varieties. The Petrosino brothers, related to the Petro-
sinos in Whitehall/Wall Street, have operated on Duane Street
since 1969 and are great seafood enthusiasts. A favorite Petrosino
menu? "Gray sole (fried or broiled) with salad, and potatoes,"
with a dash of Salerno seasonings from their father's birthplace.

*161 Duane Street. 732-8131. 8-6, Monday to Friday; closed
Saturday and Sunday. Phone orders. Delivery on orders over
$30.*

MORGAN'S MEATS is another spinoff from the great Washington Market, where Earl Morgan operated a meat stall. His market
has expanded to suit the neighborhood needs for a large grocery,
produce, beverage, and meat department, and is managed by his
son Kevin, one of four sons. Next door, MORGAN'S GRILL, in a
quaint setting that was an old butter-and-eggs warehouse in the
earlier days, is another Morgan enterprise.

*13 Hudson Street (corner, Hudson and Reade). 964-4283. 7-8,
Monday to Friday; 8-6, Saturday; closed Sunday. Phone orders.
Delivers.*

# LOWER EAST SIDE
Hispanic, Black, Jewish, Italian, Chinese, Korean,
Puerto Rican, Jamaican and other Caribbean Groups,
Asian-Indian, Pakistani, etc.

*Look not at the flask but at its contents.*
HEBREW PROVERB

**ESSEX STREET MARKET** sprawls along four city blocks of busy Delancey Street from Rivington to Stanton streets on the very ground where Peter Stuyvesant may have walked. Traffic zooms past toward and from the yawning Williamsburg Bridge, since 1902 spanning the East River to Brooklyn. People of different ethnic groups mill around the shops and old, rundown tenements. On Saturdays, lines of people form at the corner newsstand, buying Lotto chances or foreign-language newspapers. Amid the noise and confusion, one searches to find "new modernistic quarters, modern stalls, and electric lights" as *The New York Times**\* described the Essex Street Market when it opened in January, 1940, to rid the streets of colorful pushcart markets. Then Mayor LaGuardia officially opened the market to 3,500 "shivering people" and promised a continued war on pushcarts on Orchard, Grand, East Houston, Stanton, Hester, and Rivington streets. Its opening marked the end of the landmark pushcart markets and a picturesque era that some residents preferred to the new covered market. Nevertheless, 475 stalls were filled on opening day and administered by the city until the late 1960s as a public market in four buildings *The Times* characterized as "colonial rose-colored brick."

More than four decades may have dulled its brightness, but inside the first building, on the north side of Delancey, amazingly, the original stall owner, RUBIE BENICK, still operates the same produce stall!

"You want the truth? I've been here since the market opened," he announces. "The market's changed a lot since then. Oh, yes, we have all nationalities—Spanish, Irish, Italian, Jewish," explained the slight-figured man with glasses who raised two sons (including a New York attorney) while running the stand. He stocks many seasonal varieties enjoyed by his ethnic customers in the small stand equipped with a chair where he rests. "I never used to sit," he commented while selling green peppers to a Jamaican shopper and vegetables for a curried dish to a Pakistani family.

Around him, many stalls and departments function like small

---

\* *The New York Times*, January 10, 1940, p. 1.

businesses within arm's reach of each other, each with a specialty, a flavor all its own. Against the wall, Abe Stamer runs BERNIE'S DAIRY, stocking milk and cheeses. "Jewish customers buy farmer's cheese, muenster, Jarlsberg—soft types; Italians buy theirs in Little Italy (alluding to the traditional Italian marketing section around Mulberry Street); Argentinian *Queso Duro* is popular," says the young retailer, slicing off a generous square of pure white *Queso Blanco* for a customer.

EDDIE BURROUGHS, born in Norfolk, Virginia and the only black American retailer in the public market, runs his vegetable stand near Rubie Benick's. An avid cook, he enjoys using many of the tropical vegetables available in the market and compares notes on making the Puerto Rican holiday dish, *Pasteles*, with neighbor Albert Torres's recipe (page 291).

ALBERT TORRES'S enormous central tropical stand is like a bright centerpiece where shoppers can move around and pick anything from *Yautia* (root) and *Calabaza* (orange pumpkin) to dried catfish and peppers, *Recau* (an herb for *Sofrito*), *Cilantro* (fresh coriander) and football-sized papayas to cook or preserve. He cuts an enormous orange pumpkin and cradles the huge, scalloped vegetable in his arms. He stocks green bananas, plantains, banana leaves at Christmas time.

"I love *Calabaza* raw, grated," announces Eddie Burroughs, who circled around his own stall to join the conversation. At a higher level, Albert Torres energetically sells Argentinian dried beef to a shopper who plans to cut it up and simmer it with green pepper, tomato, and *Sofrito* seasoning (see recipe page 180). He also stocks green bananas, plantains, banana leaves at Christmas time, and culinary aids for Caribbean dishes *(Papel de Pasteles—* special paper to wrap *Pasteles)*, *Achiotina* (to color food, page 291), and mounds of tubers and roots; he has run the stall since 1974 and likes the spot very much. Albert Torres, a native Puerto Rican, had run a stall in La Marqueta for six years until it "burned down."

ORCHARD ESSEX MEAT MARKET, INC., against the wall, opposite the entrance, has operated since 1947 under the witty direction of Joseph Israel. The long case contains neat rows of beef, veal, chicken, specialty meats. Summarizing the community changes since he began retailing meats here, he quips, "I dance the way the music plays; change the tune of music and I change the way of doing business." He gears his stocks for Hispanics, black, and Chinese trade *(473-3363)*.

DON SONG, a young Korean, operates a superbly arranged fruit and vegetable stand near the dairy with masses of fresh seasonal greens including some oriental varieties, bright spinach and celery, chilies for your *Kimchi* (recipe, page 184), and fresh coriander for Mexican, Chinese, and Puerto Rican dishes among the herbs. Fruits are also stocked in the long stall, equipped with computerized checkout—a novelty in the public markets *(677-9539)*.

Across Delancey, in the second large market building, Florence Gross, market secretary, handles business matters from a closet-sized office. "The greatest recent change in the Essex Market has been the increasing number of Oriental stall owners. . . . There must be nine or ten Korean families here now," she notes.

ALLEN RUHALTER MEAT MARKET is run in a central market position, by Allen Ruhalter, a second-generation retailer in the Essex Street Market, and also the market president (collects rents and pays the city under a lease arrangement). Shoppers hover around the meat case as four butchers chop at their blocks and converse with the clientele.

"We cater to three different ethnic groups," says Allen Ruhalter, a tall man with glasses. "Black Muslims (who abstain from eating pork), black Americans, and Spanish. Our black customers used to eat from this side of the case," he discloses, waving toward the spareribs, neck bones, pigs' feet, chitterlings, "but with more affluence they are eating more of the better cuts now." He buys meats from the GANSEVOORT WHOLESALE MEAT MARKET (another market with ancient roots), and offers various meat "plans" to his customers. Allen Ruhalter expressed hope that the upcoming million-dollar renovations earmarked by the city would help business. "We need families to move into the neighborhood. Chinatown takes a lot of our business" *(475-6521)*.

HARRY GRUNDSTEIN runs the fish stall. He is a young retailer who summarizes the urgent need to adapt food stocks to local ethnic preferences. "When I bought the store before 1970, it did a Jewish trade. Now it's mostly Hispanic. The former owner wasn't familiar with handling conch, scungilli, live crabs—all kinds of seafoods *they* eat. Shrimp, I put in—all kinds of shellfish. You have to keep the foods that people *eat!* I eat Gefilte Fish. I'm Jewish. My customers aren't going to eat *my* soul food. They wanta eat *their* soul food," declared the enthusiastic retailer as clearly as a food anthropologist. But, he admitted, "Now, I eat shrimp . . . lobster."

The YUNGS, a young Korean couple from Seoul, operate a small fruit stand, selling tangerines, apples, pears, etc., from fruit pyramids.

WILLY stands by his small tropical stall, as he has since 1973, holding a water (jelly) coconut in one hand and a machete in the other. "Business is no good," says he, rapping the coconut. He turns it over and strikes it again and the coconut falls open, revealing white flesh. He pricks the soft coconut with the knife tip, delicious to eat for a tasty snack. Willy stocks coconut oil, papaya jam, homemade guava jelly, tamarind, sesame seed candy, and other such tasty delicacies.

MORRIS AND REBECCA RUBIN have operated an old-fashioned grocery since 1962—an unselfconscious tangle of everything from canned Jalapeno peppers (small, green, and *hot)*, to jars of Manischewitz schav (sorrel soup), bins full of aromatic spices, dried beans, grains, canned sauces, and soups. Here, a shopper finds black-eyed peas to make a New Year's Day Black-Eyed Pea Soup (recipe, page 191) or orange lentils and spices for an Asian Indian *dhal* (lentils), and soap to wash the dishes.

JOE'S FRESH MEATS AND POULTRY department is another established stand run by Joe Mevorah, offering pork, beef, chicken, turkey, sausages, and specialties. Many are displayed with Spanish signs: *Biftec de Bola* (top sirloin)—marinate and pan fry; *Chuletta de Serdo* (pork chops)—fry; *Longaniza* (hot sausage) and *Chorizo* (same, smaller size); *Gandinga de Cerdo* (pork ears); *Buche de Cerdo* (hog maws); *Mondongo* (tripe)—cut up, cook with onions and potatoes; *Cabrito* (goat's meat); *Costillitas* (fresh bacon); *Bobrelomo* (shell steak)—broil. This retailer also offers food plans to shoppers and runs another shop, LOS DOS HERMANOS, at Stanton and Orchard streets *(673-8380).*

TURKEL'S STRICTLY KOSHER MEAT AND POULTRY flourishes in the fourth Essex Street Market building (the third is leased by a furniture retailer). Robust and pink-cheeked, Frank Turkel, another original market operator, chops meat vigorously alongside his son Gary, hardly a "newcomer" after being in the business since 1957. "Our best seller is poultry; beef—for pot roast, stews, and fricassee—and veal for roasts are popular," Gary reports, stepping toward the large meat refrigerator opposite the case. Three gray-haired matrons from Brooklyn walk in, smiling, and shake hands with Frank Turkel before meat decisions are made; another butcher sells corned beef and steaks. "The future is bright," Gary Turkel comments optimistically. "Investors should come to the Lower East Side where land is more reasonable than uptown." *148 Essex Street. 477-0146. Closed Saturday.*

*ESSEX STREET MARKET. 104 Essex Street. 254-6655. 8-6, Monday to Saturday; closed Sunday. (General phone number and hours; individual stall owners' phone numbers, where available, are noted above, with the description of each stall.)*

## Neighboring Lower East Side Shops, near Essex Street Market

EDIBLE PICKLE WORKS attracts shoppers who love sour and dill pickle smells as bees swarm around a honeycomb. Seventeen tubs full of red, green, and white peppers, tomatoes, cucumbers, and more—large barrels loaded with more pickles along the back of the small stand which is located outside the Essex Street Market. What's more, there are pickles in pint and quart and gallon jars to carry home if you don't buy them in bulk weights. The stand, run by Al Silberstein since 1940, is colorful as a farmer's market.

*132 Essex Street. 475-1284. 9-6, Wednesday to Sunday; closed Monday and Tuesday.*

ANATOLY KESSLER, Moscow-born, runs the adjacent stand specializing in smoked fish appetizers—about thirty-five kinds of salmon, herring, and appetizers to please a partygoer's hunger.

*132 Essex Street. 475-1284. 8-6, Wednesday to Sunday; closed Monday and Tuesday.*

MOISHE'S HOMEMADE KOSHER BAKERY owned by C. Permutter, becomes a hive before the Rosh Hashana and Yom Kippur holidays as customers stop in for *Mandelbread* (almond-flavored sweet bread, on the cookie-dry side of cake, with fruit or chocolate topping) and *Teiglech* (clusters of dough balls pyramided and sprinkled with nuts, drenched in honey); *Hamantaschen* (triangular cakes, popular for Jewish Purim, apricot-, prune-, or poppyseed-filled), honey cakes, and the regular line of bialys, bagels, pumpernickels, challahs (braids or swirled into a graceful peaked loaf) and *Rugelach* (cream-cheese dough, filled with cinnamon, raisins, and nuts, rolled and cut up).

*181 East Houston Street. 475-9624. 7-6, Sunday to Friday; closed Saturday. Phone orders.*

*115 Second Avenue (main branch). 673-0708, 254-8290. 7:30 A.M.-8:30 P.M., Monday to Thursday; 7 to sundown, Friday; closed Saturday; 7 A.M. to 8 P.M., Sunday.*

RUSS & DAUGHTERS, an elegant smoked fish appetizer shop, could pass the white-glove test. Joel Russ, third-generation owner and professional lawyer until 1977, continues the business begun by his grandfather, Mark Russ Federman, in 1914, with his daughters—the young owner's mother and aunts. "My Dad got sick and I left my law firm to run the store. This is my first love," he exclaims, standing near the nine herring varieties, pickled lox, fresh caviar, and smoked fish which the firm wholesales and retails. Caspian Sea caviars are an all-year specialty.

*179 East Houston Street. 475-4880, 4881. 8-7, seven days. Phone orders and delivery to established clientele.*

# CHINATOWN, LITTLE ITALY
## Chinese, Italian, Vietnamese, Thai, Filipino, Burmese, Indonesian, other Oriental Groups, Jewish, etc.

Sour, sweet, bitter, pungent,
all must be tasted.
CHINESE PROVERB

Words do not make flour.
ITALIAN PROVERB

WINDING YOUR WAY toward Chinatown and Little Italy, amble into Columbus Park, a perfect spot to perch on a bench, eat your fruit snack, and gather strength for the orgy of shops facing you. Here, a circular playground is fenced with sturdy iron fencing. Chinese-American youngsters play baseball. Older Chinese watch and chat from benches on the large circular stone path around the park. All around the square the flavor is oriental—Saigon Restaurant, Thai Restaurant, Sun Kwong Lee Corp., Chinese groceries, Han May Meat Market. . . .

Two steps from the park in any direction and you are in Chinatown—another world. On Canal Street, between Mulberry and Lafayette, oriental sellers and shoppers, produce, fish, and fruit blend in a clanging, clattering frenzy, all clamoring for space in Chinatown where it seems the entire oriental New York population meets. It is astounding to visit. On Sunday mornings or late weekday afternoons, you see oriental men and women, slender and serious, smiling and gesturing—some alone, some with families—peering into baskets and stands. Hawkers sell enormous carp, and other entrepreneurs along the curb display lustrous green *Lopeh*—a smooth vegetable thicker than cucumber (the seller calls it a green carrot) good to steam or stir-fry. Bananas, ginger root, *Lo Bok* (Chinese radishes), *Malanga* (a tropical root also called *Yautia, Taro, Tannion*), asparagus beans, anything and everything imaginable when in season. By midday on Sunday, selling reaches a frenzied pitch, when Cadillacs, Buicks, and Oldsmobiles—double parked, many from out of state—clutter the streets. Enthusiasts are on a shopping jaunt in Chinatown!

As you walk through the heart of Chinatown and Little Italy, each street has its own mood. The lines between Chinatown and Little Italy are blurred and they function side by side. Groceries, meat and fish shops, and stunning vegetable displays are everywhere. You wish you could taste and buy them all. You yearn to search beneath the mystery of these incredible shops.

Walking south on Mott, you're bewitched and bedazzled by the staggering number of food shops. Between Grand and Hester streets, count no less than nineteen shops, each with its specialty to draw you into the spell of the Orient with a dash of Italy: Cheong Chain Co., Mandalay Fruit Products, Inc., Leonardo's

Groceries. . . . Then, another thirteen fruit, meat, and grocery shops nourish shoppers between Hester and Canal streets. Before you're totally engulfed by your purchases, step back to Park Street (a narrow lane leads you there near WING FAT CO., INC. at Mott and Pell Streets, page 32) and walk to Park Row. You'll see children at the playground. This, amazingly, is on the opposite end of Columbus Park where the Chinatown tour began.

Chinatown stretches out from Chatham Square like a lively octopus eager to engulf its throngs while the "throngs" flock along Chinatown's "arms," eager to devour all the amazing varieties of available foods. Doyers, Mott, Worth, Park Row, St. James Place—Bowery, Oliver, Catherine, and Division streets, intersecting at Chatham Square, all have foods for you.

Cross Chatham Square (not an easy matter), for example, and walk west along East Broadway (which is Park Row east of the square) for a few blocks and you'll see another blend—Chinese with a traditional Jewish center: Israel Beigel's EAST BROADWAY KOSHER BAKERY *(181 East Broadway)* functions next door to the WEST LAKE NOODLE CO. (page 33). At the corner of Essex and Canal streets at Jewish Passover time, you see a display stand featuring greens and a lemon-like fruit called *Eterog* ("not for eating but for blessing") and feel you are in Israel.

Catherine Street is another "arm" well worth the time to visit for the snack restaurants and seasonal varieties. Fish, fruits, vegetables, pork shops provide many choices from smooth-skinned red chilies and fragrant ginger near live catfish swimming in buckets and jumping crabs in baskets.

Obviously, many of the newer oriental groups—the Vietnamese, Thai, and many Filipinos—shop or open shops in Chinatown. Many Chinese shopkeepers told me they hear oriental languages they do not recognize! Others, such as the Koreans and Japanese, settled and opened shops in other neighborhoods.

Between 11 and 6 it may be impossible to walk, the shoppers and sellers are so abundant. But the mixture of schoolchildren and at least three generations of the childrens' elders makes this a setting unlike any other neighborhood in New York. Take money, there's plenty to buy.

## Mulberry Street

HYFUND CO., INC. has live turtles and carp swimming in the window, almost as active as the ten fish salesmen cleaning and fileting fish in the long shop. The shop, in business since 1972, probably derives its name from *Hai* which means "sea" in Chinese, and you'll find plenty of fresh and frozen seafood to whip up exotic Mandarin, Cantonese, or Hunan dishes. Shellfish have always been high on food lists that stimulate libido (among Chinese and other ethnic groups as well) and at Hyfund, crabs, clams, abalone, mussels, and lobsters are stocked; among the fin fish varieties there are plentiful sea bass, porgies, gray sole (for filet of sole), and small star butterfish (a hybrid of pompano and butterfish). Chuck Lou, one of the owners, suggests a specialty—*Jaung Bat Pan*—a large conch (available frozen), to slice and steam for two minutes; delicious with spicy dressings. Also, near the seafood department, soy sauce, sesame oil, hot red pepper sauce, and Hoisin sauce are available in the smaller grocery department alongside fresh produce.

*75 Mulberry Street. 233-8550, 8551. 8-6:30, seven days. Phone orders. Delivers in Manhattan.*

LUNG MOON BAKERY sells melon, cheese, lotus, black bean, coconut among its delectable Chinese cakes and also makes American cup cakes. Sweet rice cakes (triangular jellied cakes made of rice flour and eaten with the fingers) are also available from owner Y. H. Lum.

*83 Mulberry Street. 349-4945. 8-8, seven days. Phone orders. No deliveries.*

CARMINE CASTALDO, a third-generation Italian meat shop, is like a fish out of water among the Chinese shops. "I'm the only Italian left here," says Blase Castaldo who runs the shop with his brother Vincent. "Now, 90 percent of the clientele is oriental—Chinese, Japanese, Filipino—and customers come from New

Jersey and Connecticut," he adds. Pork, beef, and lamb are
stocked, and veal—though less of it.

*85 Mulberry Street. 962-3830, 3831. 7:30-7, Monday to Friday;
7:30-7:30, Saturday; closed Sunday. Phone orders. Delivers to
restaurants.*

UNITED SUPER MARKET, INC. may be a misleading name for
this lively center, primarily a meat shop (some dried and packaged), oils, red dates, noodles, and *Mui Tsoi* (preserved mustard
greens). Nine salesmen help shoppers and Joe Eng, one of the
partners, offers cooking tips for customers tempted by house specialties—pork sausages (red) and pork sausages with duck and
turkey liver added (darker)—made in the back room. "Cut up and
sauté red sausages with onions, add snow peas and cooked rice;
steam sausage with duck and turkey liver, then cut up." The
clientele (70 percent Chinese) also buys fresh beef and pork, pigs'
feet, tails, livers, hearts, tongue, and cutlets, and ready-to-cook
fish cakes and fish balls.

*84 Mulberry Street. 962-6440, 6441. 9-7, seven days. No phone
orders.*

CHINESE AMERICAN TRADING CO., INC., stocked with ample staple and unusual Chinese ingredients, is in its second generation with an active young man helping in the business his
mother began in 1962. He visits and buys from the annual Chinese food fair in Canton, China, from Hong Kong, Taiwan, Singapore, and other Asian markets and from Switzerland and other
European countries. The long shop is full of eye-riveting stocks
ranging from rices ("white long grain for Chinese and Cantonese
dishes, short grain for Japanese and Mandarin, and glutinous or
sticky for Thai dishes and Chinese rice cakes," says the owner),
tapiocas, flours from sweet potato to *somen* (alimentary paste),
tapioca, fresh and dried noodles, all manner of sauces, fruits and
condiments in cans and bottles (many packaged under the firm's
label) and even bamboo leaves (used to make the *May 5 Festival
Rice Cakes*, recipe, page 229).

*91 Mulberry Street. 267-5224. 9-8, seven days. Wholesale
phone orders and deliveries only.*

LA BELLA FERRARA pastry shop is a cozy haven tucked under a canopy among many coffee houses. Here you can indulge in the ubiquitous *Cannoli* and *Sfogliatella* (puff pastries derived from the Italian Sfoglia [leafy], filled with pastry cream), second in popularity only to *Cannolis*. There are fifteen kinds of cookies and eight varieties of biscuits. In business here since 1932, the baker makes all kinds of cakes to your order. Mary Compoccia has served shoppers in the shop since the late 1960s.

*108 Mulberry Street. 966-7867. 9-midnight, Monday to Friday; 9 Saturday A.M.-2 A.M. Sunday morning; closed Sunday after 2 A.M.*

ESPOSITO BROS. is an old-fashioned meat shop. A butcher block stands at the doorway by the sawdust-strewn floor. There are old hooks for the meats, the same ones used by Anna Esposito who began the business in 1926 (her name is written in bricks on the building across the street). Her son John is now in charge and veal is the specialty.

*120 Mulberry Street. 226-0050. 7-7, Monday to Saturday; closed Sunday. Phone orders. Delivers.*

## Grand Street, LITTLE ITALY

F. ALLEVA, the oldest manufacturer of ricotta and mozzarella in the country, is among the handful of very special shops still holding their own in burgeoning Chinatown. A fourth-generation business, the pristine store is white-tiled and marble-floored with green trim. Robert Alleva, Jr. carries on what his great-grandmother began. Specialties are still ricotta and mozzarella (about 2,000 pounds of each per week are made in the firm's Schenectady factory and smoked in the ovens in the shop's back room). Other cheeses include Italian *Provolone affumicate, Scamorze, Manteche, Fiaschi, Caciocavalli, Parmigiano, Romano, Pecorino.* Sausages and fresh breads are also available.

*188 Grand Street. 226-7990, 7991. 8:30-6, Monday to Saturday; 8:30-2, Sunday. Phone orders. Delivers.*

PIEDMONTE HOMEMADE RAVIOLI CO., INC., in business

since 1920, specializes in meat-stuffed *Cannelloni* rolls, *Ravioli* (cheese and meat), cheese-filled *Manicotti, Tortellini* (enriched with prosciutto)—regular and small, *Gnocchi, Cavatelli* (they look like pine nuts), *Ognolotti* (tiny half-moons), *Fettuccine, Lasagne*, gluten macaroni, *Tagliolini* (spaghetti-thin noodles), *Tagliatelle* (medium noodles)—all available in white or green (made with spinach). These specialties charm you into stocking up cupboard and freezer. Six workers bustling around in the back room factory energize the ravioli-sized shop.

*190 Grand Street. 226-0475. 8:30-6, Monday to Saturday; 8:30-1, Sunday. Phone orders. No deliveries.*

FERRARA is a well-known confectionery/coffee shop and the remodeled brick façade with large picture windows makes it look like a modern newcomer among the older buildings. Indoors, the marble floor and lusciously warm wood paneling are dazzling backdrops for the *bellissima* Italian specialties. (The shop claims to be the oldest in the United States, functioning here since 1892!) Ferrara sells its own homemade ice creams, ices, rum cakes, pastries, and a line of pasta under the "DeChico" label (the latter carried at Piedmonte Homemade Ravioli Co., Inc.). Ferrara also runs shops in Milan and Montreal, according to Vinnie Lepore, shop manager.

*195-201 Grand Street. 226-6150. 7:30-midnight, seven days. Phone orders. Delivers.*

ITALIAN FOOD CENTER is a hive—a large and varied grocery and deli. Customers line up in front for lunchmeats. In the back they choose pasta, oils, imported sardines and anchovies, tomatoes, and cheeses at the cheese counter. Joseph De Mattia, the owner since 1962, stocks truffles and caviar, "slow movers but usually in stock." Dried codfish is also available here.

*186 Grand Street. 925-2954. 8-7:30, seven days.*

## Canal Street

KAM MAN FOOD PRODUCTS, INC., a large shop, is an excellent spot to look into (especially on a quiet morning). It's usually a polite bedlam with workers unpacking boxes amid thronged aisles and counters. At the entrance, among the intriguing and mysterious ingredients sure to bedazzle you, are enormous jars of ginseng (the ancient alleged aphrodisiac, currently favored as a tea to relieve everything but taxes). Dried anchovies, oysters, shrimp, mussels, abalone, mushrooms and other fungi, are available in profusion, neatly packaged and labeled in English and Chinese. In back, at the produce department, seasonal roots and vegetables, bamboo and bean sprouts, *Bok (Pak) Choy* (Chinese cabbage) and *Kun Tsoi* (Chinese celery) are staples. *Tofu* (bean curd), young corn, octopus, and *Hoi Sam* (Sea "Cucumber," recipe, page 256)— talk about phallic foods!—are available on a row in front of the produce. Stored at eye level, frozen foods include prepared sauces, mixes, soups, meats, and fish. Also, fresh meats, preserved mustard greens, duck eggs, noodles, and other prized Chinese ingredients can be found in this amazing cornucopia.

*200 Canal Street. 571-0171, 0330, 0331. 9-9:30, Sunday to Thursday; 9-9, Friday and Saturday.*

## Mott Street

DOMINIC DE SANTIS & SONS, INC. is a meat shop. Collapse onto one of the stools provided for shoppers in the tiny space (only old-fashioned shops, it seems, encourage such civilized customs as sitting). Carmine DeSantis, a short, black-haired man with glasses and dimples, is a third-generation member of the family business, along with his brother Dominic. The shop stocks all kinds of sausages, beef, veal, pork, and poultry for the Chinese and Italian clientele. "Most of our customers live in the co-ops on Fulton Street between Gold and Pearl. The co-ops have saved our business," he declares.

*158 Mott Street. 925-4540. 8-6, Monday to Saturday; closed Sunday. Phone orders. Delivery in area.*

FRETTA BROS., an Italian pork shop in business since 1906, tempts you with spicy, smoky sausages in every conceivable shape, neatly lined up all along the ceiling and in the adjacent back room. Quiet, cool, and clean, this store will provide everything you ever wanted to know about Italian sausages.

*116 Mott Street. 226-0232. 8-6:30, Tuesday to Saturday; 9-2, Sunday; closed Monday. Phone orders.*

CANTON NOODLE MANUFACTURING CO., INC. is not a conventional shop. You walk through a door with the firm name over it (next to a fruit shop), walk directly into a long white factory—everything bright and floury. Here, sons Edward and Richard are as active as founder-father Jimmy Eng, whom I met when taking food classes on field trips to Chinatown. New York-born Eddie, a tall young man on the plump side and his wife, Lailin, born in Hong Kong, work side by side. "I've learned the business from the beginning," Eddie says. Lailin wears a Canton Noodle T-shirt with "The next best thing to rice" printed on the back. They both wear white aprons and nets to keep hair clean because the floor and their faces and hands are snowy with flour! Richard dashes back and forth between the tables. "I learned a lot about food watching other people cook," he reveals. You'll find egg roll wrappers (2-pound and 5-pound packages), wonton wrappers, *Suey Koy* wrappers (like wonton wrappers but round), fresh egg noodles, chow mein, raw mein, and dried mein, bean sprouts, fortune and almond cakes. Lailin suggests stuffing the *Suey Koy* wrappers with seasoned pork and steaming (for an appetizer) or serving in broth (for a soup). (For filling ideas, see pages 296-303).

*101 Mott Street. 226-3276, 8037. 7:30-3, Monday to Saturday; closed Sunday.*

SONICO TRADING CO., INC., a narrow, packed shop (just off Mott Street), blends Vietnamese with Chinese. The owner is Meng Hua, a tiny Chinese woman born in Vietnam. Catering to both groups, this shop is recommended by Vietnamese acquaintances. Should you need delicate rice noodle skins (called rice paper), lemon grass, sauces, chewy black tree fungus and mushrooms, and bean threads, they're all here. The owner offers her version of famed *Cha Gio* spring rolls of Vietnam (page 300).

*87-A Bayard Street. 267-1579. 9:30-7:30, seven days. Phone, mail (UPS and airmail).*

SOUTHEAST ASIA FOOD TRADING CO. stocks Indonesian ingredients—dried, canned, bottled, and bagged. Although some of the stock is not always identified, owner Chee Yip knows everything by name and since 1956 has run a tidy shop where you can hear a pin drop. Among the neatly stacked plastic bags are *Salam* (Indonesian bay) leaves, *Kemiri* yellow nuts, dried lemon leaf and lemon grass, and *Laos*, the spice root. *Trassi* (shrimp concentrate) is usually on hand as are jars with *Sambal* sauce mixtures (see recipe for *Sambal*, page 187), *Nasi Goreng* (onions, garlic and spices), *Bami Goreng*, and other pre-mixed spices to help shorten preparation time. Chinese ingredients are also stocked abundantly.

*68A Mott Street. 431-5012. 9:30-6:30, six days; closed Wednesdays. No mail orders.*

TAI PEI, INC. is handy to visit, although not the only Chinese and Japanese sake specialty shop in Chinatown. You'll find cooking and serving spirits here, of the oriental variety, and some European and domestic wines as well. Recently, a customer asked for *Mao Tai* (a powerful Chinese liquor I tasted in Beijing, China, served during banquets with the toast *Kam Pai*—bottoms up). Although usually available, it was out of stock.

*53 Mott Street. 962-1982. 10-9, Monday to Saturday; closed Sunday.*

At WONTON KING., INC., 72 Mott Street—one of several soup restaurants—Thomas Ju stimulates your appetite as he cooks wontons in the window. Indulge in a hearty snack, and try the soup at home (page 200).

CATHAY HARDWARE is the most familiar to me of the cutlery shops, specializing in oriental china and utensils, as well as cutlery. This is where I bought my woks, stands, cleavers, stirrers, wok scrubber, strainer, bamboo steamers, and Chinese soup bowls and spoons, tea cups and pot, and can vouch for their quality. The shop stocks all sorts of intriguing items you'll need to serve an eight- to fifteen-course banquet. Chinese is the major language spoken here, but someone always translates and the sellers are friendly, the merchandise neatly displayed. Victor Chin, the manager, is very helpful.

*49 Mott Street. 962-6648. 10-8 six days; closed Wednesday.*

WING WOH LUNG CO. is yet another traditional Chinese shop with many Chinese-speaking helpers (when six men take a lunch break and sit around the back table eating rice, another six or seven salesmen serve in the L-shaped shop). Well-stocked fish, meat, and grocery departments provide a remarkable array of foods.

*50 Mott Street. 962-3459. 8-7:30, seven days. Phone and mail orders. No deliveries.*

WING FAT CO., INC., importer, exporter, and restaurant supplier, is the real heart of Chinatown for me and offers the best variety of Chinese ingredients in an unchanging, old-fashioned setting. Leading from the door left, about five feet above floor level, is a windowed box for the cashier-bookkeeper. Facing the entrance, about five feet from the door, is the meat case including fresh pork cuts, beef, and poultry inside the case, with roasted poultry and pork hung on hooks above the case at the left. Straight along the top, on hooks, are varieties of sausages and dried and smoked meats. Fresh cuts in the case include spareribs, oxtails, stomachs, flank steaks, ducks, and chickens.

Lining window cases—a custom in traditional Chinese groceries—are roots, stalks, and vegetables. These include fresh *Taro* root (see recipes, pages 224 and 264), ginger root, lotus root, radish, Chinese cabbage, celery cabbage, snow peas, and continuing along the right of the store area—in boxes or bags—spinach, coriander, mustard greens, bean sprouts, scallions, and turnips. Here one finds snails and clams filling baskets in large quantities; directly behind, the fish case with fresh varieties inside and dried ones hung above. Some fresh types include smelts, sole, and red snapper. Dried sole and dried bean curd skin hang above.

Wing Fat has been in business since the 1920s, first as a restaurant supply house, then expanded to retail. Jay Lee, the manager, has been here more than thirty years and notes that lotus root and water chestnuts are usually stocked in the refrigerator. Generally, Wing Fat is an excellent barometer of available foods in Chinatown.

*33-35 Mott Street. 962-0433, 0398. 8-9, seven days. Phone orders. Deliveries only to restaurants.*

QUONG YUEN SHING & CO. has been at this address and owned by the same family for 100 years! Utensils and porcelains, gift items, and cookery-related supplies are available (this firm also sells groceries wholesale to restaurants from another warehouse).

*32 Mott Street. 962-6280, 6257. 9-5, seven days; closed major holidays. Phone orders. Delivers by UPS.*

FUNG WONG BAKERY SHOP, has cases full of almond cookies, cherry, cashew nut, egg-yolk cakes, fruit cakes, lotus seed cakes, rice donuts with black bean filling sprinkled with sesame seeds, in various shapes (fish, lion, Buddha). And a fried bowknot crinkly pastry (no one knows the Chinese name) reminds me of the Greek pastry *Diples* (except that the Hellenic variety is dipped in warm honey and sprinkled with nuts, and the Chinese version is dipped into caramelized sugar that hardens when cool).

*30 Mott Street. 267-4037. 9-9:30, seven days.*

JING CHEONG MEAT MARKET, INC., a small, tidy shop in business since the 1970s, abounds with young butchers who practically greet you at the door. Catering to Chinese shoppers, the stocks include pork butts and spareribs to barbecue. "Just go over to the grocery and buy barbecue sauce and put on the spareribs before broiling," says bilingual Hong Kong-born owner Siu Man Sat. Sausages, oxtails, chicken wings, and other meat specialties are stocked here.

*19 Mott Street. 233-0644. 8-9, seven days.*

WEST LAKE NOODLE CO., since the 1970s young and lively with thirty to thirty-five noodle experts, is the only Chinatown noodle company selling Kosher products. Ho Sing Lee, the slender Hong Kong-born manager, darts back and forth between the back room (where noodles are made and visitors not allowed) and the office near the entrance where shoppers may buy five-pound packages of the company's products: egg roll, dumpling, and wonton wrappers, fresh egg noodles (fine), dried noodles (12½" called "Chinese spaghetti"), wet noodles (about ½-inch), and fried noodles. The last are very popular with Jewish shoppers in this very traditional Jewish neighborhood. West Lake is named for West Lake, in Hangzhou, China, no doubt the most beautiful lake I've ever seen. And Rita Lam and Jennie Low in the office shared their favorite recipe (page 201).

*183 East Broadway. 677-8865-7. 8-6, Monday to Friday; 8-4, Saturday and Sunday.*

# SOHO
## International, Italian, French, Japanese, Chinese, Asian-Indian

*Bread and cheese is a medicine for the well.*

FRENCH PROVERB

WITH A "Bohemian" image created by its many artists, sculptors, musicians, dancers, and potters, Soho (an acronym for South of Houston) may be a neighborhood in transition. Even so, its food shops are multiplying and thriving. A short walk northwest of Little Italy and a few blocks south of Greenwich Village, Soho develops its own character.

Traditionally an industrial community, Soho gradually attracted artists seeking Manhattan living quarters at affordable prices. Among those drawn to Soho in the early 1970s, a young woman who asked to be identified as Francine, described her experiences and the food shops she enjoys. Around her, old factory buildings cast heavy shadows on the narrow streets. She set down her shopping bags to reminisce.

"When I moved to Soho it was a reasonable place to live—rents were low. I shopped in Little Italy, Sullivan Street, Thompson and Prince Street stores. By the mid 1970s, two-thirds of West Broadway filled with artists and the ambiance was very exciting. Gradually, Soho changed. People were forced out by higher rents. Rents skyrocketed. Buildings were sold to develop high-priced co-ops, condos, and lofts and are now selling for $100,000 to $300,000," she exclaimed. Incensed by the higher costs, she and her neighbors are in a dilemma. "I like it here, but it is very expensive compared to the 1970s." As for shopping, she enjoys Greenwich Village. "It has more of a street feeling than Soho, more relaxed, more of a neighborhood. All the shops! It has always been a residential section," she added. "In Greenwich Village I shop at BALDUCCI'S [page 45], and for fish at the BLEECKER STREET FISH MARKET [page 46]," she noted. "And in Soho I have the little bakery around the corner [meaning VESUVIO BAKERY, page 37] and DEAN & DE LUCA [page 37]. The shops are great."

Tucked in among the galleries and restaurants, the food shops draw shoppers—mostly very young and fashionably dressed ("not as punky as Greenwich Village," noted one Soho resident)—who seem to enjoy distinctiveness in food and dress.

NOBLE & BOWMAN, a cozy tea and coffee shop, displays fresh

green plants in the red brick store's picture windows. Owned since 1975 by Hugh Noble and Jerry Bowman, more than forty coffees and fifty teas (Japanese, Chinese, and Indian) are available. House blend coffee is a subtle mixture of mocha, French roast, and Mexican roast. Spicy tea blends broadcast their flavors: hibiscus flower, rose hips, orange peel, peppermint, and lemon grass, spearmint, cinnamon bark, orange peel, clove, and cardamom, among others.

*136 Seventh Avenue, South. 691-4757. 11-9, Monday to Saturday; Noon-6 Sunday. Phone, mail, and airmail orders.*

DEAN & DE LUCA's name on the window could easily be missed, but it would be a pity. Visit the scrumptious shop, one of two operated by Joel Dean and Giorgio De Luca. Tastefully and simply arranged to enhance the high-quality foods, specialties include cheeses ("200 to 500 depending on seasonal availability"), coffees and teas, fresh herbs and vegetables, baked goods, mustards, vinegars, meals and flours, nuts and dried fruits, jellies and jams. At the entrance, clusters of fresh basil, tarragon, rosemary, mint, thyme with Florida arugula, *courgettes* (finger-sized zucchini and flowers), Italian *radicchio* (lettuce), *haricot verts* (French green beans), purple beans, Italian eggplants, "All-blues" purple potatoes, and other seasonal vegetables mesmerize you. Brahms or Chopin music augments the superb taste here. Roam along the aisles of the massive, high-ceilinged shop with its original revolving ceiling fans and white tiles. Myriad copper pots and pans hang from the ceiling, and in the utensil department in back ("one third of the sales"), a spice rack arranged like lab test tubes displays forty spices, corked—just one of many temptations in the rich medley of specialties and imports.

*121 Prince Street. 254-7774. 10-7, Monday to Saturday; 10-6, Sunday. UPS mail order (delivery by outside delivery service). Catalog only for restaurants.*

VESUVIO BAKERY, a tiny loaf shop, about 8 × 10 feet of old-fashioned flavor, is *big* on Italian white and whole wheat breads, braids, *Frizelli* round toasts, pepper biscuits, four-inch sesame bread sticks, and plain biscuits. Anthony Dapolito, the original owner since 1932, bakes breads in the downstairs brick ovens. Vesuvio also supplies restaurants and hotels.

*160 Prince Street. 925-8248, 8027. 6-8, Monday to Saturday; closed Sunday. Phone orders. Delivers.*

RAOUL'S BOUCHERIE, owned by RAOUL'S RESTAURANT across the street, is a new market in a black and white tile setting designed to appear nostalgically *old*. And it does, with Gallic flair and personal service. Joe Broder, culinary instructor and butcher par excellence, bones capons (see page 277), and prepares French racks of veal and butterflied leg of lamb, among shop specialties. Other offerings: Vell & Evans poultry; varieties of patés, hams, salamis, lunch meats, sweetbreads, and calves liver.

*179 Prince Street. 674-0708. 10-8, Monday to Saturday; closed Sunday.*

SOHO FISH STORE stocks a generous supply of tuna, striped bass, and other filets sought for *Sashimi* (see recipe, page 252). Neatly displayed in cases are varieties of fin fish, fresh clams and oysters, scallops, cleaned calamari, shrimp, live lobsters, and soft shell crabs. Hyung Kim owns the immaculate shop.

*438 West Broadway at Prince Street. 925-7039. 9-9, Monday to Saturday; closed Sunday.*

# GREENWICH VILLAGE, EAST VILLAGE, AND UNION SQUARE
## Italian, Spanish, Portuguese, French, Polish, Ukrainian, Russian, Swiss, German, Chinese, Japanese, Asian-Indian, Mexican

*Of soup and love the first is best.*
PORTUGUESE PROVERB

*Sauerkraut and pork banish all care.*
GERMAN PROVERB

THE MAGNETISM of Greenwich Village lures, warms, and hugs you—stimulating without overwhelming. You feel drawn to the narrow and wider streets of Greenwich Village and East Village (nicknamed The Villages) and want to belong to them. Enjoying the fame of Paris's Left Bank and the variety of London's Soho, The Villages provide a wonderfully rich New York environment enhanced by centuries of food-shop history.

You can easily belong by sharing in the many neighborhood offerings—chic boutiques and fine theater life, intimate restaurants and old, old taverns, the culture of university life and publishing houses, and especially food stores—many second- and third-generation enterprises—and the friendly people in them.

I have always loved the zigzag approach from Astor Place to Broadway to Waverly Place to New York University on Washington Square—the heart of The Villages. From this grand, tree-studded square (which reminds me of my hometown Philadelphia's great squares), where, in warm weather, students relax and older folks play checkers while youngsters play, you can walk in any direction for fabulous food adventures. A few streets south, begin at charming Bleecker Street with its small shops pulling you back and forth in a really outdoor market setting. Here you'll meet residents who have shopped here for years, store owners running across the street for bread, coffee, or meats at a neighboring shop, the sophisticated shoppers who like the foods and like to be seen in The Villages. A short trot westward on Avenue of the Americas (Sixth Avenue), though you see the twin towers of the World Trade Center on Wall Street to the south of you and skyscrapers uptown to the north, you keep close touch with the shops. There are family stores like JEFFERSON MARKET (page 44) and BALDUCCI'S (page 45) with their well-nourished roots deep in the past. On Christopher Street, McNULTY'S (page 43) emits early-American charm with its coffee and tea scents, while LI-LAC CHOCOLATES (page 43) perfects the treats it has been making for decades. Newer shops like TUTTA PASTA (page 48), making pasta the Old World way, and traditional ones like THE PORTUGUESE-AMERICAN DELI (page 49) and CASA MONEO (page 49), tucked into other busy streets, remind you of

The Villages' ethnic heritage surviving strongly to give a flavorful food gift to us today.

Close to the Hudson River you'll see, in the wee hours, the bustling wholesale meat market. On West Street the old Gansevoort Market still functions. Pausing in his late-morning activities, Walter Harris, of Loew Avenue Beef Co., Inc. (actually a wholesaler specializing in lamb with partner Paul Daitch), is a second-generation meat expert. Following his father's trade, he remembers the open farmer's market on Little West 12th Street and heard from his elders about the nineteenth-century open-air market on ground donated by the Astor family. The city operated the market as it did the other public markets until the end of World War II.

Meanwhile, recounts Walter Harris, large packing companies (Swift, Armour, Wilson) attracted to the New York market early in the century, gradually lost their business; local companies gained control of the meat business. Loew employs some forty people handling domestic lamb and some frozen lamb from New Zealand and Australia. Commenting on the New York retail meat business, he finds prospects better, distribution advanced and, locally, Hispanic populations have "been good influences for the New York meat business." All around the narrow streets where there are large meat houses, you see meats unloaded in cobbled paths used long before the advent of cars and trucks.

Greenwich Village's links to the early public markets are reflected not only in landmarks but also in the people's devotion to small stores. Writing about this phenomenon in "Old Days and Ways of the Markets of Greenwich Village," * Nathaniel S. Olds noted:

Perhaps nowhere else in Manhattan is so much personal shopping done and certainly nowhere else are there more small stores catering to neighborhood needs. These are, along with the supers, an outgrowth of public markets, and

* *The Villager,* Greenwich Village, New York, December 17, 1942.

probably owe their origin in many instances to the break-up of the Village's market centers.

That the most famous of all Village markets was Jefferson there can be no doubt. All local residents except the more recent generations can remember its stalls and its busy activity and the meat market men in straw hats.

He refers to the public markets built primarily to serve the Villagers: first, the Greenwich Market, built in 1800 on Brennan Street (now Spring); the Clinton Market, opened in 1827 on the site of the Holland Tunnel entrance; Weehawken Market, at West Street and Weehawken "where the public took things in their own hands and called it Greenwich Market (since the forerunner had already closed down). But the most famous of all was Jefferson Market, opened on Sixth Avenue in 1832, where six butcher stands were sold at public auction (bringing from $575 to $1,405), and Thomas F. DeVoe, author of the fine study, *The Market Book: A History of the Public Markets of the City of New York*, was a butcher in that market. In typical Village tradition, the current privately owned JEFFERSON MARKET (page 44) adopted the name of the famous old public market. And the spired brick New York Public Library a few blocks from it is called the Jefferson Market branch, another reminder of the nineteenth-century market.

On the east side, at Astor Place, more reminders of food-shop history, again, of course, with contemporary touches. Young musicians often play their instruments in the shadow of Bernard Rosenthal's huge cube sculpture. Across Fourth Avenue at Cooper Square, the pink stone Cooper Union, a landmark since it was built by Peter Cooper in 1859, dominates the area. Gone from the square since 1911, however, is the old Tompkins Market on Third Avenue. From this market, viewers could look down into the Third Avenue Trotting Course where steeds were trotted every afternoon. This disappeared as cobblestone pavements were laid for the omnibus traveling uptown to Yorkville and Harlem.

Today when you cross this enormous square and walk eastward on St. Mark's Place, you see the many old clothes shops that attract the young and avant-garde fashionables, resident artists, writers, and dancers to the Villages. Along Seventh Street, don't miss McSorley's Old Ale House (15 E. 7th St.), built in 1854, with its sprinkling of sawdust indoors and original green barrels at the front door.

And in the East Village, the Polish and Ukrainian sausage shops await you, since the silent movie days, with their fabulous spice and garlic aromas and Old World techniques. Aware of the ethnic influences, old timers admit changes in the populations. "There used to be more Italians," one resident said. "But the Polish and Ukrainians settled here." Now you'll find Russian, Swiss, German foods in addition to those of the early settlers.

## Christopher Street

LI-LAC CHOCOLATES, owned by Ed Bond, features delectable chocolates in a lilac setting. Chocolates are prepared in the back room factory by hefty Jimmy DiLorenzo, who has been with the firm since 1932. Best seller: French Assortment (64 chocolates in a box); also, fruit and nut, cashew, pecan, or walnut clusters, fudge, French mints, and other ravishing specialties from hazelnut truffles to butter crunch. Manager John Rath, wearing a lilac apron, suggests a perfect homemade dessert (recipe, page 331) using the shop's bulk chocolate.

*120 Christopher Street. 242-7374. 10-10, Tuesday to Saturday; Noon-8, Sunday and Monday. UPS mail orders and air mail (catalog).*

McNULTY'S TEA & COFFEE CO., in business since 1895, currently owned by Tai Lee, has been at this spot since 1942. In this irresistible shop you will hear Bach and Debussy music, see an aged wooden counter and floor, wonderful antique bins, and will smell the aroma of coffee—American, French, Italian—as well as seventy kinds of black, oolong, green, blended, and flavored teas. Bins, jars, and bags are clearly labeled. I found Lung Ching Dragon Well green tea, a flavorful variety from the tea commune I visited in Hangzhou, China. Anton Pavlovski, curly-haired manager, helps undecided shoppers. Usually, "after-dinner coffee should be medium strength," he suggests. "A stronger coffee roast climaxes a French dinner, such as a French or New Orleans roast, and a Colombian/Italian style roast is fine following Italian food." Coffee makers are also stocked.

*109 Christopher Street. 242-5351. 11-11, Monday to Saturday; 1-7:30, Sunday. Mail orders (catalog).*

## Avenue of the Americas

At the JEFFERSON MARKET, vigorous salesmen filling orders and local shoppers create a contagious hustle-bustle in the very large store. In its heyday, the *old* Jefferson Market was a Greenwich Village center and the butchers received center-stage attention. Today, John Montuori and his son John, Jr., along with four or five butchers, are supremely jovial—enticing shoppers to their stellar attractions. You'll find meat in a wide assortment and the spicy aromas permeating from the cold-cut counter will tantalize you until you succumb and buy. In the adjoining section, there are nineteen trays brimful of fish and a lively Maine lobster, weighed, clambers over the scale. The central grocery department is a treasure chest of baked goods, canned specialties, and twelve shelves full of cheeses. Seasonal fruits and vegetables are always featured on the outdoor stand. Unpretentious, fresh and wholesome, the Jefferson Market is a joy to visit.

*455 Avenue of the Americas. 675-2277, 8, 9. 8-9, Monday to Saturday; 9-8, Sunday. Phone orders. Delivers.*

GREEN VILLAGE FRUIT AND VEGETABLES GROCERY beckons you with a dazzling pavement display created by Hyong Kim (pronounced Hong Keem) and many helpful relatives. For the mixed ethnic clientele, fresh produce is the shop's major focus. There are also sixteen types of coffee beans and oriental condiments, instant soups and staple ingredients on indoor shelves.

*468 Avenue of the Americas. 255-4728. 24 hours, seven days. Phone orders. Delivers.*

YOUNG FISH MARKET, a flourishing new shop, open since 1979, stocks Florida shrimp, cleaned calamari, scallops, fresh tuna, filets for *Sashimi* (recipe, page 252), and a dozen more varieties displayed along the green-framed window. Young Ko and his son, James, replenish the chipped ice and fish for Korean and other mixed ethnic clientele. James offers a tasty recipe: "Brush filet of sole with milk, broil, season with salt, pepper, and lemon juice."

*491 Avenue of the Americas. 924-7912. 10-7:30, Monday to Saturday; closed Sunday.*

BALDUCCI'S is another world if you can find the door to enter into it. Enticed by the elegant exterior signs, "Prime Meats and Sea Food," "World of Fresh Fruits," "World of Fine Cheese," "International Delicacies," *and* its reputation, you pull at the locked doors. Then the security guard inside motions you to a door at the left. Once inside, face-to-face with the enormous, curved seafood department, you hear piped-in Muzak, an impersonal voice calling through loudspeakers for Bill Bowers (manager of some of the departments) and salesgirls urging "Get your number for service." Your first reaction may be to label the shop a department store and "big business." Quickly, however, the varied departments— all those promised on the signs plus more—and the quality of the foods—fresh Matisse colors, impeccable garnishes and displays— draw you closer, as paintings do in a museum. And you discover the uniqueness of the store. In the meat case, fresh quails, calf's brains, liver, veal kidneys, chicken livers, and breakfast sausages are displayed on oval white platters; a tidy row of green watermelons lines the floor along the case. In low baskets, nine kinds of legumes are lovely to behold below a five-tiered aisle display of heaped fresh fruits. There are whole shelves of imported varieties of chestnuts, honeys, bins of golden pasta, fourteen kinds of sauces including *Prittanesca* (clams), *Marinara* (tomatoes), *Forestiera* (mushroom). Another five-tiered ceiling-to-floor display contains seasonal fruits, oils and vinegars, and tempting olives. The bakery department is superb, and the huge deli section features homemade foods (like *Scungilli* [conch] salad, Tripe *Fra Diavolo* [winy-herb sauce] and Artichokes Vinaigrette) that seem to be made in heaven. "Mama" Balducci shares a recipe (page 225). Black truffles, *Sopressata* salami, paté, Norwegian smoked trout, and wild *Porcini* mushrooms are among specialties (available through the mail order catalog). Excited by the marvelous array of foods, you move from exhibit to exhibit until you pull yourself away again into the real world . . . if you can find the exit.

*424 Avenue of the Americas. 673-2600. 7-8:30, Monday to Saturday; 7-6:30, Sunday. Phone orders. Mail orders (catalog).*

## Bleecker Street

ROCCO'S is a friendly pastry and coffee house where you can relax over a pastry and espresso. Then you beam over the Italian pastries, Milanese style *Panettone, Torrone,* and eight flavors of homemade ices. Franco Generoso, an Italian ice specialist born in Calabria, Italy and member of Rocco's family, suggests dessert ideas: "Following any dinner," fill parfait or stemmed goblets with chocolate, lemon, and cremolata ices; or, for a fruit combination, try layering cherry, lemon, and pineapple ice flavors. Serve with pine nuts.

*243 Bleecker Street. 242-6031. 8-11, seven days. Phone orders. No deliveries.*

BLEECKER STREET PASTRY SHOP has been at the same location since the 1930s. Donato and Lucia Di Saverio, an amiable and talented couple, have run the shop since 1966. Their young son and daughter help out in summer. From the bakery in the back room emerge cookies and cakes (plain and fruit), *Panettone* (Milano style with raisins and nuts in 1-, 2-, 3-, 4-, and 5-pound sizes, and the smaller Genovese type packed with light and dark raisins, aniseed, pine nuts, and fennel seeds). The Di Saverios also make delectable fruit tarts and coffee cakes. Sample some of their delicious pastries at the little tables where rich wood paneling and a superbly designed hexagonal tile floor in rust and gray colors visually sweeten your snack.

*245 Bleecker Street. 242-4959. 7:30-7, Monday to Thursday; 7:30-7:30, Friday and Saturday; 7:30-4, Sunday.*

BLEECKER STREET FISH MARKET'S slogan is "If it swims, we have it." A wholesaler and retailer, the little shop is stocked with all kinds of seafood and has been run by the Ruggiero family since 1937. The current owner, Francesco Ruggiero, will sell you fish for everything from *Cassolette* (page 260) to *Sha o Pokkum* (page 281).

> *253 Bleecker Street. 929-8789. 8-6:30, Monday to Thursday; 8-7, Friday and Saturday; closed Sunday. Phone orders. No deliveries.*

FAICCO PORK STORES, INC. is so rich in sausages and salamis, the scents ensnare you at the door. Established in 1900 and now run by brothers Joseph and Eddie Faicco, Faicco also makes smoked mozzarella daily. "Italian sausage is our specialty," declares manager Tony Cetta. Salamis are available in three sizes, spicy or mild, and the fat and thin sausages are made with seven seasonings including hot, fennel, cheese, and mild. Plenty of fixings for antipasto parties. Faicco also runs two shops in Brooklyn.

> *260 Bleecker Street. 243-1974. 8-6, Tuesday to Thursday; 8-7, Friday and Saturday; 9-2, Sunday; closed Monday.*

ZITO & SONS BAKERY, INC. bakes white and whole wheat Italian bread in nine sizes. Frances Zito with her four brothers runs the old shop, open since 1925, and finds that local customers are keener than ever about Italian bread. Zito's may be tiny, but downstairs, in the bakery, there are two large brick ovens where four Portuguese, one Cuban, one Argentinian, and one Spanish baker bake the Italian breads! (A 1939 photo of this charming shop's window in the New York Central Research Library archives features round and long loaves for 5 cents.)

> *259 Bleecker Street. 929-6139. 6-6:30, Monday to Saturday; 6-2, Sunday. No phone orders.*

At GREENWICH VILLAGE FISH CO., Vincent Gurrera cries "Eat fish, live longer!" promoting the salmon, halibut, swordfish, and shellfish in the shop. The fish shop has been run by father and son Anthony and Joe Gurrera since 1967. Anthony's brother and helper, Vincent, tells his perfect dinner: Broiled swordfish steaks seasoned with garlic and parsley with a dash of lemon juice, served with broccoli florets, fresh peas, *Insalata*, crusty bread, and red wine, finished off with ice cold watermelon.

*265 Bleecker Street. 929-8042. 7-8, Monday to Saturday; closed Sunday. Phone orders. Delivers.*

O. OTTOMANELLI & SONS meat market has many specialties, but filet of veal seasoned with garlic, prosciutto, and other seasonings, ready to roast, is the *pièce de résistance. Osso Bucco* and other veal roasts are also prepared by American-born Jerry and his brothers who help father Onofrio, who was born in Bari, Italy. The Ottomanellis also sell their homemade sausages, wild boar, and venison (in season), wild game, pork, lamb, and beef.

*281 Bleecker Street. 675-4217. 8-6:30, Monday to Friday; 7-6, Saturday; closed Sunday. Phone orders. Delivers in Greenwich Village and Soho.*

APHRODISIA is a shop with a contemporary air. Hundreds of herbs, spices, and oils are stocked in bins and eighty jars are full of culinary spices and herbs for Oriental, Asian, Indian, French, and Spanish cuisines. Each side of the central aisle holds twenty-four bins with herbs and there are sixty jars more full of leaves, barks, flower herbs, and seasonings. In back, there are fifteen kinds of wheats, grains, and flours, a dozen varieties of dried fruits, nuts, and orange blossom and wildflower honeys.

*282 Bleecker Street. 989-6440. 11-7, Monday to Friday; 10-7, Saturday; Noon-5, Sunday. Mail order & catalog available.*

## Other Streets in the Neighborhood

TUTTA PASTA, INC. is exactly that—pasta, pasta, and more pasta. Black-haired Signora DiNatale packages homemade *Tortellini* (green and white) and black-eyed daughter sells ravioli, *Cavatelli, Manicotti, gnocci*, shells, and lasagne all made by "Maestro" DiNatale, an inventive pasta maker. The DiNatales also run TUTTA PASTA II, a take-out shop two doors away.

*22-24 Carmine Street. 242-4961. 7-8, Monday to Saturday; closed Sunday. Phone orders. Delivers.*

THE PORTUGUESE-AMERICAN DELI increasingly stocks many Brazilian foods for Brazilians living in Manhattan. Portuguese oils, cheeses and *Linguica*, a mild smoked sausage, are also available. Owners Sam and Isabella Garnecho moved to this spot in 1980 after twenty-five years at 323 Bleecker Street ("When Bleecker was all Portuguese"). The industrious couple, born in northern Portugal, stock palmitos, dry black beans, *Farinha de Mandioca* (cassava flour), Dende Oil (palm oil), Brahma beer, and 12-ounce size *Guarana* (an unforgettable beverage made from the Brazilian fruit *Guarana*) and everything you'll need to cook the national dish *Feijoida* (black beans and meats, recipe, page 239). Brazilian coconut milk, olives, jams, smoked meats, beers and ales are among the specialties. At night, for their supper, the Garnechos enjoy the Portuguese cheeses *Casteloes* made from cow's and goat's milk (Brie-textured, yellow, with rich flavor) and *Queso de Sera* (all available at their shop) with bread and fresh fruits. They also stock Portuguese sweet bread rolls.

*112 Greenwich Avenue. 255-7868. 11-midnight, Monday to Saturday; closed Sunday. Telephone, mail, and airmail orders. Delivers.*

CASA MONEO bids you a real *Buenos Dias* when you visit it. Miniature bags of herbs, seeds, and spices fill the left wall at the entrance—a prelude to the Spanish, Mexican, Portuguese mood and tempo throughout the long shop. The aisles are filled with many varieties of dried corn and *Masa Farina* (corn meal) for tortillas and many Mexican, Argentinian, Brazilian, and Colombian dishes. Inca foods include dried clam meat, dried potatoes, powdered ginger, and hot pepper. There are oils, olives, sauces (several styles of *Mole Poblano*), diced cactus, beans, *Chorizos en Rama* (sausages in small to 6-pound cans), cream and jellies including *Jalapeno* and guava. Jesse Moneo, manager and son of the Spanish-born owners, darts back and forth filling orders. Employees converse in Spanish and a *Gracias* (thank you) or *Por Favor* (please) draws a warm response from the friendly helpers. In the back deli department, there are six sausage types, twenty cheeses including *Monchego Panella* Spanish cheese; five kinds of fresh chilies; *Tomatillos*, always available along with fresh guavas. *Malanga* is available frozen, fava beans dried and frozen. And there are fresh cactus paddles to scramble with your eggs and some dried corn husks to wrap your *Tamales*. In its Bazar Moneo department, there are utensils: Mexican *Molcajetes* (for grinding corn), paella pans, grills, and *Casserolas* (low-sided pans for braised and stewed dishes).

*210 West 14 Street. 929-1647. 9:30-7, Monday to Saturday; closed Sunday. Wholesale phone orders only; Mail and airmail (catalog, $2).*

A.V.D. INTERNATIONAL FOODS AND GLOBE PARCEL specializes in Russian, Ukrainian, and Polish foods and gift items. Rosa and Noum Zagorsky have run the shop since 1976. They stock caviar, canned eggplant, sprats, sturgeon, honey, oil, jellies (red and yellow cherry, strawberry, and blueberry), teas, and candies. Polish mushrooms are strung on threads (to be softened in water before chopping into dishes); nearby is a selection of canned imports. Dried and smoked herrings are sold in bulk.

*101 First Avenue. 982-7864. 8:30-7, seven days, except closed Sunday in July and August. Mail and phone orders.*

B & C MEAT MARKET, is a tiny Polish sausage shop formerly called KERSHNOWSKY & SON (the name is still on the window). Chester Marszalek (the "C" in the partnership) is proud of the sausages and head cheeses he makes. He suggests as a perfect dinner *Gowumpki* (stuffed cabbages made with ground pork and beef with rice, topped with mushroom or tomato sauce). And for dessert? *"Wyborowa"* (Polish vodka) calls partner Bob Zawisny (the "B") from the back room!

*111 First Avenue. 677-1210. 8-6, Monday to Saturday; closed Sunday. Phone orders.*

At BRODY MEAT PRODUCTS, INC., Steve Brody, born in the Ukraine, has spiced his sausages and cold cuts in the back room factory since the 1950s. The rest of the time he slices meats alongside six serious butchers who also serve shoppers promptly at the counter. Among the specialties are the familiar Polish

*Kielbasa* variations. Hung in rows on the wall hooks, sixteen-inch slender *Kabanosy* pork sausages vary in color from orange-red (when freshly prepared) to a deep wine (dried after a week). Hang them in your kitchen to slice and eat for a quick snack. *Kabanosy*, spicy but not hot (delicious after drying a week) lasts indefinitely. A sign above the butchers' heads suggests, "If you don't see it, ask for it" which is a good idea if you like sauerkraut (supplied by Eddie's Pickles, Maspeth). Out of sight, but always in stock: barrel sauerkraut, half-sour pickles, and horseradish. In sight are black, rye, and light Lithuanian bread (from Silver Bell Bakery, Corona, Queens) and a full line of fresh meats as well.

*96 Second Avenue. 475-5052. 8-6, Monday to Saturday; closed Sunday; closed Monday in August.*

EAST VILLAGE DELI-MEAT, INC. radiates European Old World charm. The smoked hickory smells emerge from specialties made in the shop by expert owner, Julio Baczynsky. These include variations on the *Kielbasa* theme since Polish sausages are the outstanding items. *Krajana* (pronounced Krayana) is a ready-to-eat, garlic-spiced sausage, mostly pork with some beef, about 1¾ inches in diameter. Sold by links or sliced (eat cold or heat chunks in boiling water for 10 minutes). *Siekana* sausages are made of finely ground meats. *Kabanosy* are slender sausages nicknamed *TV Kielbasa* for snacking. Jarek Rottermund, an East Village resident born in Poland, buys *Kabanosy* to eat with rye bread. *Mazurka*, a pork cold cut about 4 inches in diameter, is flecked with dill seeds, pepper, and garlic. *Kishka* is a dark pork and beef blood sausage speckled with buckwheat, about 2¼ inches in diameter, tasty sliced thinly for a Polish buffet. There are numerous liver sausages: for example, *Pashtet*, a square loaf rich with fat flecks. *Salceson*—another favorite as an appetizer to serve with bread—is a white head cheese made from pigs' feet jelly, full of rosy pork bits. It perks up when sliced into chunks with a little lemon juice or vinegar. Choices are endless, graciously described by Pavli Witold, tall counterman born in Poland, and his colleagues. What do they enjoy for breakfast? *"Kielbasa*, sliced and fried with eggs." And for lunch? *"Kielbasa*, just plain with bread." For dinner? *"Kielbasa* with sauerkraut and potatoes and beer!" "Too much *Kielbasa!*" says Julio Baczynsky, laughing, and slicing *Krakowska*, a heady ham bologna.

*139 Second Avenue. 228-5590. 8-6, Monday to Saturday; closed Sunday. Summer, closed Monday.*

KUROWYCKY MEAT PRODUCTS, INC. has flourished since the late 1920s and now third-generation Jerry Kurowycky spices the *Krajana, Siekana, Kabanosy,* and other *Kielbasa* specialties. The homemade pork and ham favorites are flavor-brightened with pepper, caraway, garlic, and the indispensable spice of enthusiastic expertise. The large and airy store also stocks fresh meats and dairy products. The aroma of smoky sausages lingers, rising from the butcher paper and bag you carry home, titillating you until you indulge your appetite. *Gin ku ya!*

*124 First Avenue. 477-0344. 7-6, Monday and Saturday; 7-6:30, Tuesday to Thursday; 7-7, Friday; closed Sunday.*

DE ROBERTIS PASTRY SHOPPE suddenly turns your thoughts to sweets in a neighborhood dominated by pork shops. In the shop, still sparkling with the original 1904 white tile walls and tile floor, you can sample thirty cookies or *Biscotti,* pastry delicacies. Or, if a party or wedding, anniversary or birthday looms, order a cake from John De Robertis or his son, John, Jr. This shop offers an astonishing assortment of creamy, fancy cakes in a refined atmosphere for nostalgia lovers. Among the scrumptious Italian specialties is *Pastiera de Grano* (rich cake of ricotta cheese and peeled, whole wheat kernels), and the French delicacies include many with mocha butter cream fillings including the famed *Pyramid* (spongecake base with hazelnut butter cream).

*176 First Avenue. 674-7137. 9-midnight, Sunday to Thursday; Open to 1 A.M. Friday and Saturday. Phone orders for customers. Delivers in the area.*

The BLACK FOREST PASTRY SHOP window full of fruit-topped pastries and chocolate cakes will dazzle your eyes. Inside the tiny, brick-walled shop is an astonishing array of imaginative cakes. Owner Dieter Fuss, using the expertise he developed in his birthplace in the Black Forest and his subsequent years in Switzerland, creates classic favorites such as Black Forest Cake and voluptuous Linzertorte. He also invented an Apple Pizza (thinly layered apples over cake with glazed topping) and fresh banana cake (a halved banana on cake topped with chocolate). A peaked concoction of coconut layered with chocolate cream and covered with chocolate thicker than a creamsicle's is called Mount St. Helens. And there's Fruit Strip (puff dough topped with freshly glazed fruit) and Othello (chocolate over macaroon) and poppyseed strudel and cheese sticks (popular among the locals to slice for appetizers with wine) . . . and . . . the house specialties go on and on, each more fresh and original than the other.

*177 First Avenue. 254-8181. 8-8, Monday to Saturday; closed Sunday.*

RUSSO & SON DAIRY PRODUCTS—a cozy shop and another relic of the early part of the century—specializes in homemade mozzarella and ricotta, fresh curd and slicing. ("I can smell the cheese smoking every day," a customer told me.) Mozzarella varieties include smoked, salted, and unsalted and *Scamorze* (cow's milk cheese made in pear shape) hung to dry for a few weeks. They also sell prosciutto. Shoppers huddle around the counter as though visiting. Savino Russo, who opened the shop in 1921 and was joined by son Tony in 1972, maintains his quality in an unchanged, old-fashioned ambiance.

*344 East 11th Street. 254-7452. 8-6:30, Monday to Friday; 8-6 Saturday; closed Sunday.*

VENIERO'S ITALIAN PASTRY SHOP, has been in business since 1894 and has won many awards during that time. The shop is a dazzling sight with mirrors all along the right wall. White branches are woven to make a lattice on the ceiling and the old tile floor is lovely. If that isn't enough, the staggering array of cakes and pastries leaves you breathless. Looking closely, one finds the Italian standbys—the *Anisette* and *Quaresimale* (almond-cinnamon biscuits), the *Biscotti* and *Cannoli* by the dozens and *Sfogliatella* (flaky pastry) lined up like soldiers ready to be attacked. And all around, people sit at tables sipping *Cappuccino* as if they were in Roma or Milano or Firenze. House specialties include wedding, birthday, and anniversary cakes, *Torrone, Gelati,* and *Spumoni.*

*342 East 11th Street. 674-4415. 8-midnight, seven days. Phone orders.*

## Union Square

MAYS, UNION SQUARE, the department store, offered an unexpected find—a "gourmet" department in a first floor corner. It consists of ten round floor tables full of packaged foods. These range from chocolates, crackers, and cookies, to canned mussels and clams, nuts, pumpkin seeds, snacks, and soup mixes. And there are herb teas, oils, and dressings near the Hungarian acacia honey and Israeli bitter orange jam and a few bottles of "alcohol-removed wine"!

*14th and Broadway. 677-4000. 10-7, Monday to Wednesday; 10-8, Thursday and Friday; 10-7 Saturday; 12-5, Sunday.*

# GRAMERCY, LITTLE INDIA, MURRAY HILL
## Little India—
Asian Indian, Pakistani, Armenian, Iranian,
Indonesian, International, Bangladeshi, Chinese,
Mexican, other Middle Eastern groups
### Gramercy, Murray Hill—
British, International, Oriental

*His bread is buttered on both sides.*
BRITISH PROVERB

FLAVORS BETWEEN Gramercy and Murray Hill melt like chocolate on warm cake and spices in hot *Ghee*. Amiable shops, colorful fish and flower stores and restaurants blend with the quiet, elegant brownstones.

Where the ground levels off after the hill of the mid-30s and the buildings slim down to the nineteenth-century and early twentieth-century heights, where the spicy shops smell like historic old India and you yearn for an aged mortar and pestle, you are in the "Little India" section of Gramercy. Specialty Asian-Indian shops are primarily clustered on Lexington and Third Avenues and on East 28th Street. Usually small and unpretentious, these shops' stocks are utterly fascinating and amazingly rich for a variety of cuisines.

The shopper seized by an urge for a Continental food trek can trot to B. Altman's food department (page 59) or smaller neighborhood shops catering to epicurean tastes. There's a remarkable neighborhood feeling in the fruit and meat shops from the warm and friendly shopkeepers; one has the sense of being in exotic lands in one of the quietest sections of New York.

## Little India

INDIA FOOD AND GOURMET has supplied Indian, Pakistani, and Bangladesh shoppers since 1967. The small shop carries a range of spices, three kinds of rice, pulses, split peas, pickles, chutneys, nuts. Kishor Gosalia, of Gujarat, India, is the owner. In the produce department, you'll find staples for curry dishes and cabbage, cauliflower, and seasonals including an unusual item (even for Asian-Indian shops), *Amba Haldi* (fresh white and yellow turmeric)—for salad. *Naan* (light-textured bread) is fresh (made in Queens); no frozen breads here.

*110 Lexington Avenue. 686-8955. 7-7:30, seven days. Phone orders. Deliveries to restaurants.*

GOOD FRUITS AND VEGETABLES where spectacular fruits glow is a corner shop with seasonal offerings and house plants (often on the sidewalk) with some groceries (including some oriental) indoors.

*118 Lexington Avenue. 686-4317. 24 hours, seven days. Free delivery.*

FOODS OF INDIA SINHA TRADING CO., INC. is a large seven-step walk-up store. Neatly and extensively stocked with 200 kinds of Asian-Indian pickles and chutneys and twenty varieties of pulses (best sellers), numerous spices, groceries, snack foods, nuts, and flours. A shopper bought *Chapati* flour to make cupcakes! Why not? From the refrigerator, refresh yourself with fresh mango drink. *Chapati* and *Naan* are available among the breads. In the produce department, you'll see the favorite long green squash. Arun Sinha, the shop operator since 1972, also stocks utensils and records (under the large picture window overlooking Lexington Avenue).

*120 Lexington Avenue. 683-4419. 10-8, Monday to Saturday; 10-6, Sunday. Phone and mail orders (UPS or airmail).*

KALUSTYAN'S and TASHJIAN'S cater to Asian-Indian, Pakistani, other Middle Eastern, and Armenian cooks, offering staple groceries for almost any dish and fresh produce used in many of these cuisines' dishes. Displayed simply in boxes at the left at the entrance: *Taro* (called *Arbi,* in Armenian), hot chilies, bitter melons *(Loofah* in Chinese) and long, skinny asparagus beans (also a Chinese favorite), fresh coriander *(Cilantro* to Mexicans), and seasonal delights such as papaya. Don't miss the pulses, spices, and pickles available on shelves on both sides. See manager John Bas's delectable candy recipe on page 330. KALUSTYAN'S divided the shop in November 1983 to include its neighbor, TASHJIAN'S. TASHJIAN'S, fifteen years on Third Avenue before moving in, is still an Old World charmer. Karnig Tashjian, an Armenian man born in Aleppo, Syria, runs the shop with his son Viken. It could be the hundreds of items stacked neatly on the narrow shelves all the way up to the high ceiling that give shoppers such pleasure. Or, it may be the antique touches: wooden drawers with glass windows with twenty-eight kinds of coffee beans, fifteen teas (including an aphrodisiac tea) Karnig can explain to you; brass and wooden mortars and pestles, couscoussiers, and many imported treats such as quince, sour cherry, rose petal, and apricot jams (sold in bulk from gallon jars) that make the shoppers come back again and again. And there are Indonesian ingredients here and Middle Eastern favorites from *Tahini* (for Creamed Tahini Salad, see note on page 353) to spicy spices.

*123 Lexington Avenue. 685-3451 (Kalustyan's) 683-8458 (Tashjian's). 10-5, Monday to Saturday; 11-6, Sunday. No mail or phone orders. Wholesale delivery only.*

SPICE & SWEET MAHAL, a lively corner shop, has attracted shoppers since 1975 to the extensive seasonal produce in stock (okra, eggplants, *Kauda* squash, hot chilies, ginger root, garlic, Chinese radishes, and Haitian mangos in season. Creamed coconut (for *Goan* and other South Indian dishes) with *Chapati* and *Naan* (on Fridays), fifty spices, pulses *(Channa Dhal*—Bengal gram, *Kabuli Channa*—chick peas, *Moong Saboot*—green gram or mung beans, *Malka Masoor*—lentils, *Toor Dhal*—red gram, *Urad Dhal*—black gram split and husked, and more). There are pastes *(Vindaloo*, fish, curry, green *Masala* [spice mixture], and mulligatawny), many pickles and chutneys, dried fruits, flours, and rice, thirteen oils and butters, teas, twenty-two essences and more.

*135 Lexington Avenue. 683-0900. 10-8, Monday to Saturday; 11-6, Sunday. Phone and mail orders.*

ANNAPURNA INDIAN GROCERIES offers spices (chili powders, turmeric, coriander, cumin, mustard, and other indispensables for Asian-Indian and Pakistani cuisines), rices *(Basmati*, long- and short-grained, brown), South Indian pickles and chutneys. If not overwhelmed by incense fragrances at the door, you'll see 7-inch *Chapati* bread rounds (packed in plastic bags) available singly or in large quantity. Owner Thomas Thoppil, born in South India and particularly knowledgeable in that region's cuisine, also runs a crafts emporium (on an upper floor) and stocks cooking utensils.

*127 E. 28th Street. 889-7540. 10:30-7, Monday to Saturday; 12-5, Sunday. Mail orders.*

NADER'S GROCERY STORE attracts locals with window boxes of roasted pistachios and fifteen other seed and nut varieties. On narrow shelves along the walls and aisle are spices, grains, and legumes for the Persian *Ashe* (soup), *Polo* and *Chelo* (rice), *Khoresche* (sauce) and *Sabzi* (vegetable) dishes. *Panir* (cheese) is stocked as feta. *Naan*—flat Persian bread, 18 inches long and about one hand wide, sprinkled with sesame—is available fresh (it sells out early), from a Queens baker. Middle Eastern, Armenian, and Asian-Indian ingredients—from sesame oil to Israeli *Gefilte* fish (10½-ounce cans) are here. Iranian Nader Aboutalebi said he caters to many Iranians living in the area and to adventuresome cooking buffs. His sister, Shedi Aboutalebi, who helps in the store, shares a recipe, page 288.

*1 East 28th Street. 686-5793. 8:30-7, Monday to Saturday; closed Sunday. Phone orders.*

## Murray Hill

B. ALTMAN food department, a gracious invitation to foods of France, England, and Ireland; a meat department tipping toward Northern European hams and salamis, topped off by cheeses from Scandinavia and France. The food section is refined and roomy, tempting one to cavort among the utensils and kitchen gadgets— an entire wall covered with cooking aids. *À la français* flavors include Fauchon *Vinaigré Vieux* and Maxim's Walnut Oil and Red Sherry Wine Vinegar, *Moutarde à l'Ancienne* for contemporary cold meats, shallot wine vinegar, and the elusive *Beurre d'Écrevisse* (crayfish butter). British condiments glorify holiday and special tables with Fortnum & Mason apricot and almond preserves, and the luscious jasper-toned gooseberry preserve. From Crabtree & Evelyn there are melon and ginger preserve, and walnut ketchup. Among the stocks, a shopper finds Brazilian palm hearts or demerara sugar, Japanese rainbow trout and Danish musssels or Swiss *Spaetzle* and the pre-mixed Irish Brown Bread (originally baked in an open fire) to bake at home. John Gilmartin serves at the meat counter, slicing Shaller & Weber Black Forest and Westphalian hams, and any of the twenty-five cheeses including best sellers Jarlsberg, Danish Havarti, and Holland Gouda. This genial Irishman also shares his favorite stew (recipe, page 273).

*Fifth and Madison Avenues at 34th Street. 689-7000. 10-6, Monday to Saturday; closed Sunday. During Christmas holidays: 10-8, Monday to Friday; 10-7, Saturday and Sunday.*

SWIFT MEAT MARKET, the Fiumefreddo family meat business, was begun in the 1920s on 29th Street between Second and Third Avenues by grandfather Philip. Son Frank moved to 32nd and Second and adopted the name Swift, then relocated to this long narrow shop, now run by his sons Tony, Jr. and Pete with cousins Frank and Phil—all excellent meat experts. Tony, a tall, serious man with thick, slightly graying hair, reports his clientele has not changed during recent years. Stocks include beef tenderloin and roasts, for Roast Beef and Yorkshire Pudding, page 263, veal for cutlets, butterflied lamb, or leg of lamb for Irish Stew (page 273), pork and veal chops, chicken breasts stuffed with prosciutto and mozzarella ("Spread with butter or margarine, bake, covered, for 30 minutes, uncover the last 5 minutes.") "Customers are interested in gourmet and specialty dishes, not the 'homemade stews' of my childhood," Tony Fiumefreddo declares. A wholesale meat expert described the shop as "the best in the business—real choice meats."

*146 East 34 Street. 532-0796, 0682. 8-6:30, Monday to Saturday; closed Sunday. Phone orders. Free delivery.*

V & F SEAFOOD Shop features specialties and specials handwritten in chalk on a blackboard at the entrance. Filets (flounder, sole, and scrod) are most popular requests; also whiting, brook trout, porgies, red snappers, and sea bass are displayed sedately on ice. A line of prepared seafoods includes stuffed sole (stuffed with crab, shrimp, onion, garlic, spices [pepper, paprika], wine and butter sauce); Shrimp Scampi and others. Vincent Napolitano, the young owner, has four helpers and reports clientele has not changed since 1977 when he opened his business.

*519 Third Avenue. 725-1833. 8-6, Monday to Friday; 9-5, Saturday; closed Sunday. No phone orders.*

VERDE'S MARKET, established in 1898, was bought in 1977 by Ohjon Le and his wife, Eunil. Varied offerings range from groceries including oriental staples, fresh fruits and vegetables, coffees (a specialty) from Kenya, Brazil, Venezuela, Guatemala, Colombia, France, and Denmark. There are also dried nuts (eighteen varieties) stocked in jars.

*534 Third Avenue. 532-2267, 8, 9. Open 24 hours, Monday to Saturday; closed Sunday. Phone orders. Free delivery.*

K. T. FRUIT AND VEGETABLE MARKET, a large store, buzzes with relatives of owner Soon Ja Kim (president of the K.T. Fruit Corp.), running back and forth unloading cartons and replenishing stocks. Sliced fruits are displayed in dainty, lidded containers among the whole fruits. Among the groceries, you'll see Wonton Soup mix featured next to Maggi soups and Gulden's mustard, dried Korean anchovies, and many ingredients for Western and Eastern dishes. Soon Ja Kim also runs another shop at 44th and Second Avenue.

*555 Third Avenue. 686-4510. 24 hours, seven days. Free delivery.*

*821 Second Avenue. 697-3322. 24 hours, seven days. Free delivery.*

LEXINGTON FRUIT AND VEGETABLES is an abundant and fragrant shop with outdoor displays that pull you like magnets. Seasonal offerings may include St. Clause melons, golden honeydews, Casaba melons, Canary melons, cantaloupes, pineapples, grapes, peaches, mangos, strawberries, bananas. Indoors, fresh greens—spinach, cress, parsley and dill, Oriental bottled and canned foods, *tofu* sprouts and okra, a medley of nuts, seeds, and fruits in jars are attractively displayed by Lee Ly, slender owner and his pleasant wife.

*325 Lexington Avenue. 679-6392. Open 24 hours, Monday to Saturday; closed Sunday. Free delivery.*

# MIDTOWN, GARMENT DISTRICT, THEATER DISTRICT
International, Korean, Japanese, other Oriental, Jewish, Swedish, Italian, Argentinian, Greek, Chinese

*Eating is half one's food, sleeping the other half*
SWEDISH PROVERB

*When put to sprout, bad beans grow only roots.*
KOREAN PROVERB

MIDTOWN PERSONIFIES to the world New York's complex image. Noisy and frenetically active, Midtown, adjoining the Garment and Theater Districts, presents breathtaking and/or harrowing social, cultural, and business contrasts. Food shops, though diversified, may not dominate the scene although food vendors compensate, unendingly promoting their ethnic favorites to the hungry passersby. And among the wealth of shops and buildings crowding the neighborhoods, there are well-established as well as newer food shops to search out.

The Garment District, which abuts Midtown and hums as a significant business artery for it, offers splendid variety. MACY'S Herald Square "Cookery" and "Marketplace" (page 65) for instance, attracts food lovers with a magnetism equal to Europe's finest. Where bead, novelty, and accessory wholesalers are featured, where handcarts with racks of shrouded ready-to-wear are scurried onto delivery trucks, several Korean shops sell fresh oriental vegetables, groceries, varied meats and seafoods for Korean, Japanese, and other oriental dishes. SAM BOK, the "original" Korean food store in Manhattan (page 66), swells with oriental ingredients at the rim of the Theater District, a lone food shop in a district famed for its eateries.

Certainly, the Swedish influence is strong. NYBORG-NELSON operates a shop in the Citicorp Building (page 67). Bakeries at Grand Central Terminal and the Citicorp Building please the ever-increasing commuters' appetites. Citicorp "Market," in fact, enriches the neighborhood as a vivid, lively food center, providing a charming *free* plaza where visitors may sit and enjoy their lunch or a pastry snack from the many colorful food boutiques surrounding it.

One of the city's oldest delicacy shops, MAISON GLASS (page 68), continues to pamper exotic-loving gourmets. And on First Avenue between 51st and 52nd, gourmets have a triple treat— three specialty shops a short skip from each other: A. FITZ & SONS, INC. *(944 First Avenue, 753-3465),* its original marble shop sign in the window since 1867, is a cozy meat market. A few doors away, PISACANE MID-TOWN *(940 First Avenue, 758-1525, 7560)* sells fish, oysters, and other seafood to a mixed clientele including Jewish, Swedish, and Italian customers. Across the avenue, ELYSÉE *(939 First Avenue, 755-5858)* bakes croissants, brioches, apple turnovers, orange tarts among its many pastries and also is a caterer.

But it is the street snack vendors, umbrella-topped and emitting spicy aromas from their wagons—bravely weathering the cold and rain—who constantly evoke food thoughts. Within a ten-block radius you can sample grilled frankfurters (with or without sauerkraut), roasted chestnuts, hot giant pretzels, *Falafel*, Argentinian wine sausage on oversize hot-dog rolls, *Tempura*, egg rolls, *Souvlaki*, *Latkes*, *Gyro*, Afghan hamburger on Indian *Chapati*, beverages, Middle Eastern sesame bread rings nicknamed "Holy Bagels," *Gyoza* (Japanese dumplings), dried fruit and nuts, an array of fresh seasonal fruits from bananas to tangerines, candies, and more (see *Street Snacks*, pages 341 to 358).

## Garment District

BROADWAY GROCERY CO., like other nearby Korean groceries, has more foods and activity per inch of floor space than a village festival. Adding to the excitement, shoppers and sellers speak Korean and Japanese, but someone always pops up to help out in English. Crammed full of groceries, produce, meats, and utensils, the shop, operated by Hyuk Rae Kim, spotlights ready-cooked Korean dishes and condiments in neat rows in the entrance refrigerator case.

*38 West 28 Street. 696-9678. 9-9, seven days.*

DONG DAE MOON MARKET, INC. flourishes, selling foods amid the novelty shops. Peter Byun, a New York resident since 1975, has operated the shop since 1980, catering to Korean, Japanese, Chinese, and non-oriental customers and is fluent in English. The shop specialty: twenty-four and sometimes more kinds of spicy, homemade Korean dishes, including three to four kinds of *Kimchi* (available in bulk, or pint, quart, or gallon jars). In the meat department, there are fresh, frozen, and marinated beef slices (soy sauce, sesame, scallion marinade) ready to grill. Grocery shelves hold sauces, rice and rice products, soy beans and other pulses, dried fish (including large cuttlefish), and a fresh produce department provides radishes, sprouts, celery, napa cab-

bage, and oriental staples for stir-fry and steamed dishes.
*12 West 32 Street. 564-6312, 6313. 10-9, seven days. Phone orders. Deliveries to restaurants.*

DAE WOO ORIENTAL FOOD MARKET stocks huge stacks of twenty-five-pound *Kokuho Rose* rice in the entrance window. A large store, the atmosphere is casual and very friendly with busy workers unloading cartons, fresh meats, bright greens, and crispy Japanese radishes and bagging fresh mung and soy bean sprouts in the produce department. One long section stocks many utensils, china, and novelties. One freezer exhibits oysters, cooked mussels, jackknife clams; another freezer stores the pigs' feet, oxtails, tripe, beef hearts, chicken gizzards for Korean *Pokkum* (stewed and braised dishes) and *Kuk* (soup) and other specialties. Large refrigerators hold the preserved foods—especially *Kimchi* in many styles and combinations (radish, leek, mixed cabbage). There are supplies of bean mash, baby croaker, salted anchovy, salted shrimps, and seasoned green hot pepper—condiments prized to eat with the national beef dish *Pulgogi* (see recipe, page 266) and meat or seafood dinners. Kim Chung Un, the manager, also explained that *Poll Biung Tea* in the freezer is fish roe (he used the Korean-English dictionary in the book section to look it up!).
*42 West 36 Street. 695-0843. 10-9, seven days.*

MACY'S is a major Manhattan retailer and its COOKERY shop is a joy for food lovers. Along a really wide yellow brick road beginning at P.J. Clarke's delightful restaurant-saloon, on the right hand the Cookery stocks everything from copper and crockery to appliances. On the left, in the MARKETPLACE, there are ingredients for sublime menus. Accented with a strong European flavor, the meat, smoked fish, cheese, condiments, patisserie, and bonbonniere departments offer a wide variety of selections. In the produce department where 30 kinds of fresh seasonal vegetables, tubers, roots, and herbs are available, you can plan any salad from Nicoise to Brazilian avocado. Nearby, ten kinds of coffee beans and a dozen kinds of packaged teas (including *Typhoo*) are stacked. There are 140 bottled herbs and spices; 55 essences and sprinkles are available for baking whims. PASTA + CHEESE shops (page 94) manages the pasta section. Bakery departments are run by VIVE LE FRANCE and ECLAIR Pastries (main branch at 141 West 72 Street). There are shelves and displays to entice and lure—crackers, jams and jellies, mustards, olives, butters, and 36 flavors of jelly beans. In the cheese department there may be 300 different cheeses. At the adjacent smoked fish department where Nova Scotia salmon is the best seller, there are smoked eel, mackerel, sable, chubbs, trout, sturgeon, as well as Irish, Norwegian, Scotch, Columbia River salmon and Yugoslavian caviar. On Macy's Seventh Avenue side, the huge meat department stocks vast quantities of beef, pork, veal, chicken, rock cornish hens, ducks—anything you may need—in large or small quantities.

*Herald Square. 971-6000. 9:45-9:30, Monday, Thursday, Friday; 9:45-7, Tuesday, Wednesday; 9:45-6, Saturday; closed Sunday.*

## Midtown

SAM BOK ORIENTAL GROCERY & GIFT SHOP, a bit out of the neighborhood, but well worth visiting, at the edge of the theater district, next door to Town Hall, orchestrates Korean and Japanese foods. In fact, the vast shop owned by Sang Oh since 1972, is a chorus of exotic aromas and tastes. Crates may be stacked casually in aisles; open crates may simply exhibit unusual foods such as *Ya Ma Ee Mo* (10-inch-long roots) in fine sawdust, where shoppers can pick them up and carry them to the doorway cash register. Seasonal fruits and vegetables are displayed in boxes just as they arrived. Refrigerator cases are always crammed full of jars of *Kimchi*, alongside pickles and preserves eaten as condiments with Korean dishes, and many kinds of *Miso* pastes. There are steamed buns and ample fresh supplies daily of bean sprouts and tofu. Ice-packed fresh fish is available for prized raw fish specialties and also fresh meats, especially rib roasts. In back there are stacks and stacks of dried anchovies and seaweeds, neatly divided by sizes and types—anything you'll ever need to know and use for Korean and Japanese cuisines.

*127 West 43 Street. 582-4730. 10-8, seven days. No phone orders. No deliveries.*

ZARO'S, in Grand Central Terminal under the stairs leading to Vanderbilt Avenue, is where a hungry commuter learns the joy of a hot sesame bagel. The ovens turn out thousands of breads and rolls daily. If you can approach a counter and shout your order, you may choose from a wide assortment of Irish, French, Jewish, Italian, Austrian breads, cookies, specialties on one side and ready-to-eat foods on the other. Aside from the quick service, you will be amazed by the courtesy of the counter people and manager George Lopez. Even in hot weather when steamy ovens behind them create a Turkish-bath atmosphere, they smile. Zaro's, a Bronx-based bakery, has several shops—owned by Phil Zaro and son Andy.

*Grand Central Terminal, 42nd Street between Vanderbilt and Lexington Avenues. 595-1515. 7:30-10, Monday to Saturday; closed Sunday. Phone orders.*

*Zaro Bake Shop, Inc., 181 Dreiser Lp., 379-9670; 29 H.J. Grant Circle, 822-9181; 1321 Oak Point Avenue, 589-1700 (Bronx); check hours locally.*

ARTICHOKE, a fragrant, fresh-looking shop, boldly prints its name in bright green over the door. Well situated between David Wan II and Paparazzi restaurants Artichoke stocks cheeses, smoked salamis, breads, and a melange of ethnically inspired cooked dishes—Bombay Chicken, Indonesian Rice, pasta. Owner of the shop is Bob Greenfield.

*968 Second Ave. 753-2030. 11-7, Monday to Thursday; 10-6, Friday and Saturday; closed Sunday.*

NYBORG-NELSON window signs—"Danish Havarti," "Norwegian Jarlsberg" hint at the stream of Scandinavian foods to be found indoors. The Swedish owner, Hans Booge, knows the business well, having worked with the original owner before buying it, lending an authentic Swedish flavor to New York, since 1921. Swedish lingonberries (fresh and canned), soups, pancakes, mustard sauce, coffees, *Glog* and *Arrak* beverages are among the specialties. Maggi and Bahlsen food lines are found amid the variety. For the holidays, Swedish Yule *(Schinke)* (ham tinged with the house mustard sauce and whole cloves) is on hand. Available

daily, among the prepared specialties: Fried Swedish meatballs
(ground beef, bread crumbs, eggs, salt, and pepper), *Gravlax* (see
recipe, page 176), and salads. Pete Mandakas is manager, and Mia,
a Swedish lass, is in charge of the deli.

*One Citicorp Center—153 East 53 Street. 223-0700. 11:30-9,
Monday to Saturday; 12-6, Sunday.*

MAISON GLASS is the place for you if you share George Washington's penchant for "savory steaks." No matter where you live,
you may order boneless New York sirloin strip steaks and have
them airmailed to you. Specializing in delicacies since Ernest
Glass opened the shop in 1902, the current owners pamper highly
developed tastes with hundreds of items featured in a 116-page
color catalog. Most, but not all, of the foods are usually available
in the shop. A "classic" store with wall and floor displays brim-
ming with cans, bottles, and baskets, salespeople, wearing uni-
form coats, walk around the shop with customers, filling and
selecting orders. More than a dozen countries are represented in
the offerings—wild birds and boar meats, twenty-six patés and
thirty-two pickles and relishes including pickled quail eggs,
mango chutney from India, Chinese spices and sauces, Thai chili
sauce. The basics—flours and grains, oils and vinegars, herbs and
spices, cheese, seafood and meats, fruits and vegetables—are well
represented as well. Frozen steaks and double-Frenched lamb
chops are newer offerings. Marvin Goldsmith, one of the owners,
suggests a menu for a special event: Fresh Beluga caviar on toast
points with Dom Perignon champagne; Roast Pheasant with Wild
Rice and Petits Pois (peas) to be followed by Crêpes Suzettes with
Cointreau topped off by Espresso coffee. Don't forget the fresh
fruit and brie (Brillat Savarin). For another of his suggested
menus, try Gravad Laks with Mustard Dressing with black bread
and Aquavit (liquor); Quail Veronique with white crêpes, baby
Belgian carrots, Babas au Rhum (dessert), café Marquis (French
roast coffee) and fresh fruit with Saga St. Andre (Danish cheese).

*52 East 58th Street. 755-3316. 8:45-5:45, Monday to Saturday;
closed Sunday. Phone, mail, and airmail orders. (Catalog).*

# NINTH AVENUE
## PADDY'S MARKET, CLINTON, HELL'S KITCHEN
West African, Filipino, Hispanic, Italian, Greek, Middle
Eastern, Cuban, International, French, Asian-Indian,
Jewish, Irish, Japanese, Korean, Black, Spanish,
Nigerian, Sicilian, Thai, Indonesian, Caribbean, Puerto Rican

*Taste is in variety.*
CHILEAN PROVERB

ON A SHOPPING TOUR of Ninth Avenue (a fantastic food avenue with many nicknames) it is easy to recapture the vibrancy of "Paddy's Market," a Ninth Avenue market of 200 food stalls that flourished between 37th and 42nd streets during the early part of the century. The pushcart market was eliminated in 1937 by construction of the Lincoln Tunnel. As cars whiz by toward the Tunnel, retailers today still vividly remember that the vendors were all Jewish or Italian serving Irish shoppers, primarily, and their own ethnic groups.

Despite some retailers' nostalgia for the "old days," Ninth Avenue is still an exciting food center with an unmistakable spirit— especially during the May "Ninth Avenue Festival" when the street bulges (with visitors) and cascades (with food snacks and treats). Races and cultures mix imperceptibly in one of the city's richly diverse neighborhoods. Catering to newer waves of immigrants, no one ethnic food dominates; many people find their food needs fulfilled here. And the retailers also cater to many swank city restaurants.

Yet an image problem lingers. The area is still known as "Hell's Kitchen," named for the gangs and interracial fights when the area teemed with poor, living in wretched conditions during the nineteenth century. Long gone is the "vale of flowers" when it was called *Bloemendael* and a stream ran along 42nd Street in the eighteenth century. "Paddy's Market" was probably named for the Haymarket area of Sydney, Australia. Now the name "Clinton" is promoted for the neighborhood west of Eighth Avenue between 34th and 57th. Whatever it's called, Ninth Avenue is special. . .

LOPEZ FRUIT STORE transports the fruits and roots of the Caribbean and Central America to the sidewalk. *Malangas, yuca* (cassava), bananas, and plantains are featured at the door. Inside, owner Ralph Lopez, who speaks Spanish, deftly cuts a small opening in the top of a water coconut and trims back the fibrous shell. The shopper smiles contentedly eating the soft coconut flesh from the "cap" and another man cries "What a coconut—full of juice." Then the purchaser pours the coconut liquid into a tall cup and drinks it bottoms up. Available all year, water coconuts are always cut for the customers (so carry a jar if you prefer to save the liquid). Other specialties here, depending on seasonal availability: mangos, oranges, grapes, several kinds of *yuca* (darker-skinned types are produced in mountainous regions), sweet potatoes, and yams.

*454 Ninth Avenue. 564-7193. 6:30-9:30, seven days. Free delivery.*

TRIO FRENCH BAKERY, specializing in Italian and French bread, is the first of many Ninth Avenue bakeries. The "trio" of brothers ran a bakery on Bleecker Street in Greenwich Village for twenty-nine years and relocated to this address in 1981. Now the shop is run by Mario De Giovanni, one of the original brothers (another left the firm and one died), and his wife and twenty-year-old son. Available are six kinds of rolls, seven kinds of Italian and French breads, sixteen varieties of biscuits (mostly Italian) and cookies (including French bow ties). House specialties are the long bread sticks and "Riviera" toast, in demand by restaurants. The latter are thinly sliced toasts about 6" by 1"—very crisp and hinting of oil and salt.

*476 Ninth Avenue. 695-4296, 4735. 7-6, Monday to Saturday; closed Sunday.*

EMPIRE COFFEE AND TEA COMPANY is a tiny shop where scintillating aromas are thick enough to stir with a spoon. It's on the Northeast corner of 37th and Ninth Avenue, next to a small fruit stand and a secondhand clothing shop. Bushel bags of hickory and chestnut-colored beans fill floor space, and shelves are packed solid with fifty-five kinds of coffee beans and sixty tea varieties. If you can squeeze through the narrow aisle to the back, you'll probably see owner Dave Mottel at his small desk while two energetic salesmen help shoppers on both sides of the counter. "Empire changed hands only once since it opened in 1908," he notes. "After I bought the company in 1965, I moved here from West 42nd Street." He reports lively consumer interest in fresh and loose teas and coffee beans. "People want to grind and mix their own." He classified coffee drinkers into the "powdered and larger ground types." Middle Easterners, Slovaks, Arabs, Hellenes, Jews, and Turks order powdered coffee and they all ask for "Turkish coffee" except the Greeks who call it "Greek coffee," he says with a laugh. When shoppers seem overwhelmed by the profusion of beans, the salesmen ask how they enjoy their coffee so preferences can be classified and suggestions made. "Usually Italians opt for Colombian or African mellow, dark coffee; Jews select Turkish and Arabic beans; Anglo-Saxons prize American light-roasted, black and mellow coffee, while Caribbean customers favor Colombian and Central American blends. Tea drinkers are also distinctive. "Big tea drinkers—the British—prefer Indian, Sri Lanka (Ceylon) teas. China and India, the big tea producers, are well represented here. And Empire increasingly imports tea from Africa and Brazil."

*486 Ninth Avenue. 564-1460. 9-7, Monday to Friday; 9-6, Saturday; closed Sunday. Mail (catalog). Phone orders. Delivers.*

PUSAN FISH MARKET, a sparkling shop with much floor space to walk about in, is named for the Korean city where the tall owner, Ik Sang Kim, was born. Cases are full of fresh water and sea foods for an avid mixed ethnic clientele planning food from raw to cooked. "Spanish-speaking customers like octopus, kingfish, and shrimps; Japanese and Koreans buy tuna, fluke, octopus, tile, and calamari and other types of fish to make *Sashimi* (recipe, page 252); Greek shoppers love the smelts and anchovies and the U.S. Post Office workers (from the 31st and 32nd Street Ninth Avenue branch) pick everything," points out the retailer, who will pack the fish with ice for you on hot days and give you recipes (page 249).

*498 Ninth Avenue. 947-5711. 8:30-7, Monday to Saturday; closed Sunday. Phone orders. Delivery only to restaurants.*

GIOVANNI ESPOSITO & SONS, a corner pork shop, has Smithfield hams and salamis hanging from hooks along the counter from the door to the rear. Behind the counter where four butchers chop at their blocks, another row of hams decorates the wall. Cases are stocked with everything from cold cuts and sausages to poultry and red meats. "We have all kinds of customers and carry every kind of meat," explains Tony Esposito. His family began the family business in a pork shop on Mulberry Street in Little Italy in 1898; moved into this shop in 1933. "Our black customers buy chitterlings, pigs' feet, smoked knuckles, tails, and other specialties; Italians choose sausages, steaks, chopped meats for meatballs, pork for their gravy, cutlets and beef; Filipinos prefer pork shoulder; Spanish-speaking customers enjoy suckling pigs; and Greeks lamb," declares Tony Esposito. Tripe, livers, and other innards are always waiting to be sold, but the homemade sausage—six types from sweet to hot—is the specialty of the house (recipe, page 271).

*500 Ninth Avenue. 279-3298. 7:30-7:30, Monday to Saturday; closed Sunday. Phone orders. Delivery in the area.*

MICHAEL'S AND SONS MEAT MARKET is small and sawdust-sprinkled. Radio music accompanies the sounds of cleaver on chopping block. Michael Ameno, the owner since 1967, works energetically serving shoppers from huge quantities of meat and poultry in the case or stocked in the back room refrigerator. Cases exhibit mounds of chicken parts, pork chops, pork shoulders, smoked pork, roast beef, chuck cuts—name it, it's here. An Asian-Indian man buys two shopping bags full of meats including beef blood to curry ("My wife won't have to shop every day"); another selects a succulent whole calves liver. A sign reads QUAIL, DUCKS, GOOSE, SQUABS, GUINEA, PARTRIDGE, PHEASANT, WILD DUCK, WILD RABBIT, DOMESTIC RABBIT, VENISON LEGS, CHOPS AND BONELESS. Michael is a black-mustached man with flashing eyes who speaks with a Neapolitan accent. As he cuts meat nonstop, he names his favorite dish—*Pasta e Fagioli* (pasta and beans)—*not* meat!

*516 Ninth Avenue. 279-2324. 9-7:30, five days; closed Sunday and Wednesday. Phone orders. No delivery.*

CUZIN'S MEAT CO., LTD. has been owned and run by three cousins—Sidney Horowitz, Murray Doktor, and David Goodman since the mid-1970s. Walking back and forth to the walk-in refrigerator where meats are stored, the butchers hammer away at blocks while joking with customers and each other in the casual sawdust-strewn ambiance. "We have all kinds of customers— Hispanic, Caribbean, blacks, Italians, and other Americans—but we specialize in short ribs for Koreans who like to cook *Pulgogi* (national beef dish, recipe, page 266), explains Sidney Horowitz. Goat meats, smoked pork, pork chops, and beef filets are always available, so ask; little is in sight.

*515 Ninth Avenue. 736-5737. 5:30-6, Monday to Friday; 7-6, Saturday; closed Sunday. Minimum phone orders.*

VINNIE'S runs two shops within a block of each other. Vinnie DiMaggio stocks staple fruits and vegetables for Mediterranean menus and some for Caribbean tastes. Indoor and outdoor displays are varied; bags of shallots and garlic braids are hung indoors. Outside, Saber Mostafa, a young Egyptian who has worked at the shop since 1978, picks up his favorite fruit, mango. Saber explains how to choose a fine one: "It must be just soft to the touch, but not too soft." Then he lifts it to the shopper's nose. "With a sweet aroma, it is ripe and good," he says with a persuasive smile.

*496 Ninth Avenue. 563-0545. 523 Ninth Avenue. 563-0687. 24 hours, seven days (both shops). Phone orders. Free delivery.*

CENTRAL FISH COMPANY sells everything but flying fish. Ten salesmen—Italian, Santo Dominican, Cuban, Afro-American, Puerto Rican, and others—sell sharks and skate, *Lalotte* (monk fish) and red mullets, rare species near the whiting and smelts. There's Louis Riccobono, owner here since 1936, wearing a navy sailor's cap, and son Tony in a green jumpsuit helping shoppers select octopus; partner Dominick Oliveri talks to a customer from Italy about the *pesce* business. White as marble, carnelian bright, silvery blue, and pink as the finest coral, the fish and shellfish pause on ice shavings ready to be stewed by Nigerians and Italians, by Asian-Indians and Hellenes, Koreans, and Filipinos who walk through the large shop calling "Louis" and "Tony" and are also addressed by name. In this roomy store you can walk along two side aisles and simultaneously see displays on each side and across to the wall stalls. The fish cleaner stand is toward the back and the fish salesmen know the fish names in several languages.

*527 Ninth Avenue. 560-8163; 279-2317. 8-6, Monday to Saturday; closed Sunday. Delivery to restaurants.*

INTERNATIONAL GROCERY STORE AND MEAT MARKET is true to its promise. It has an international flavor and typifies the best in old-fashioned person-to-person retailing. Brothers Panagiotes and Sotirios Karamouzis bought the business in 1956 from the Simis family who had run it since 1930. College student Andreas, Panagiotes' son, helps out in the store. Stocks are constantly turned over and replenished but styles and displays haven't changed in the seventeen years I've known the shop. You'll feel soft sawdust under your shoes and smell the spices. Foreign conversations grab you from the sidewalk. Outdoors, it could be a Greek island grocery with food displays in burlap bags, a colorful three-deep display of spices. At the entrance right is the meat department, run by blond, blue-eyed Sotirios ("Sam") who bakes the delicious stuffed quail for the Ninth Avenue Festival (see recipe page 276) and sells them along with fresh lamb, red meats, poultry and, to order, all kinds of specialties (for *Kokoretsi, Souvlakia,* roast lamb, and pork). At the entrance left, the olive, oil, and cheese counter begins and continues in a mouth-watering extravaganza stocking twelve varieties of olives in bulk, fifteen types of oils, and a dozen kinds of Greek, Italian Cypriot, and French cheeses (the shop's specialties). A remarkable department awaits you from the center to the back (a perfect place to study legumes and grains)—twelve rows, four deep, of bags heaped with grains (burghuls, semolinas, whole wheats, rices, barley) and pulses (beans, peas, lentils) for any cuisine from Peru to China. A kaleidoscopic bouquet of herbs and spices (more than thirty-five) and nuts are available (including dried Italian chestnuts). In bins, all manner of noodles, spaghetti, *Kritharaki* (orzo), and other pasta (bulk and packaged) plus a full line of canned goods and sweet, sour, bitter, and salty foods from grapevine leaves to Hymettus honey and rose water, with West African ingredients such as dried cassava and *Egusi* (melon seeds) sold by three or four friendly salesmen.

*529 Ninth Avenue. 279-5514. 8-6, Monday to Saturday; closed Sunday. No phone orders or deliveries.*

GIUSEPPE'S FRUIT MARKET display joins INTERNATIONAL'S to create a nonstop food bazaar typical of Ninth Avenue, especially of this block. All kinds of choice fruits and vegetables are stocked, especially inside the small, cluttered shop. On a warm day, the scent of cooking attracts me to the back where owner Giuseppe Vitale (who has been here since 1972), wearing shorts and sandals, stands before his aromatic pot, stirring his sauce and calling for "a buncha basil" for the *Zuppa di Pesce* (Sicilian Fish Stew, page 250). "In summer, I eat light," he explains, taking the basil sprigs, washing them, and slicing them into the pot full of delicious smells. Two sellers serve shoppers inside and outside the shop.

*531 Ninth Avenue. 564-1682. 24 hours, seven days. Free delivery.*

GOLDEN SWEET FRENCH PASTRY, in business since 1980, makes and sells pastry and cookie specialties. Run by Un Kon Kim, and his charming wife, Choon Joo Kim (they own the fruit market two doors away as well), their most frequent requests are for French Egg Rolls—soft roll-twists of light texture and egg-yolk color—stocked in huge quantities in the window to attract local workers. Coffee is served at tables in back.

*568 Ninth Avenue. 695-8790. 7-7:30, Monday to Saturday; closed Sunday. Phone orders.*

KIM'S MARKET'S fruit aromas draw you like bees to honey. Halved honeydews and cantaloupes make for a refreshing snack. There are thirty varieties of vegetables, juices, as well as hot, spicy sauces and *tofu*, but fruits are the main attraction in this tempting store run by the Un Kon Kim family since 1975.

*572 Ninth Avenue. 736-7280. 7-7:30, Monday to Saturday; closed Sunday.*

ORIENTAL GROCERY, a hub for Filipino ingredients, also stocks foods for Thai, Indonesian, and Korean cuisines. For the Philippine dishes, there is *Alamang* shrimp paste and *Patis* anchovy sauce; *Bangus* (frozen milk fish), *Tinepa* (smoked fish). Rosenda Torres, born in Rizal, Philippines, has run the store since 1972, with her mother frequently helping at the barbecue where skewered pork attracts the hungry passersby into the long, well-swept shop. For Thai shoppers there are fish pastes and sauces, coconut milk (frozen or in jars). Indonesians buy the green "yard long" beans (also called asparagus beans), sweet soy sauce, and sambal. Here you'll find *Chorizos* (sausages) to last all winter, and *Balut* (fertilized eggs) from Long Island duck farms (you'll hard-cook them at home before enjoying them as the Philippine people do). And many more dry and frozen specialties; among them preserved red mongo and kidney beans, coconut preserves, and sweet jackfruit for *Halo Halo* (recipe page 330).

*526 Ninth Avenue. No telephone. 10-7, Monday to Saturday; closed Sunday.*

BULAKLAK MARKETING, INC. attracts shoppers to its Philippine and Oriental foods with a supply of fresh bean sprouts, eggplants, radishes, taro, ginger, and seasonal produce set out by the door. Maria Cristina Manaloto, born in Victoria, Tarlac, Philippines, has run the shop since 1970, working inside and outdoors at the barbecue, grilling her delicious barbecued pork on skewers (recipe, page 347). In greatest demand are noodles, fresh and dry *Pancit* or *Misua* (Chinese bean thread) for *Pancit* or *Lo Mein* dishes, appealingly blending fresh vegetables, pork or shrimp, and noodles. If uncertain, ask Maria; she's an expert cook.

*532 Ninth Avenue. 947-0170. 8-7, Monday to Saturday; closed Sunday.*

WEST AFRICAN IMPORTS CO. is a well-stocked store run by Korean Sunny and Anny Kwak, an energetic couple, concentrating on West African foods with a good supply of ingredients for Philippine and West Indian cuisines as well. Salesman Amadu Dallo, born in Guinea, speaks French and excellent English and knows the native foods extremely well. In addition, West African graduate students stop in frequently to buy groceries and willingly help explain uses of their foods for which they have exuberant enthusiasm (see recipes, pages 218 and 258). An entire aisle is stocked with pure palm oils, coconut oils, *Egusi* (melon seeds, whole and cracked for the specialty *Egusi Soup* (recipe, page 194), ground hot pepper, dried shrimps, *Gari* (ground or grated toasted cassava known in Brazil as *Farofa)* (page 215) palm nut pulp, yam *Fufu (Foofoo,* page 214), dried red chilies, dried mushrooms. Imported from Korea, Japan, Philippines, and Africa, these ingredients indicate the versatility of use in the dishes of geographically diverse ethnic groups. Outdoors, large yams, *Malanga*, tamarind, six varieties of dried, salted fish, two types of dried beef and preserved pork feet in large barrels are stocked for Caribbean and West African customers. Also, extensive spice supplies include bay leaves, mint, brown African sesame (not the white or black kind), sage, allspice, and many grains and flours.

*535 Ninth Avenue. 695-6215. 8-8, Monday to Saturday; closed Sunday. Phone, mail, and airmail orders.*

WASHINGTON BEEF CO. OF NEW YORK, INC. is a busy hive with trucks unloading meats at the door and inside, black, Hispanic, Jewish, Italian, Filipino customers lined up at the long cases with twelve multiethnic butchers on the other side filling orders. Isadore Frank founded the business in 1904 and moved to this spot in 1922. Sons Herbert and Jimmy continue the business with Herb's son, Lee, who is now an active vice-president of the firm. Specialties always in stock here are beef chuck, boneless shinmeat (for a tasty Goulasch Soup, Hungarian style, page 198), roasts; all manner of lamb, pork, and veal cuts and poultry choices. When asked separately to describe their perfect meal, Herb and Lee Frank had the same reply: "Rare steak with French-fried onion rings!" (Now that's an American meal with English and French influences.) Lee added, "A fresh salad with blue cheese dressing, beer and no aggravation."

*575-583 Ninth Avenue. 563-0200. 6:30-5:30, Monday to Wednesday; 6:30-6:30, Thursday and Friday; 6-5:30, Saturday; closed Sunday. Phone orders. No deliveries.*

JOE'S FRUITS AND VEGETABLES may be closed in winter during very cold weather, but in other seasons the shop spills its colors onto the sidewalk stands. Fruits are angled for maximum eye appeal—cherries, watermelons (quartered or halved), tomatoes, potatoes, peaches, in season. Joe Nebbia, owner since 1958, selects peaches as his favorite dessert. His helper, George Pyles, shares his favorite South Carolina "soul food" recipe: "Boil ham hocks in water, add lots of peeled potatoes, green beans, season with salt and pepper and serve warm."

*609A Ninth Avenue. 247-4541. 7-7, Monday to Saturday; usually closed Sunday.*

POSEIDON BAKERY stimulates appetites for pastry desserts. Then there's the homemade filo leaves to whip up your own *Baklava* and *Galaktoboureko* and filo sweet and savory pastries. Best sellers, however, are *Spanakopita* (spinach savory pies), according to John Anagnostou, son of the founders. His Albanian father and Trieste-born mother specialize in Greek delicacies, filo varieties, and hand-rolled cookies: *Kourambiedes* and *Melomakarona* and "dunkers" for coffee such as *Paximadia* and *Koulourakia.* A wide ethnic clientele—including Moroccan, Jewish, Middle Eastern, Greek—seek filo (both homemade here and packed commercial brands) for their native specialties and some cooks use the fine pastry leaves in their Beef Wellington!

*629 Ninth Avenue. 757-6173. 9-7, Tuesday to Saturday; 10-4, Sunday; closed Monday. Phone orders. Delivery in one-mile radius.*

P. CARNEVALE & SON, INC., is a small shop for retail and restauranteurs, specializing in European sausages and cheeses. Paul Carnevale opened the shop in 1942 and his son, Paul, Jr., helps. Stocks include French *Saucisson à l'Ail* (garlic sausage), Toulouse sausages, *Paté de Tête* (head cheese), and *Paté Maison* and *Paté Campagne* (which are in greatest demand). Cheeses include *Rollatini* (prosciutto rolled in mozzarella) and you'll also find coffees and teas. For a supper or brunch, try French sausage, potato salad, and rosé wine, suggested by Paul Carnevale, Jr.

*631 Ninth Avenue. 765-0640. 9:15-5:30, Monday to Saturday;*

*closed Sunday. In summer, closed Monday and half day Saturday.*

BRUNO THE KING OF RAVIOLI CO., INC. exudes superconfidence from the outdoor sign emblazoned over the blue and white awning. Unfortunately, Rigo Cavalli, the founder, died in 1978, but his lovely widow, Evelyn Cavalli, who also has fabulous pasta ideas, runs the business. The shop produces a complete and superb pasta line: *Manicotti, Ravioli* (meat, cheese, spinach), *Agnolotti* (raviolets), best sellers *Capelleti* and *Tortellini, Cannelloni, Gnocchi* (potato), *Fettucini, Cavatelli, Lasagne*. Ricotta, unsalted mozzarella, and *Sfoglia* (sheets of dough) are stocked along with grating cheeses.

*653 Ninth Avenue. 246-8456, 8668, 8643. 6-5, Monday to Friday; 8-5, Saturday; Summer, closed 4 P.M., Saturday; closed Sunday. Phone orders. Delivery ($25 minimum).*

SPANISH FRESH FRUITS AND VEGETABLES specializes in tropicals. Lucy Arizaga, her husband, and their young daughter, Lori, create artistic fruit cups and greens cut for salads displayed on the outdoor stands. Melons, plantains, Spanish pumpkin, and seasonal vegetables and fruits (water coconuts) are on hand for enticing tropical dishes.

*661 Ninth Avenue. 582-9634. 9-8:30, Monday to Saturday; 9-4, Sunday.*

CAPTAIN PARK FISH MARKET is a seabreeze of a fish shop. Many dark-eyed Korean maidens bustle about serving customers, wrapping seafood and fresh-water fish. The owner, Captain Park, a quiet man but quick to smile, refills stocks on finely cracked ice. Whiting, flounder, salmon, bluefish, trout—to serve with a hot *Sambal* (page 187)—shad roe, crab, cod, king and tile steaks, plus a cluster of shellfish from clams—for *Clams a la Marinara* (page 177)—to oysters, are fresh and appealing in the pleasant surroundings. Try Minhee Jang's recipe of Korean Fried Rice with Shrimp and Pork (page 281).

*679 Ninth Avenue. 757-6528. 8-8, Monday to Saturday; closed Sunday.*

POZZO PASTRY SHOP, INC. is a refreshingly sparkling shop with prized specialties. Established in 1932, the bakery business was bought in 1950 by the Bianchi Brothers. With a rich baking family background from Piedmont, Italy, John and Bruno Bianchi have created cakes for Presidents Truman and Kennedy, for Pearl Bailey and Betty Grable, and for *Sugar Babies'* anniversary on Broadway for Mickey Rooney and Ann Miller (you'll see their photos on the walls). Now the younger generation, Joe and Mario Bianchi, help in the business. At the counter, a bilingual French woman sells Italian *Anisette,* one- and two-pound *Panettone, Palmieri, Sfogliatella,* twenty-five kinds of cookies, French croissants, and American-style apple pie, pineapple upside-down cake, and crumb coffee cakes. On an uncluttered work table in the bakery behind the shop, curly-haired, graying Bruno, a courteous, mild-mannered man, decorates four cakes with butter icing. Then he pipes red jelly through a pastry tube and writes "Happy Birthday," and garnishes the cakes with pink roses and green leaves. Cakes are boxed and whisked off for delivery by a young Bianchi.

*690 Ninth Avenue. 265-7530. 7-6, Monday to Saturday; closed Sunday. Phone orders. Delivery to restaurants.*

MAZZELLA'S MARKET—specializing in choice fruits and vegetables, many imported—is run by Carl Mazzella, a third-generation family member. His mother, two sisters, niece and, occasionally, his son, help in the retail and wholesale business that extends over several stores (one store is for wholesale supplies). In the large retail store, be sure to see a wall frieze of old Paris ("I bought it from a restaurant in the East 60s that went out of business."). A disorganized array of crates and boxes clutters the floor space, but Carl Mazzella, who took over in 1967, proudly shows the specialties (between answering the phone and questions from helpers and produce truck drivers who may drive up to ask if he can use a truckload of surplus watermelons!): French melons, very slender, tender green beans, shallots, Italian *radiccio* and fennel, Israeli long-stemmed garlic. "Asian-Indians ask for okra; Italians crave dandelions, eggplant, zucchini, French dandelions, and cranberry beans (summer); Irish like potatoes, lettuce, tomatoes, celery, carrots; blacks seek collard greens, cabbage, okra; Greeks prize all the Italian favorites plus green peppers and okra." So Mazzella stocks them all!

*694 Ninth Avenue. 586-1448, 0368, 0369. 6-6 Monday to Saturday; closed Sunday. Phone orders. Delivers.*

LA GRAN CACHITA PANADERIA Y DULCERIA, a Cuban bakery in business since 1968, may be unpretentious in size and decor, but you'll hear enough Cuban language and music and see enough Cuban specialties to think you're in Cuba! Though he speaks little English, Havana-born Sergio Clavijo knows his breads and pastries and makes them himself. Cuban breads he makes are crisp, golden-crusted, and very soft-textured. There are bright egg-yellow sweet breads *(Pan Dulce)*, braids, and round swirls. You'll find cream or guava-filled pastries with chocolate glazes, *Caracoles* (cream-filled pastries) with chocolate or *Caramelo* toppings, and savory *Pasteles de Carne* (spicy beef in flaky pastry).

*695 Ninth Avenue. 581-1290. 8-7, Monday to Saturday; closed Sunday. Phone orders. No delivery.*

PARK'S FRUITS AND VEGETABLES, a large store, brightens the rather drab block of antique and hodgepodge shops. Here, varied tubers are stocked for making your *Cocida* or *Suppe* or *Kuk*, and there are leafy varieties, sprouts, herbs, and dried fish for Spanish, Mexican, black, Italian, and Puerto Rican customers. Mr. Park also carries lots of fresh ginger, papayas, and mangos in season along with the other colorful fruits.

*817 Ninth Avenue. 489-1964. Open 24 hours, 7 days. Phone orders. Delivers.*

At J. DEMARTINO SEAFOOD MARKET, Joseph DeMartino is the third-generation owner and remembers the neighborhood when "It was all Irish with just a few Jews and Italians." Now, with son Joe, Jr., helping, DeMartino has a much broader ethnic clientele and stocks to suit every shopper. "Italian preferences—squid and whiting; Spanish-speaking folks—Spanish mackerel, kingfish, red snapper, octopus; Jewish customers—whole or filet flounder, whitefish (from Michigan lakes), salmon, halibut;

Greeks—porgies and other Mediterranean favorites; blacks—porgies, whitings, Virginia spots (a porgy-sized fish that resembles snakeskin)." Seasonal varieties include soft shell crabs from Maryland (summer), boned shad and shad roe from Delaware (winter)—all fresh; lobster tails are frozen. Joe DeMartino's favorite dish? "Fried filet of sole: Dip filets first in beaten egg, then in plain or seasoned bread crumbs and again in egg. Fry in hot, 'swimming' [meaning plenty] oil briefly on each side. Serve with fresh broccoli and baked potatoes and, yes, red burgundy wine for this Italian dinner."

*821 Ninth Avenue. 265-3813, 3832. 8-5:30, Monday to Thursday; 8-6, Friday; 8-3, Saturday; closed Sunday. Phone orders. Limited delivery.*

# UPPER WEST SIDE
## Jewish, Hispanic, Scandinavian, Russian, International, French, Italian, Thai

*Love and eggs should be fresh to be enjoyed.*
**RUSSIAN PROVERB**

DAY AND NIGHT on the Upper West Side, Broadway traffic screeches to a halt at cross streets. Oblivious to the noise, casually dressed people, many wearing jeans and jogging shoes, amble up and down the sidewalks, crossing streets, moving in and out of the parade of stores. People walk steadily; they seldom window-shop. As if listening to invisible "Walkman" music, they seem propelled by inner resources, played out and resigned to the jarring sounds and varied sights around them. Even more oblivious to traffic, a few elderly folks bravely perch on benches along the central island dividing the north- and south-bound traffic.

Upper Westsiders' support of their food shops is anything but nonchalant, however, continually attracting new stores in the business districts. French bakeries selling the ever-popular croissants are easy to find. Columbus Avenue ripens quickly into an abundant food center—everything from outdoor fruit stands, caterers, minuscule shops to ultra-suave palaces like the DDL FOODSHOW (page 87) and one-of-a-kind spots like The Great American Cone Company (288 Columbus Avenue, 873-5238) featuring ice cream cones.

Upper Broadway's ethnic flavors are often hard to trace among the many chain and service stores that seem impersonal. But there are some gems, as though lifted whole from a foreign land like a great temple in the art museums. Mejia Spanish-American Foods (2585 Broadway between 97th and 98th) is a large grocery store. At Choi's Farm Fruits and Vegetables (99th and Broadway) the seasonal fruit salads and striking pyramids inspire fruity beverage ideas. A.M.Z. Corp. (2652 Broadway) touts "Grocery En General" and "Productos Tropicales" that intrigue you even if you can't read Spanish. And SIAM GROCERY (page 89) is quite Oriental.

But smoked fish departments are probably the liveliest attractions of all, especially on weekends. ZABAR'S (page 86), BARNEY GREENGRASS "THE STURGEON KING" (page 88) and MURRAY'S STURGEON SHOP (page 89) offer many salmon and sturgeon varieties and phone and mail order services as well. These departments have built wider and wider clienteles for most of the century, giving the flavor to this neighborhood that you immediately feel inside the shops. You may like to shop by phone once in a while or from a great distance by mail. But when you're in Manhattan, be sure to walk into these shops. You'll enjoy the intensity, the food enjoyment and responsiveness of shoppers, choosing from the rich assortment of cheeses, fish, condiments, breads and pastries, specialties of all kinds that arouse the people from the nonchalance you may perceive on the less exciting noisy avenues.

BEAUDESIR, a French baker, specializes in French breads and everything is in French including posters and French spoken at the register. *Fantastique!* Baskets full of breads—*Baguettes* (the classic long, skinny breads), *Ficelle*, small *Baguettes*, *Epis* (long wheat-seed shaped), *Petit Pain* (rolls—small, medium, and large) and large *Boule* (round loaves)—dominate the scene. Pastries, too, are well represented: *Croissants* (raisin version called *Pain aux Raisins* is sprinkled with cinnamon and chocolate variation is called *Chocolatine*), *Brioche* (the famed specialty sweetbread and *Brioche Crème* (filled with cream), Tarts, *Mille Feuille* (flaky pastries such as *Napoleons*), *Eclairs*, and *Cornet Crème* (cone-shaped). Rather new, the shop is run by a bilingual French brunette, Marie Pierre Bacques.

*2143 Broadway. 873-1191. 8:30 to 8, seven days. Phone orders.*

ZABAR'S, since I've known it, reminds me of a giant food circus bringing back oldtime Ashkenazy Jewish flavors, such as gefilte fish, plus dashes of Swedish herring, Hungarian salami, Danish blue cheese, Irish blarney, Italian gorgonzola, Norwegian ship biscuits, Welsh caerphilly, Russian black bread—foods adored by almost everyone. Pots, pans, baskets undulate on the ceilings (and a second floor "Wares Fair" lures you from above). Traffic is heavy. Sidewalks are crowded with cartons; hand trucks move mountains of cheeses, zigzagging through the shop among customers. The loudspeaker keys up the audience. Handmade, un-uniform signs—"Yes, we make our own CRÊME FRAICHE"; "GOAT CHEESE!!!"; "Absolutely NO Samples" (placed over the Danish crumbles of raisins and nuts)—shout more vociferously than a circus barker. Bedlam on a busy day, enveloping baking smells from the back room, Spanish chatter as young workers unload cartons, Murray Klein, with shirtsleeves rolled up, coaxing shoppers, "Come try the bread, just out of the oven." European cheeses from fifteen countries jam the refrigerators, counters, aisles. In back, Ivan Almont presides over twelve huge burlap bags of coffee beans. "Customers have favorites," he explains. "Jews like Zabar's (a secret blend); French buy Vienna roast; Italians—French/Italian roast (dark espresso); Mid-Easterners mix Colombian and espresso or Jamaica blue mountain; Hispanics—Italian espresso or Vienna roast." Frenzied activity pulls you to the meat department where butchers slice cold cuts; a half dozen salesmen sell smoked fish (the store specialty). Along the walls and aisles are vinegars, dressings, preserves, syrups, and pasta. Baked goods behind four queues at computerized checkouts. Confused by the acts? A central display lists all cheeses in stock, smoked fish, caviars, salads, coffees, teas, *"en croute"* specialties, picnic ideas . . . For a delightful menu, Murray Klein recommends: "Fresh caviar with a bottle of champagne followed by Scotch salmon. And then, not steak! My wife makes a great *Cholent* (bean and meat casserole)," he suggests brightly. Edith Klein shares her delicious recipe, page 284.

   *Broadway at 80th Street. 787-2000. 9-7:30, Sunday to Thursday; 9-10, Friday; 9-midnight, Saturday; in summer closes Friday at 7:30 and Sunday at 6 P.M. Phone orders (special orders 2 to 3 days in advance).*

At DDL FOODSHOW a ten-year-old girl shopping with her mother asks, "How about cheddar?" "Everyone has cheddar. I want to try something *different!*" decides her mother scanning soft *Taleggio di Monte*, goat cheeses including *Gatine Buche*, semifirm *Crottin Poivre*, and triple cream *Explorateur* among the 250 cheese varieties. This craving for new, exotic flavors is typical of shoppers roving the immense, skylighted food store opened in December, 1982. Dino Di Laurentis, Italian film producer, owns the store, stocking classic Italian as well as other European and domestic American foods in a lavish, ultramodern setting. Among the departments are fresh pasta (2-inch ribbons for lasagne; ¾-inch strips for *Pappardelle* (game and poultry stews); ¼-inch *Tagliatelle*; ⅛-inch for *Fettucine Romano*; ¹⁄₁₆-inch for *Linguine* and even finer *Capelli d'Angelo*), fresh fruits and vegetables, salumeria favorites (salamis, bacons, pickles, etc.), groceries (condiments, soups and syrups, dried fruits and nuts), chocolates

(Peyrano from Italy and DeLoisy from France) coffees from six countries, smoked fish and caviars in abundant arrays. But the breads may be the real show-stoppers. Delivered on eight-foot bread boards to the bread counter, there are herb and seed breads (such as rosemary, sage, and fennel), vegetable and fruit-tinged specialties (like zucchini, tomato, artichoke, banana, and walnut) and old-fashioned *Pagnotta Pugliese, Romana*, and *Napoletana* loaves as if fresh from the Italian countryside. In the "Gastronomia" department of ready-to-eat foods, salads, soups, and specialties like *Stracotto di Manzo al Barolo* (Italian pot roast with wine) are featured on immense stainless steel platters.

*Columbus Avenue at 81st Street. 787-6644. 10-9, Monday to Thursday; 9-10, Friday and Saturday; 9-8, Sunday. Phone and mail orders. Delivers.*

BARNEY GREENGRASS "THE STURGEON KING" is such a large, high-ceilinged store, you may, for a few minutes, feel dwarfed and somewhat confused about where to look first. At the left, an art deco style white and black mirrored case boldly frames the old-fashioned cheese counter; right of the entrance, a long case informally stocks Faroe Island smoked salmon, sturgeon varieties, salads, caviars, homemade *Borscht*, many other smoked fish and herring specialties, ready to eat. Centrally placed, barrels full of coffee beans on the floor attract attention under a faded photo of Barney Greengrass, who founded the business in 1908. The founder's son, Moe, his wife, Shirley, and son, Gary, now move around the store filling orders; they also run the adjacent dining room (open daily 9-4, except Monday; especially busy on Sundays). Herring in cream sauce is smooth and comforting on the tongue after the Greengrass family has soaked the Iceland herring several days, marinated it in vinegar and flavored it with heavy sour cream, sugar, and spices. Canadian lake sturgeon (skinned, boned and smoked) and Gaspé Nova Scotia (also called "Eastern") wood-smoked salmon are best sellers.

*541 Amsterdam Avenue. 724-4707. 8:30-5:45, Tuesday to Saturday; 8-4:30, Sunday; closed Monday. Phone and mail orders (will Express Mail perishables packed in dry ice—order form available).*

MURRAY'S STURGEON SHOP, using maximum planning, routes shoppers along the long, narrow terrazzo aisle in front of the refrigerator case running the length of the shop. Meticulously arranged containers inside the case highlight colorful smoked fish—kippered salmon, smoked whitefish, sable plate, lake sturgeon, Eastern and Western Nova Scotia (a mild smoked salmon), as several countermen slice and wrap fish. In back, behind the "Order Department" sign on the rear door, you may see the owner, Arthur J. Cutler, working on phone order slips covering the entire wall. "Impossible to keep up with orders," he exclaims as a customer rattles off an order list to be picked up in three days. "Atlantic and Eastern salmon, sturgeon from Lake Winnipeg (mild with very little salt) and homemade pickled herring are our specialties," he emphasized.

*2429 Broadway. 724-2650. 8-7, Tuesday to Friday and Sunday; 8-8, Saturday; closed Monday. Phone and mail orders. Free delivery.*

SIAM GROCERY, a small shop with narrow shelves stocked with food cans and packages, wooden elephants and cane hats in the window, has three-tiered baskets hanging from the twenty-foot ceiling. You will see many Thai newspapers and periodicals wrapped for delivery (this is also a Thai news agency), hear Thai spoken, and you'll feel transported to a past era, another place. Merchandising is quaint and may even appear a bit helter-skelter. But Chichi Paleewong, born in Thailand, knows where to find every tantalizing ingredient in the mysterious stock and shares a recipe (page 277). Among the canned curries, choose from green and red curry pastes (indispensable to Thai cooking) or ingredients to grind your own, including mortar if in stock (or use a Mexican *Molcajete).* You'll find *Kapi* (shrimp paste), *Nampla* (anchovy fish extract), chilies, lemon grass, *Kha* (looks like ginger root, available dried), ten kinds of rice and rice products, a dozen sauces, fifteen chili products, preserves, spices, syrups, and kitchenware. The Paleewong family also imports *Sigha* and *Amarit* Thai beer.

*2745 Broadway. 864-3640. 11:30-8, Monday to Saturday; 12:30-7:30, Sunday.*

# UPPER EAST SIDE, YORKVILLE, LITTLE HUNGARY

German, Hungarian, Czechoslovakian, Polish, Irish,
French, Japanese, Scandinavian, Mexican, Greek,
Austrian, International, Korean, Italian, Asian-Indian,
Hispanic, British, Sicilian, Yugoslavian,
South American, Swiss

*Good coffee should be black like the devil,*
*hot like hell and sweet like a kiss.*

HUNGARIAN PROVERB

LIKE THE TREASURES, wonders, and mysteries of the antique shops around them, East Side and Yorkville/ Little Hungary shops are encrusted with scents and flavors. In a neighborhood endowed with the world's most spectacular museums, galleries, and boutiques, the many shops await you with cosmopolitan elegance and the charm of old Europe. Yet you will never doubt you are on New York's Upper East Side. Discovery of its wonders is easier than digging up a buried treasure. You need only walk from 59th Street along Madison, Lexington, Third, Second, and First Avenues up to the high 80s, with senses intact.

The mood is leisurely and manicured, an atmosphere where *"S'il vous plait"* and *"Schön"* seem at home with Hungarian meats, Swedish Hot Sauce, and Irish bacon; Austrian and continental baked goods comfortable in a *Patisserie* and *Konditorei,* where a *jicama* (root) may be stocked near rosy *Radicchio* (lettuce) and Belgian endive. You can relax, European style, over a coffee and flaky pastry and continue your amble among the superb fruit shops—rapidly blossoming into vibrant produce centers—and multiethnic bakeries where the stomach is pleased as easily as the eyes. Amid the many continental stores catering to sophisticated tastes, don't miss the specialty shops focused on Hungarian, German, Irish, Czech foods, even though many of the older traditional German shops have expanded their wares to embrace more cuisines. Notably present are the seafood and meat shops for planning oriental or occidental meals.

Not for the jaded, these neighborhoods are for the lively, the upscale, affluent who like unexpected surprises like biting into a chocolate-dipped morsel and tasting the bursting juices of a fresh strawberry or stepping into a meat shop to be engulfed by smoky pork aromas. Here, a glimpse into an elegant caterer's window stimulates impulsive plans for a champagne party to be topped off with the coffee described in the proverb above.

**BLOOMINGDALE'S** 59th Street entrance (near Lexington) begins at the window displays of MICHEL GUERARD COMPTOIR GOURMAND (sixteen *nouvelle cuisine* dishes and twelve desserts) and THE PETROSSIAN SHOP (four types of caviar, salmon, foie gras), new boutiques divided by a wide aisle leading to the new deli department. The latter features fresh and smoked meats and cheese, where you may also see fist-sized garlic displayed in baskets. Fresh beef is supplied through Old Homestead Steak House and the smoked ribs through Smokey's. French and Italian cheeses are also included along with fresh salads in this department (formerly on the Lexington side). Down a flight of steps, in the "Delicacies" department, are the vinegars, oils, teas and coffees, crackers, plum puddings, and jams (don't walk into the smoked mirror) and also MARCELLA HAZAN'S ITALIAN KITCHEN selling pasta (part of the Fresh Food department). Activity mounts with shoppers, demonstrations offering samples, and the inevitable circling from one boutique to another. At the 59th Street entrance (near Third Avenue), the BAKERY (breads and pastries) continues to stir up the excitement of the original department, expanded in October, 1981. Albert Prato is manager here. Brick-oven baked bread includes French country (two sizes), rye, whole wheat, and walnut bread, among others, and pastries vary considerably, with emphasis on the French specialties. Winding your way through the food boutiques, you'll surely whet your appetite and your taste buds with something you buy.

*59th Street from Lexington to Third Avenue. Deli: 705-2957; Delicacies: 705-2958; Bakery: 705-2954; Michel Guerard: 705-3177; Petrossian: 705-3176. 10-9, Monday and Thursday; 10-6:30, Tuesday, Wednesday, Friday, and Saturday; closed Sunday.*

RAINBOW GOURMET, at its 59th Street entrance (opposite BLOOMIE'S) has a rainbow of fruit colors in its sidewalk display, drawing you in to more fruits—fruits for salads in a melon cup, fruits to make a fruit beverage (page 337) or to poach in wine. Vegetables rival the fruits in colors and freshness, to cut up and stir-fry to crisp brightness. At the Lexington Avenue entrance, in refrigerator cases, prepared specialties for lunch snacks, dried fruits, for *Anousabour* (page 316), dairy and grocery departments are appealing.

*735 Lexington Avenue. 752-1280. 7-9, Monday to Friday; 7-8:30, Saturday; closed Sunday. Phone orders. Delivers.*

KATAGIRI is a classic example of survival, like the huge ancient, wooden *Uso* (mortar) and *Kine* (pestle) displayed in the umbrella-dotted window. Since 1907 at this same location, the large shop specializes in Japanese foods. Also, gifts (many food-related) are available along with open-stock china for the Japanese and non-Oriental clientele. Jun Tonegawa, the courteous manager, keeps on hand a wide variety of ingredients for the beauteous Japanese cuisine. For *Sashimi*, tuna, yellow tail, octopus, calamari, tile fish; for *Sukiyaki*, thinly sliced beef; for *Shabu Shabu* (recipe, page 264), even more thinly sliced beef. Fresh produce, and a refrigerator full of *Miso* (eight kinds), and preserved eggplants enhance shopping choices. In addition, there are freeze-dried vegetables and *Kimchi* for Korean customers.

*224 East 59 Street. 755-3566. 9:30-6:30, Monday to Friday; 10-6, Saturday; closed Sunday. Phone, mail, and airmail orders. No deliveries.*

HOT & CRUSTY BREAD AND ROLLS shop is impossible to pass. Like flags waving, red and white printed signs and blinds grip your attention and freshly baked bread your olfactory nerves. So many loaves in bins and baskets make selection difficult: whole wheat, rye, Vienna, French, Portuguese, Challah (poppy or sesame), pumpkin date, walnut loaf. Also, there are pastries, rye, and whole wheat rolls. Everything is roped off, museum style, preventing shoppers from approaching the loaves while two salespersons circulate to select their choices. Owner Peter Lobell, who supplies Tavern on the Green restaurant, bakes his health bread flecked with pine nuts and sprinkled with cracked wheat.

*1201 Second Avenue. 753-2614. 8:30-7:30, Monday to Friday; 8:30-6, Saturday; 9-5, Sunday.*

"THE GRAPEVINE" FOOD HALLS create a village market ambiance with lustrous vegetables for Western and Oriental cuisines. The innovative greengrocer adjoins a chocolate, tea, and candy shop and the corner FAY & ALLEN'S BAKER-KONDITOREI for pastries and coffee. In "The Grapevine," a shopper finds *Jicama* for a Mexican dish and long green squash for an Italian dish or an Asian-Indian curry; there are black and white radishes, *radicchio* lettuce imported from Italy, plantains for Caribbean dishes stocked near the New Zealand *tamarillos*, cranshaw, sharleen, and casaba melons. The popular Salad Bar features ready-to-dress salad greens for whipping up your own combination; and there are foil-wrapped potatoes and cheeses in plentiful array. Owner Billy Iarrobino has enthusiastic and energetic employees, including manager Sal.

*1237 Third Avenue. 249-9550. 7-Midnight, seven days. ("The Grapevine")*

*794-1101. 8-11 P.M., Monday to Friday; 8-12:30 A.M., Saturday and Sunday. Phone orders (Bakery).*

WILLIAM POLL—a food magnet for those with continental cravings where a chocolate-colored marquee covers the sidewalk and a spinning pastry display fills the window. Stanley Poll, tall son of founder William Poll, runs the business (there since 1922) alongside his parents. "Poll" is shortened from the Greek Pappadopoulos. (William was born in Macedonia and his wife in Sparta) which explains the numerous Greek varieties available: frozen dishes *(Moussaka, Pastitsio)*, desserts and pastries *(Trigona* and *Saragli Saraïli)*, imported canned specialties. Yet there are enough French (Paul Corcellet and Soleillou) and British (Tiptree from Wilkin & Sons and Dundee) brands—vinegars, jellies, caviars, fish delicacies, escargots, chestnut spreads, oils, olives, and nuts to please selective taste buds. Ideas for dips: "Cheddy" (cheddar cheese, sour cream, chutney); "Prosciutto" (prosciutto, cream cheese, and spices).

*1051 Lexington Avenue. 288-0501. 9-6, Monday to Saturday; closed Sunday. Mail and phone orders (catalog).*

PASTA & CHEESE, a refreshing green and white shop, has knee-deep baskets full of pasta shells inside the large windows at 72nd and Madison, one of the pasta & cheese shops opened by Henry Lambert. Catering to pasta lovers, there are also French, Swedish, English, and Italian cheeses, oils, and salamis for homemade pasta dishes with zesty red sauces.

*31 East 72 Street. 249-2466. 10-7, Monday to Friday; 9-7, Saturday; 11-6, Sunday. Phone orders. No deliveries.*

*Other shops: 756 Madison Ave., 570-0884; 1198 Madison Ave., 369-2980; 1312 Second Ave., 628-1313; 1375 Third Ave., 988-0997; 1896 B'way, 977-8782. (Some branches close later weekdays and open later on Sunday.)*

BAKERSFIELD MARKET, INC. "We try to bring more variety, more Oriental vegetables to our customers," owner Jaesup Ro explains. With his wife, Mayong, he relocated here in 1981 from their former 82nd Street and Lexington Avenue shop where they developed a clientele for their fresh produce. Customers pick from European and Kirby cucumbers, Mexican mangoes, Hawaiian pineapples, Jamaican ugli, Canadian strawberries, and California apricots. A large central display of crisp staple vegetables make selection pleasant and the seasonal fruits broadcast their delicious scents. Twelve fresh or dry herbs are available daily.
*1081 Lexington Ave. 744-4133. 8-8, seven days.*

SUCCES LA COTE BASQUE announces *"Patisserie Français,"* on the sign over the stucco front. A large picture window faces Lexington Avenue. Inside, a dozen small tables packed with pastry tasters fill the floor space.
*1032 Lexington Ave. 535-3311. 7:30-8, Monday to Friday; 7:30-9, Saturday; 7:30-7, Sunday.*

LES DELICES DE GUY PASCAL, run by Guy Pascal, founder of the chain formerly called DELICES LA COTE BASQUE, includes four pastry shops.
*1231 Madison Avenue. (with a tearoom), 289-5300. 9-10, Monday to Saturday; 9-8, Sunday.*
*939 First Avenue. 371-4144.*
*Olympic Towers bakery, 645 Fifth Avenue. 935-2220.*
*Guy Pascal at Zabar's, 80th and Broadway. 874-5400.*

LILY FRUIT CO., has brilliant fruit displays which spur thoughts of fruit salads (recipes, pages 323, 324). The shop is owned and run by Joe Young and named for his sister Lily, who works nonstop at the cash register. The Korea-born greengrocer opened this well-stocked shop in the summer of 1982, relocating from a smaller one across the street which he had operated for three years. Greatest demand? Seasonal grapes, cherries, fresh orange juice (made on the premises). There are also coffee and nut departments.
*1389 Second Avenue. 879-4761. Open 24 hours, seven days. Phone orders. Delivers.*

E.A.T., run by Eli Zabar, is primarily a caterer offering everything from airplane meals to feasts that sound Lucullan. But at the large store's tables, shoppers can pick Cavaillon baseball-sized melons, or *cepes* mushrooms displayed in small baskets near seasonal fruits. There are French-style homemade breads, smoked fish, and Provençal specialties.

*Madison Avenue at 72nd St. 879-4017. 7-7:30, Monday to Friday; 7-7, Saturday; 7-6, Sunday. Phone orders. No mail orders. Delivers.*

FRASER MORRIS is "international," says Oscar Brumberg, one of the owners, glowing over his Rodel imports from France (seafood, vegetables, jams, preserves), England (Minicheshire, Minicaerphilly, and other cheeses), Denmark (Baby Samsoe, Baby Cream Havarti, Baby Esromi) and Russia (Giant Malossol Beluga Caviar). "Our smoked salmon is from Scotland and Nova Scotia, sliced carefully, the English way; we carry coffee from Germany," he says proudly. Smoked brook trout (filleted and rewrapped in its own skin) is another house specialty. In the meat department, boneless shell steaks and filet mignon, blast frozen and packed in dry ice, are airmailed to order. Fraser Morris specializes in catering and gift baskets in two shops. What does Oscar Brumberg enjoy most? "Fresh fruit." And there are about eighteen varieties in the fruit department at the left of the entrance.

*931 Madison Avenue. 988-6700. 1264 Third Avenue. 288-7717. 9-6, Monday to Saturday; closed Sunday. Phone orders. Mail and airmail (catalog). Delivers.*

HARANT PORK STORE is quaint, early twentieth century. It is a tiny shop with an eye for Czechoslavakian meats—a novelty in New York. Tucked in the cases and mirrored, white enameled antique icebox, are smoked pork chops and kielbasa, ham salami and head cheese, smoked and fresh ham, rib bacon and spareribs. Jolly and hefty owner Steve Harant, Slovakia-raised, makes *Jitrnice* sausage (pork liver, rice, bread crumbs, garlic, pepper, and marjoram) for the holidays. Small, quiet wife, Mary Harant, likes a Czech dinner "with homemade knedle" topped with rich gravy. Just enough customer space for shoppers to step in off Second

Avenue, find a picnic bench to rest on, and read the admonition over the salami-slung old hooks, "WHEN YOU EAT SOMETHING GOOD REMEMBER WHERE YOU GOT IT." And there's enough shelf space for imported syrups (morello cherry, raspberry) and teas. Sauerkraut and pickles are stored in the refrigerator.

*1363 First Avenue. 744-4497. 8-6, Monday to Saturday (closed Wednesday and Sunday). Phone orders. Delivers.*

At SALAMONE & SONS, INC. (in business since 1900) you walk down three steps and into a world of fish. Owner Al Salamone, stocks fresh and smoked fish, for everything from *Sashimi* to *Paella* as well as sole, shrimp, salmon and scrod; also clams and oysters (to tuck into a steamy pilaf) among the shellfish.

*1410 First Avenue. 861-2662; 838-4100. 7:30-6:15, Monday to Saturday; closed Sunday. Phone orders. Delivers.*

MONSIEUR PHILIPPE'S CHARCUTERIE features French Brie from Lorraine (cow's milk), goat *Bucherme, Fromage Chevre,* topaz-hued *Asigo* from Italy, and Havarti from Denmark. Holland Westland skim milk cheese is gaining ground, says new owner Arden Portakal, a dark-haired and mustached Armenian. For the breads and rolls stocked from the Forgione Bakery there are patés, calves liverwurst from Schaller & Weber, and butters from France. To team with the teas and coffees in stock, choose from the chocolate tarts, truffle chocolate rolls and croissants from Viola, a Brooklyn-based bakery.

*1022 Madison Ave. 861-0920. 10-7:30, seven days. Phone orders. Free delivery.*

## Yorkville, Little Hungary

MATTIE HASKINS SHAMROCK IMPORTS is the friendliest Irish shop this side of Dublin. Amid Irish newspapers, records and tapes, food, and snack-related gifts, stop in to seek the sauces and jellies, toffees, fig rolls, and ginger snaps. For a breakfast of ol' Ireland, pick Irish oatmeal and marmalade, black (blood) pudding,

bacon, and sausages. And at Christmas time, to be sure, there's
Thompson's Christmas cakes and plum pudding from Cork, Ireland. Manager Kathleen suggests a zesty mint sauce for the lamb
roast, "It'll take the tears out of your eyes!"

*205 East 75th Street. 288-3918. 10:30-6, Monday to Saturday;
closed Sunday; summer, close early Saturday. Phone, mail,
and airmail orders.*

STAR MARKET shines like a star across from the Pahir Afghani-
stan restaurant with oriental vegetables and fruits heaped on outdoor stand and huge varieties of dried fruits and nuts, carefully
labeled and bagged, on the indoor shelves.

*1422 Second Avenue. 628-9782. 8-9, seven days. Phone orders.
Free delivery.*

FRANK AND TONY FISH MARKET has, at its entrance, a Chinese tile painting depicting a fish jumping for a butterfly. But the
catch is already on chipped ice in cases here. When eager for
Sicilian recipes and straightforward talk, come in and chat with
Frank Licata and Tony Maniscalco—in business together since
1946 and still talking. There's swordfish, halibut, sardines, cod,
mackerel, and porgies, and there may be Mowi salmon from Nor-
way, clams and mussels to steam, and calamari and octopus for a
winy sauce. There's always a daily special. Frank and Tony's
perfect meal? Fish filet, breaded and fried, served with vegetables
and, of course, Chianti wine. Their tip to bread fish filets: dip first
in flour, then in beaten egg, last in bread crumbs and fry for just a
few minutes in a generous amount of hot oil. They enjoy calamari, sauteed in tomato sauce, served on linguine with cheese.
*Molto buono! Gracie!*

*1486 Second Avenue. 288-9032. 7-5:30, Monday to Saturday;
closed Sunday. Phone orders. Free delivery.*

TIBOR MEAT SPECIALTIES' entrance is enlivened by a red and
white awning and the spicy, smoked meat scent lures you inside
the shop. Charming owner Barbara Vajda (pronounced Voy-do),
with her husband, Tibor, bought the shop in 1979. They specialize in no less than thirty-four varieties of Hungarian franks,

bologna, and salamis. These pork and veal succulents are strung
and smoked over hardwood sawdust in the back kitchen. The air
is also peppered with Hungarian, the national language of half the
clientele. Shoppers hang hungrily over the case in the three-foot
aisle as Barbara Vajda offers tidbits of salami and bread. For a
snack: garlicky, spicy salami and dark bread; or the mild orangey
sausage in large or small link sizes. To serve yourself and a very
special guest: one pound sausage, one pound sauerkraut, and two
smoked pork chops sprinkled with caraway seeds and bay leaves.
Simmer 10 minutes for a heavenly Hungarian meal. Another
tasty recipe is on page 295.

*1508 Second Avenue. 744-8292. 7-6, Monday to Saturday;
closed Sunday. Phone orders. No deliveries.*

At ORWASHER'S, you can almost smell the bread baking in the
original hearth ovens built by Abraham Orwasher in 1916 as
shoppers buy hearty ryes and pumpernickels, whole wheat breads
and rolls. Now son Louis and his son, David, carry on the bakery
business. The mood is quiet in this Austrian shop with white
tiled floor and marble counter still intact. Elizabeth Nemeth at
the counter sells breads representing many lands: Ireland, France,
Russia, Switzerland, and many studded with Danish or Dutch
caraway seeds. If you've planned a menu around the bakery's
Hungarian potato bread, come early; it may be sold out before
noon. Or better, call to order a loaf of it or other specialties including cranberry, walnut, and wreath loaves to name a few of the
fifty-five bread and roll features. The cheese counter is convenient for impulsive choices from an extensive stock.

*308 East 78th St. 288-6569. 7-7, Monday to Saturday; closed
Sunday. Phone orders.*

PAPRIKAS WEISS'S fetching windows—grains and nuts, spices
and herbs—stimulate ideas for paprika-strewn dishes, especially
Hungarian. Inside, the long shelves and counters are stocked with
more Hungarian foods and ingredients in cans, bottles, and bags.
Also, there are more imported cheeses, vinegars, dressings, and
patés than Louis the Great ever dreamed of. Edward Weiss, third-
generation owner and cookbook author, takes pride in the 95-

year-old family business, which until 1956 was a Hungarian specialty shop. Now the clientele and stocks include French, British, German, Czech, and Austrian. But Hungarian egg-grain products are still called by their Old World names: *Tarhonya* (barley-sized); *Nokkedli* (lima bean size); square noodles, *Kockatenta* (large squares) and *Spaetzle*. Like other ingredients, these specialties can be cooked "long" (in a soup) or "short" (drained, with butter or sauce), to quote the terms coined by Ed Weiss's father. (Ed shares a recipe, page 198).

*1546 Second Avenue. 288-6117. 9-6, Monday to Saturday; closed Sunday, except before Christmas. Phone and mail orders (catalog).*

The 82ND STREET FRUIT AND VEGETABLE MARKET parades fresh fruits all around the corner, just to ensnare you from either side. Four workers place greens in the central display along with tofu, bean sprouts, and tubers (taro and cassava), neatly arranged in a rich assortment offered by the large shop. Hs Kim, owner since 1976, says *"An Yung Hashimnika"* ("Hello" in Korean).

*1576 Second Avenue. 737-5977. 24 hours, seven days.*

LEKVAR BY THE BARREL (H. ROTH & SON) a corner shop with richly stocked windows, features foods, knives, forms, and griddles by the thousands. Begun by "great grandma Roth" as a "little shop in America that would cater to those yearning for a taste of their homeland," today it appeals also to those yearning for cuisines from Indonesia to South America via Hungary, Holland, and Mexico. Bobby Roth (now a mother with a child of her own) has been in the shop "since I was a little girl." She can suggest uses for each diverse item in the crammed shelves and aisles (a cozy place for wandering and dreaming up menus by the dozens). There are foods honeyed and preserved, dripping fruits, and heady chocolates, spices, herbs and herb teas and baking essences from anisette and arrac to *waldmeister*, walnut, and vanilla. But poppy seed and three kinds of "real, red paprika" are spicy highlights. Bobby Roth offers a delectable recipe (page 313) from Hungary.

*1577 First Avenue. 734-1111. 9-6:30, Tuesday to Saturday; closed Sunday and Monday. Mail and phone orders (catalog).*

YORKVILLE PACKING HOUSE, INC. lovingly makes "European-style meats," and Michael Lovinger is a second-generation owner. Sweet, hot, and garlic-spiced sausages and homemade bologna varieties are produced. Many Hungarian, Polish, and Yugoslavian shoppers pore over the garlic-spiced, "torched" and deep-fried bacons. A typical mild Hungarian sausage made here, molded of pork and beef and gently spiced with pepper, paprika, and coriander cooks in five minutes. It keeps up to eight days in the refrigerator. Hotter, heavily spiced kinds keep indefinitely. Michael Lovinger's "recipe for happiness" is Hungarian garlic-smoked sausage, sliced diagonally, with Bermuda onion and washed down with sips of Debroi Harslevelu wine (sold in Yorkville Hungarian wine shops). Niebylsky bread, Globus (Hungarian) and Krakus (Polish) items, including jams and jellies are also available.

*1580 Second Avenue. 744-5936, 628-5147. 7-7, Monday to Saturday; closed Sunday. Phone orders.*

SCHALLER & WEBER has featured German-style meats and flavors in this large, airy shop since 1937. An established mail order business and supplier to Bloomingdale's, Gimbels, and other retailers, the firm processes its specialties in the Astoria, Queens plant. Lined up in rosy formation on its display cases are: *Fleischwurst* (German bologna), *Jagdwurst* (coarser textured bologna), *Gelbwurst* (veal and pork studded), *Speck Blutwurst* (beef blood sausage with fat). The pageantry of cold cuts includes delectable Black Forest bacon, smoked goose breast, *Nuss Schinken* (small Westphalian ham), *Bauernschinken* (farmer's ham). Always in stock are the familiar frankfurters and wieners that have fed New Yorkers since the "gobble-and-go" lunches first flourished on street corners before this century. To further tempt shoppers, there are German-style wieners, Polish sausages, salami (with garlic), cervelat (without garlic), and Oldenburger onion liverwurst. And for slicing, try Braunschweiger liverwurst. To bake and stew, pick a *Kassler Rippchen* (smoked loin). Fresh meats include pigs' feet, hocks, ribs, butts, shoulders, veal, beef, and lamb cuts. According to Joe Knau, the American manager born of German parents, top sellers in the store are Gold Medal liverwurst (for spreading) and Black Forest ham and *Lachs-schinken* (smoked, cured, boneless pork). Like many Yorkville retailers, Joe Knau clings to personal favorite ethnic dishes. His favorite: Sauerbraten with red cabbage and dumplings.

*1654 Second Avenue. 879-3047. 9-6, Monday to Thursday; 8:30-6:30, Friday and Saturday; closed Sunday. No phone orders. Mail orders (catalog available).*

BREMEN HOUSE, INC. opened shop in 1950 as a German food center and now encompasses the whole world of international foods. A very large store with record, china, and gift departments, the German deli at the entrance tempts the shopper with its European flavors. John Schweiger, Austrian manager of the food department since 1952, stocks favorite German wursts, cold cuts, breads, and preserves, and expanded his offerings as neighborhood clientele changed. South American chilies and Asian-Indian chutneys, all manner of coffees and teas, nuts and honeys, mustards and crackers give variety to the shelves. A "happy" dinner for John Schweiger: Pre-cooked knockwurst cooked in ten minutes with sauerkraut. "Heat and eat," he says, "with *Schinkenbrot* (coarse bread) or *Bauernbrot* (dark) and German wine or beer."

*220 East 85 Street. 288-5500. 9-8, Monday to Saturday; 11-7, Sunday. Phone and mail orders. Delivers.*

KARL EHMER, a Brooklyn-based 54-store chain, spurs ideas for hearty German, Swiss, and Austrian meals. Wolfgang Weisshaupt, manager of the Yorkville shop since 1955, suggests menus for the 100 sausage and salami varieties. Seek out fresh pork cuts, veal, beef, and lamb. Niebylski ryes, pumpernickels from Silver Bell (a Queens Lithuanian sourdough bakery), and stone oven baked breads (delivered Wednesday, Friday, and Saturday) are always on hand. *Bueckling* (white smoked fish) is another specialty here. Wolfgang Weisshaupt, born in Bodensee, Lake Constance, describes his favorite supper: Headcheese salad or *Presskopf* (pressed brawn), cubed or thinly sliced with chopped onion, oil and vinegar dressing and served with *Bauernbrot* and German beer. For a special German dinner, he suggested "sauerbraten beef roast (marinated from 2 to 6 days in wine, vinegar, and spices), potatoes and carrots."

*230 East 86 Street. 535-2129. 8-6, Monday and Tuesday; 8-6:30, Wednesday to Saturday; closed Sunday. Phone orders. No delivery.*

*246 Third Ave. 676-8480; 730 West 181 Street. 928-7770 (check shop hours locally in Brooklyn and Queens).*

ELK CANDY COMPANY is a candyland where marzipan and chocolates delight youngsters and adults. In business since the 1940s with the Elk name ("They were looking for a short name"), the shop changed hands several times, and is now run by Swiss-born Albert W. Hadener. Merken's American chocolate drips into and over the almond paste for marzipan molded into kringles, fairy acorns (pistachio marzipan half-dipped in chocolate) and dominoes for the lucky tongues. For the primarily German customers, good luck at New Year's means candy of mushroom and piglet shapes; special shapes for other holidays.

*240 East 86 Street. 650-1177. 9-6:30, Monday to Saturday; 11-6:30, Sunday. No phone orders.*

# SPANISH HARLEM
## Hispanic, Black, Jamaican, Dominican, Haitian, Barbadian, West African, Korean, South American, Italian, Jewish

Give me today's meat, yesterday's bread,
and last year's wine, and the doctor can go.

JAMAICAN PROVERB

DESERTED BUILDINGS, broken windows, neglected streets—more than other neighborhoods . . . How difficult it is to imagine Harlem in its heyday, alive with social organizations and white-collar and working-class people. Russian-Jewish, Irish, German, and Italian immigrants were among the earliest populations.

> By 1900 Harlem was home for an economically diverse Russian-Jewish community of approximately 17,000. Although numbers of immigrant Jewish families could be found scattered throughout Harlem, their major concentrations were in the predominantly Irish-German East Harlem neighborhoods south of 110th Street. Most of the more affluent Russian Jews joined their Irish and German counterparts in settling the mixed tenement, brownstone apartment-house section west of Lexington Avenue. Their poorer brethren crowded into the densely populated working-class tenement district east of Lexington. Few Jews settled in East Harlem's growing "Little Italy" . . . by the East River and Third Avenue between 105th and 120th Streets.*

Along with the black settlers, numerous ethnic groups demanded local foods and necessities. Outdoor markets flourished during the early decades of the century: the two largest on Park Avenue between 99th and 106th Streets; another on Park Avenue between 111th and 116th Streets. New markets for Harlem were requested in 1930. The first enclosed market, *The Park Avenue Retail Market* was opened in 1936 and the 450 stands were filled by many of the 700 pushcart operators from the open-air markets.

Talking to many of the original stall owners today becomes an instant link to the past. Retailers nostalgically speak about the early days, the colorful stall owners—specialists in their own food fields—and especially the community changes that forced adjustments in their retailing practices (like those in *Essex Street Market*, page 16).

Currently, Hispanics, blacks, Haitians, Africans, and Caribbean

* Gurock, Jeffrey S. *When Harlem Was Jewish.* New York: Columbia University Press, 1979. p. 36.

peoples from Barbados, Jamaica, and other islands are avid shoppers supplying indoors the color lacking outdoors.

While for decades LA MARQUETA (see below) has dominated food retailing in the area known as Spanish Harlem, many individual shops remain open. For instance VALENCIA BAKERY, INC. (page 110) has developed into a multistore operation, beginning in Spanish Harlem as a small Spanish bakery. Giving new vitality to the neighborhood, several Korean retailers offer fruits and other tropicals, fish and seafood along Second and Third Avenues. Stimulating thoughts of food anytime of the day and evening, food shops offer hope for a resurgence and revival in this once-elegant community of "little worlds," where "affluent live in dignity and splendor." The apartments facing Central Park, where the professional classes resided, were called "The Golden Edge" and "Sugar Hill." *

**LA MARQUETA: PARK AVENUE MARKET:** *"Paga, Paga, Paga," "La Mia es de Masa Nadamas!" "La Carne de Masa," "La Patitas!" "Molleja!"*
Inside La Marqueta at the 111th Street and Park Avenue entrance, shoppers call in Spanish to *paga* (pay) or to order meat cuts on a busy Saturday morning. They stand at a long meat counter owned by ALAN GLANTZ. His helper Alan Mazza, treasurer of Park Avenue Enclosed Market Merchants Association, Inc., serves customers in the market where he practically grew up. His parents, MEYER and SOPHIE MAZZA, run the adjacent stall where they have sold vegetables since the market opened in 1936—first of six covered public markets (in Manhattan, Bronx, and Brooklyn) built by the city to house pushcart vendors. Shoppers crowd the aisle that runs lengthwise through the food section of the entire building including grocery, produce, and meat stalls, *botanico* (herb and spice shop), and tropical stands providing a mass of variety and color. On the opposite parallel side, soft-goods departments feature clothing items and novelties.

Children call their parents, butchers crack cleavers and talk

* *New York City Guide:* American Guide Series. New York: Octagon Books, 1970 (reprint from 1939), chapter on "Harlem."

spiritedly with shoppers, radio music fills the air and, overhead, a train roars by—as one does 120 times daily—but no one notices it. The din is too heavy here in La Marqueta's Building #1.

You can walk through five buildings, tucked under the railroad bridge, all the way to 116th Street and hear more Spanish, West Indian, and Southern United States English, than anywhere in New York and see more tropical roots and fruits, vegetables, groceries, meats, and poultry, fish and shellfish prized by local ethnic groups than in any other market. As you walk through on a weekend when the aisles are full, the interesting foods and the shoppers' liveliness create such an exuberant atmosphere that you hardly notice the dingy surroundings, without paint, better lighting, improved plumbing, or other renovations since the market opened. Only the third building, burnt in 1974 and rebuilt in 1981 by a city grant, has new stalls. If you shop on a quiet day, however, you can stop and ask retailers about the foods they sell. The buildings have never been graphed and stalls change so frequently that you may be somewhat perplexed about which building you are in. At the "fish house" (115th to 116th streets), the hilly ground produced an interesting market arrangement with a maze of fish, poultry, meat, and shellfish stalls divided by three, four-step intervals. At no time, however, will you ever doubt you are in LA MARQUETA, a market specializing in local needs. There were 450 stands when the market opened, but as the traditional neighborhood ethnic distribution changed from Italian, Jewish, and Irish the retailers and products have reflected the change. Nevertheless, among the current stall owners, amazingly, a large number of original operators continue to sell from the same stall. Many learned to speak Spanish, and learned new foods during the adjustment period. THE MAZZAS are excellent examples of cultural and business adjustments.

"My father, Marcus Mazza, he had foresight, he saw people changing, saw the Hispanics coming in, in the 1940s," Sophie Mazza explains. "I was born on 114th and Madison Avenue," she adds. Recalling the old days, she continues, "That's when our market was outdoors, right under the bridge. We warmed our hands over our little fires. It was more white then. Now if you walk around you see mostly tropicals," she said, referring to Spanish Harlem. Her father became one of the largest importers of tropical foods and was among the first to learn how to handle *Platanos* (plantains). Alan, one of her two sons, followed in the elders' footsteps.

A shopper, José Velasquez, born in Ecuador, buys kidney beans across the aisle from a grocery stall and plans to buy fish to cook with the beans. "Cook them with garlic, onions, oil, and *no* hot peppers," he advises.

In the second building, JEAN and AL LAPP, another original Mom–Pop grocery stall, sell thirty kinds of beans and grains, dried codfish and canned goods. "I used to live in Harlem when the population was German, Jewish, and Italian," Jean says, serving a shopper. She wears a white apron over her skirt and sweater. "Then we were all Jewish and Italian vendors; now, only a few Jewish left and most are Spanish." The Lapps consider retirement a probability soon.

In the newly renovated Building #3 (why don't they give these market buildings more interesting names?) there are small vegetable stands, a *botanico* and LA LECHERIA (dairy) that sells milk, white cheese, and guava jelly (a favorite dessert). Pass a meat department and at the left corner, JOE SOLOMON, original owner and market historian presides. "We've got it. You want it," he hawks, selling dried shrimp and *Gari* (ground cassava) to a Nigerian shopper and sugar to a Spanish-speaking woman. Nostalgically, Joe Solomon, a dapper man with carefully groomed hair and sports clothes, recalls early market days. "We had such sellers . . . talk about Hollywood! They had a story for every food and spice they sold!" When shown a 1950 article from *New York World-Telegram and Sun* which I had discovered in the New York Central Research Library, he almost broke down at seeing the photo of Inspector John J. Kelly (formerly a market inspector for twenty-six years) holding an octopus from VIVIAN CE-RASUOLO's stand (her nephew runs her former stall in the "fish house").

In Building #4, newer stand holders provide a contrast. For example, high above the floor level of the Haitian stall, ELLI

BEAU SEJOUR, standing on a high platform, is visible from the waist up. Surrounded by piles of *Balanaro yams* (log-sized, can be 20 pounds!), glossy avocados, *Yautia* roots and *Calabaza* (pumpkin), she speaks French, Spanish, or English depending on her customer's needs. In the aisle, her husband, JOSEPH BEAU SEJOUR, a tall man, greets the public. Coconuts and plantains are stacked among the roots while spherical breadfruit, some large as basketballs, bob in water (to delay ripening). The Beau Sejours often stock dry black Haitian mushrooms. A shopper orders *yam*; Joseph hands it to Elli who lops off a huge chunk with a quick hit of the knife blade and wraps the cut section for the shopper (you can request any weight you need, cut to order). Like other produce owners, Joseph Beau Sejour buys his foods (most imported from Costa Rica) from the Bronx Terminal Market, transporting crates to La Marqueta in his own car.

ELIZABETH FEBLES, at a nearby tropical market, specializes in mangos, *Quennepas*, coconuts, avocados, all seasonal fruits, and tiny *Ajicitos* with *Cilantro* and *Recau* to make *Sofrito* seasoning. She sells banana leaves at holiday time. Her teen-aged brother, Heriberto, helps out on Saturdays. *(369-6756)*

At the end, Domenick Lassandro, second-generation owner, runs LASSANDRO'S GROCERY & DELI, catering to West African and West Indian shoppers. A Jamaican customer buys Irish sea moss and linseeds, to cook for a beverage, reputedly a sexual stimulant, muscle strengthener and also a thickener in foods. Or, for a snack, cook the sea moss with water and linseed for 1½ hours; add milk, sugar, nutmeg, and vanilla. It will be thick and jelly-like. Lassandro's also stocks *Egusi* (melon seeds), palm oil, and other West African products.

ISMAEL ATEIWI has owned a stall since 1972 carrying eighteen kinds of beans, codfish, oil, canned specialties, *Couscous*, and African semolina.

In the fish house, octopus, shrimp—from finger-size to almost hand-size—can be found at SAL'S SEAFOOD, run by Sal Serasuolo. Live crabs move around the deep tubs. Sal's brother, "Junior," hoses down the shrimp to aid thawing; water slushes over his boots into the drain. "They built the fish house on the hill so the water could run down," he says. *(427-9300)*

Opposite Sal's stall, D.C. POULTRY stocks turkeys, ducks, rabbits, cornish hens. "D" stands for Frank DeSario, partner of Sal Serasuolo in this department where turkey parts, chicken wings, and other parts are popular among Afro-American and French Moroccan customers. *(427-9300)*

Hymie Rosa, grandson of the original owner, runs PARK MEATS, a long department in the fish house. Here, offerings range from goat and pork to smoked meats and chitterlings, hog maws, pig tails, and other special meats. *(831-5547)*

SALVADORE MORALES runs a finfish department where red snappers, kingfish, porgies, and whitings are among the popular sellers *(410-9885)*.

After stepping down to lower levels, you'll see another third-generation meat department, this one run by LES AROUH. An extensive stock of beef, fowl, goat, and smoked specialties fills the long case. South Carolina-born Loretta Faust, shopping with a friend, describes how she makes okra soup with okra, fresh corn, tomatoes, tomato sauce, green pepper, and onions. *(289-0180)*.

HORN & EISNER, INC. specializes in poultry in the maze of stalls. Sol Halfon and Gerald Fuchs are partners. *(289-6130)*.

LASKY MEATS is a pork specialist. Sam Lasky runs the business, catering to Hispanics and Afro-Americans. Fresh and smoked pork, sausages, pork chops, and *Tasajo* (Argentinian dried beef) are available. *(369-3244)*

*La Marqueta, On Park Avenue (Bet. 111 and 116 Streets). (Al Namer, Pres.) 722-3633. (Office phone; some stall owners have individual phones, noted above.) 7-6, Monday to Saturday; closed Sunday.*

VALENCIA BAKERY, INC. in the same neighborhood since 1932, has expanded into a multishop operation and still whets your sweet tooth. Founder Joe Riboll, born in Alincanti, Spain, bakes Spanish-style cakes with tropical fruit fillings to order: guava, custard, strawberry, or pineapple fillings; sponge cakes in any imaginable shape. The shop, near the original location at 1365 Fifth Avenue, Harlem, displays four large cabinets full of wedding, birthday, engagement, and party cakes (one-, two-, three-tiered, hearts, book shapes, horses, dolls, drums). You can suggest your own design or choose one of the samples for a freshly made cake.

*1869 Lexington Ave. 991-6400, 1, 2, 3 (central switchboard at 801 Edgewater Road, Bronx main office and bakery). 9-7, seven days. Branch shops in Manhattan: 245 E. 14 Street; 538 W. 181st Street; in Bronx: 1042 S. Boulevard; 499 E. 138 Street; in Brooklyn: 132 Smith Street; 1676 Pitkin Ave.; in Queens: 96-04 Roosevelt Ave. 9-6, seven days.*

KIM'S TROPICAL FRUIT SHOP, on Third Avenue, is an oasis among furniture and clothing stores. Staples such as chilies, cassava, *malanga*, and other root vegetables, mangos, papayas, plantains, and seasonal produce are available. More Spanish and Korean than English is spoken here.

*2272 Third Ave. 8-7, Monday to Saturday; closed Sunday. No phone.*

PAK'S FISH MARKET, a block farther east, features two counters with many helpers behind each one in the large, airy shop. At the right, orders are filled for cooked fish to take out; at the left, the fresh varieties include butterfish, shrimps, clams, octopus, red snappers, mullets, croakers, tile, and kingfish displayed on crushed ice. Jong S. Pak, the jovial owner, points out that both black and Hispanic customers prize whitings and porgies above other varieties. He personally enjoys all kinds of fish, especially raw salmon (recipe, page 176).

*2337 Second Avenue. 831-5095. 8-7, Monday to Saturday; closed Sunday.*

# BRONX

# NORTH BRONX
## Italian, Yugoslavian, Puerto Rican, Hispanic, Albanian, Black, etc.

*Coffee from the top (of the cup) and chocolate from the bottom.*

VENETIAN PROVERB

ARTHUR AVENUE shopping district, in the vicinity of the Bronx Zoo and Botanical Garden, is a most exciting food neighborhood—a touch of old Italy. It is promoted, in fact, as "Little Italy in the Bronx." One visit and you'll see why. Catering to Italian-Americans who adore their ethnic favorites, small shops bustle from Fordham Road to the most concentrated (and hectic) section near the great stone walls of St. Barnabas Hospital where Arthur and Crescent avenues converge with 184th Street. It has been a nonchalant, unpretentious residential neighborhood since the early part of the century—mostly row houses with apartments above the never-ending stores like similar structures in other boroughs.

Winter and summer, the shops open daily, except Sunday. Fruit stores set up their displays on the sidewalk along the entire storefronts, where shoppers pick from baskets—green olives (to pickle at home), artichokes, baby eggplants, Avvelino chestnuts, golden-orange zucca squash, dandelions, and spinach by the bushels. Fish and pork chops, bakeries, a live poultry market, pasta, cheese, and pastry shops offer enough selections, it seems, to feed the entire 7 million inhabitants of New York.

At the center of this abundant display, the ARTHUR AVENUE MARKET can be found. Like the other public markets on city property (see pages 16 and 106), it was enclosed early in the 1940s to house the street's pushcart vendors. Mario's famed Italian restaurant prospers next door to the public market, and in the opposite direction, a few paces away, the Enrico Fermi Cultural Center Library opened early in 1981.

## Arthur Avenue Market

Inside the newly renovated **ARTHUR AVENUE MARKET**—an airy market a city block long from Arthur to Hughes Avenue and about three stores wide—shoppers find seasonal produce, meats, meat specialties, and groceries. Like the other public markets, each stall is run by an individual or family. There are eighteen stalls—all selling foods except for one that sells utensils. Sunlight streams through overhead skylights. Sellers and shoppers who recall the pushcart days of the '30s mingle with newer residents. You could hardly tell who is buying and who is selling, if most of the stall owners did not jingle change from their apron pockets, their heads the human adding machines.

Recently, two avid cooks shopped in this popular market for ingredients to make their homemade sausages (although there are a dozen sources for homemade sausages all around them). Entering the market from the Arthur Avenue entrance, they stopped at JOSEPH LIBERATORE'S specialty greens and herbs stall, operated since his parents had a pushcart on the avenue in 1935 when he was seventeen years old. The shoppers looked over the chard and cress, dandelions and rabe, Belgian endive, and long beans and chose garlic, leeks, and parsley from the array of aromatic seasonings. "My customers are 90 percent Italian with some new customers from Albania and Yugoslavia," says the stallkeeper. "Okra (bought by Yugoslavians) is the only new food I've carried since the market opened."

The shoppers moved through the aisles to the left wall where TERESA MARCESE runs a village-style grocery. Buckets teem with beans, grains, nuts, seeds, and spices. At the counter, Teresa, a brunette in her twenties and the youngest stall owner in the market, sells imported pasta, olives, oils, and sauces from Naples and Sicily. "I like the shop . . . but a lotta work. When not busy, I like to hear stories from the old ladies." She smiles as she sells sausage spices to the sausage lovers.

Then the shoppers move diagonally across to the opposite wall, passing several Mom–Pop produce stalls. They stop at a large fruit stand run by BOB, CARMINE, NICK and AL CARPENTIERI brothers—a business begun by their father, Samuel. Vertical fruit displays glow with oranges, grapefruit, pears, and grapes. All around the roomy stall, fresh vegetables entice the eyes and nose—fennel or anise, celery, cardoons, mushrooms, asparagus, onions—anything for *Zuppe* and *Insalate*. Bob Carpentieri, who wears a Greek sailor's cap, sells navel oranges to the two shoppers who plan to chop the rind into the stuffing.

The air fills with a tenor voice singing *Pagliacci*—the voice of MIKE GRECO, blue-eyed owner since 1954 of the savory deli (opposite the Carpentieri stall). Mike Greco's pepperonis, dried sausages, and cheeses fill the air with aromas and keep four sellers running during peak selling times—weekends and holidays.

At the meat department, owner PETE SERVEDIO grinds pork

for the sausage creators. Everything from beef to veal for scallopini is among the fresh meat stocks. *(367-3136)*.

Next to the meat department, a unique stall, run by MARIO RIBAUDO, is worth a visit. "I specialize in *Rognone* (kidneys), *Cuore* (veal, beef or lamb heart), *Animella di Vitello* (veal sweetbreads), *Lingua* (tongue), *Fegatini* (liver), *Cervello* (brains) and *Capozzella* (lamb's head)," he says, pointing out the fresh parts in his spotless case.

Farther along the aisle, near the entrance opposite the Liberatore stall, ISIDORE BERENSTEIN, president of the market, operates the only variety stand piled high, hung over, and loaded down with kitchen utensils, cutlery, coffee makers, ravioli cutters, and pizzelle makers—enamel to aluminum. "Izzy," as his colleagues call him, is joyful over recent renovations of the market (completed in spring, 1983) and for future prospects. His best seller? Exactly what he sells to the two shoppers—the hand-operated funnel for stuffing sausage.

*2344 Arthur Avenue. 367-5688 (Arthur Avenue Market; some stalls have phones as noted above). 7-6, Monday to Saturday; closed Sunday. Phone orders vary according to department.*

## Other Neighborhood Shops

On weekends, by 9:30 A.M., Arthur Avenue business is in full swing, cars double-parked. (Needed parking now exists in a lot across the street from the public market.) This tour begins at the corner of 184th Street (near the Arthur Avenue Market):

CALANDRA CHEESE SHOP with dry, gourd-shaped mozzarellas hanging in rows over the counter; Josephine (Jo) Longarino and son, Joe, behind the counter selling fresh ricotta, *Formaggio Fresco*, *Pecorino* (for grating), *Ricotta Salata*, *Provolone*, *Formaggio Siciliano* to a row of shoppers in the cheese-white shop. Ricotta and mozzarella are made fresh in the back room; other specialties are made in the firm's factory in Nazareth, Pennsylvania. Jo dispenses tips as she slices cheese: "Ricotta makes a delicious cake (see recipe, page 308). Eat *Formaggio Fresco* sliced; when it dries, grate it, or egg and flour it and fry it; great with a salad. Dice the dry mozzarella into a salad, into mashed potatoes;

store it, uncovered, in the refrigerator." Owner Sal Calandra, here since 1959, moved his shop from 115th Street (Bronx) where he made cheeses for twenty-nine years.

*2314 Arthur Ave. 365-7572. 9-6, Monday to Saturday; closed Sunday. No mail or phone orders.*

RAFFAELE SANTELLA's small shop is unusual in this largely Italian neighborhood. Run by him and his family, it specializes in tropical vegetables and fruits. "My customers are mostly Puerto Ricans and Albanians," says the Naples-born owner as he sells *Yautia* roots to a Hispanic shopper, while his wife, Maria, and sons Luigi, Pasquale, and Gennaro set up *Malanga*, cassava, green bananas, coconuts (water and dry), collard greens, and sweet potatoes on the sidewalk stands.

*2318 Arthur Avenue. 365-8876. 7-6, Monday to Saturday; closed Sunday.*

CALABRIA PORK STORE has been open since 1971, but is considered a newcomer in this neighborhood. Nick Parrotta is no newcomer in the business, however. He learned his specialty in Calabria, Italy, his birthplace. Even in winter when the small shop's door is closed, the aromas seep onto the sidewalk. Indoors, the entire ceiling, hung with drying sausages of various lengths, widths, and colors, becomes a magnificent, edible sculpture. Cases and window displays, filled with all kinds of pork, reflect the shop specialty: *sausages*. Nick Parrotta makes three kinds of *Calabrese* sausage (hot, garlic, sweet), two kinds of *Abruzzesi* (hot or sweet), *Sopesada* (gentle orange and peppery), delicious sliced paper-thin for antipasto. Serve with *Paysano* red wine and crusty Italian bread. Breakfast sausages (four or five kinds), smoked pork, tripe, fresh pork roasts, pork rind, and ready-to-broil fresh pork hamburger patties (seasoned with cheese and parsley) win the shoppers at Calabria in "Little Italy in the Bronx."

*2338 Arthur Ave. 367-5145. 7-6, Monday to Saturday; closed Sunday. Phone orders. Delivers ($50 minimum).*

FRANK RANDAZZO'S SONS FISH MARKET, opened by their father, is run by Mike and Joe Randazzo. With many helpers, they take turns refilling fish stocks, selling and cleaning jumping crabs, mussels, conches, and oysters for a *Bouillabaisse* or fish stew using bluefish, cod, eels (the latter live in the red tubs). As Mike wraps her order of fresh calamari, a blond customer shares her own method of serving it raw (page 177). Other shoppers choose their purchases from the long stalls and pavement displays.

*2340 Arthur Avenue. 367-4139. 7-6, Monday to Saturday; closed Sunday.*

MADONIA BAKERY is a three-generation family enterprise that continues to blossom. In the back room, Mario Madonia, grandson of the originator, and two helpers pat satiny dough into loaves and set them on trays to rise before baking them in the stainless steel ovens. Tina Bagatta, born in Calabria, Italy and Elizabeth Bhiodi, both in their early twenties, sell whole wheat and white breads—long, round, twists, rolls—and cookies, *Biscotti, Quaresimale,* pizza dough, and toasts from the large stock. Madonia also does wholesale business.

*2348 Arthur Ave. 295-5573. 7:30-6, Monday to Saturday; closed Sunday.*

COSENZA'S FISH MARKET has been a standby since patriarch Joseph Cosenza opened the store in the early 1920s. Now his grandsons run the wide shop specializing in all kinds of sea food, clams, and oysters, wholesale and retail. For Mediterranean or Caribbean dishes, salmon, cod, mackerel, tile fish, trout, flounder, octopus, and calamari—all seasonal catches—are found in the ice-packed displays.

*2354 Arthur Avenue. 364-8510. 7-6, Monday to Saturday; closed Sunday. Phone orders.*

ARTHUR AVENUE POULTRY MARKET specializes in live poultry and rabbits in the heart of Arthur Avenue shopping center. Ducks, turkeys, bantams (small soup chickens), guinea hens, pullets (female spring chickens), *Gallinas* (for a chicken stew), and white king pigeons are always in cages waiting to be chosen. Oriental shoppers travel from other boroughs for chicken and duck.

*2356 Arthur Avenue. 733-4006. 9-5, Tuesday, Wednesday, Thursday; 8-5, Friday and Saturday; closed Sunday and Monday. Phone orders. No deliveries.*

TIM'S SAVOY MEAT MARKET is a classic butcher shop, in business since 1917, with five or six butchers cutting beef, veal, lamb, pork, chickens, rabbits, and goats with Tim Polito, the second owner of the shop, at the helm. The original walk-in refrigerator is still in great shape; the long case full of plump chops, steaks, roasts, shoulders eager to be broiled, baked, roasted, fried, or braised. Buy a whole lamb and Tim Polito and his expert butchers will slice it to order for your freezer. This is where I buy a whole baby lamb for Easter barbecue on a spit, marinated with oil, lemon, and oregano.

*600 East 187 Street. 733-3637. 8-5:30, Monday to Saturday; closed Sunday. Phone orders. Delivers.*

DE LILLO PASTRY SHOP bakes fifteen types of Italian pastries, twenty-five varieties of cookies, and eleven biscuits. Five bakers work in the back room, but up front Vickie Persiano packs cookie trays, takes orders for cakes, her expert fingers never pausing to rest. She has worked in the shop since 1959 (founder's daughter Rose owns the business). De Lillo also makes spumoni.

*606 East 187 St. 367-8198. 7:30-8, seven days. Phone orders. Delivers.*

At BORGATTI'S pasta shop you'll see noodles drying, fresh noodles sliced into any of seven widths, fresh noodles and ravioli sprinkled with cornmeal from a huge mound at the counter opposite the door. You'll see acres of noodles and find them all hard to resist. Third-generation owner Mario Borgatti grins behind his bushy brows and salt-and-pepper mustache, as he cuts dough on the long counter under his Bologna-born parents' yellowing photos hung on the wall. An avid pasta maker since 1935 and cook (see his recipe, page 235), highly recommended by other Arthur Avenue retailers, he says there's a lively new interest in spinach, carrot, whole wheat, and tomato noodles, the shop's "specialty" noodles. BORGATTI cooking tips: If frozen, don't thaw pasta before cooking; drop it into a very large quantity of rapidly boiling, salted water, stirring steadily. Watch the clock after the water returns to the second boil, and boil noodles five to six minutes (boil manicotti squares and lasagne strips only one minute). Instead of draining in a colander, run cold water into the pot until you can handle the water and pull pasta out with fingers. Drop pasta on a dry kitchen towel to absorb excess liquid, then continue layering, stuffing, and baking, according to your recipe.

*632 East 187 Street. 298-6105. 9-6, Tuesday to Saturday; 8-1, Sunday; closed Monday except before major holidays. Phone orders from customers. No deliveries.*

TINO'S SALUMERIA *(609 E. 187th)*, PEDOTA'S MEATS *(616 E. 187th)*, EGIDIO PASTRY since 1912 *(620 E. 187th)*, and DANNY'S PORK STORE *(626 E. 187th)* are delightful to visit for their ambiance and food specialties, all clustered around Mount Carmel Church. And on Arthur Avenue, there are many, many more wonderful shops like BIANCARDI'S, a superb meat market owned by brothers Tony and Dominick *(2340 Arthur Avenue, 733-4058, 7545)* and others you'll discover on a shopping trip.

# BROOKLYN

# ATLANTIC AVENUE
Arabic, Hispanic, Pakistani, Syrian, Lebanese, Russian,
Armenian, German, Egyptian, Middle Eastern, Greek

Better to have bread and an onion with peace
than stuffed fowl with strife.

ARABIC PROVERB

FESTIVE COLORS brighten Atlantic Avenue during its annual October street carnival, and an air of celebration remains in shoppers and sellers of many food shops all year long. Travelling from other boroughs or from nearby homes, shoppers—of many ages and ethnic groups—seek fascinating available foods that they obviously enjoy buying. Amazingly, people will stop and tell you interesting stories of their lives and foods, divulging favorite recipes.

As you walk along the west side of Atlantic Avenue near the East River facing downtown "old" Manhattan, the neighborhood evokes a bit of nostalgia for the early New York days as well. Before bridges were built, locals traveled across the river on boats and ferries to shop or sell their foods in the famous Fly Market (see page 7). During these seventeenth- to early nineteenth-century days the village called "Breucklen" was renamed "Brookland" and then "Brooklyn." Recalling the difficulties of Brooklyn farmers and marketman transporting their foods by boat, Thomas F. DeVoe in *The Market Book* wrote in 1862: *

The manner of bringing the market productions to the FLY [market] and other markets at this period was usually by water. . . . The boats were propelled either by a fair wind or rowed across, usually three or four times a day.

To take advantage of the tides, most of the boating took place in the evening. Then the farmers had to remain outdoors until morning, without covering or shelter. In addition, they had to pay a fee. "Some of us pay quarter of a dollar for the privilege of standing in the street unprotected, and selling a single calf or sheep, and on other things in proportion," DeVoe wrote. Brooklynites petitioned for years to lessen their burden of hauling produce and meats to the Fly Market. "People of Brooklyn are interested in the removal of the Fly Market to Fulton Slip." * *

---

* DeVoe, Thomas F. *The Market Book* (1862). New York: Augustus M. Kelley, Reprints of Economic Classics, 1970, p. 489.
* * DeVoe, Thomas F. *The Market Book*, p. 488, quoting the *Long Island Star*, February 7, 1821.

In 1821, their wish was granted and the Fulton Market was erected (surviving today in an expanded form; see page 9). Within the following century, Brooklyn population grew from 10,000 to 2 million, streetcars supplanted stagecoaches; the Brooklyn Bridge, built in 1883, replaced the old ferry. Today, reversing its role, shoppers travel in the opposite direction, *to* Brooklyn. Ethnically rich Atlantic Avenue attracts Staten Islanders, Manhattanites, residents from Queens and other Brooklyn communities and Westchester suburbs. Along the wide avenue lined with brick buildings with ubiquitous bric-a-brac and antique shops, ethnic restaurants, there is a strong Arabic flavor in the food shops. Yet within an hour, you will meet shoppers from diverse backgrounds. For example, shopping with her two youngsters, Marie Hildebrandt, a Brooklyn-born woman of Hispanic roots, bought red beans and rice to cook with hot peppers for a spicy stew. A Pakistani woman with three children sought ingredients for an Asian curry dish. Brooklyn-born Gladys Lanese, of Lebanese descent, explained that her delicious Lebanese-Syrian rice dish is made with rice (white or brown) and fine noodles and seasoned with butter and allspice. An Egyptian man from Queens described his favorite dish called *Koshari* (macaroni, rice, lentils simmered in a garlic-tomato sauce lashed with vinegar). Two sisters born in Azerbajan shopped for grapevine leaves to make *Dolma* (stuffed grapevine leaves with ground beef, rice, and fresh mint, and sprinkled with salt, pepper, and lemon juice).

At NEAR EAST BAKERY, it's worth the effort to walk down steep, uninviting steps into the quaint shop with its heavenly bread and pastry aromas. Standing in the few feet reserved for shoppers, you can look over the counter into the huge brick oven on the left-hand wall—a reminder of a Syrian, Lebanese, or Greek village bakery. Eddie Kanatous, son of the owner, thrusts his giant-sized spatula into the oven, rotating enormous pans filled with savory meat (ground meat and onions) and spinach (onions and spinach). To the right, at a large table, his mother pinches seven-inch dough circles into triangular pies. And there's more activity in the large back room. In cases around the counter, pastries await decisions: *Baklava* (nut and filo pastry glistening with syrup and pistachios), round apricot tarts, *Berraza* (sesame and pistachio flat rounds), nut clusters (long), butter cakes (rings and ovals) appeal to the eyes, while the hot pies tempt the olfactory nerves. The Kanatous family from Lebanon bought the late nineteenth-century bakery in 1960, and specialize in Syrian delicacies. While you observe and your appetite mounts, another shopper buys all the spinach pies, pickled turnips ("Even if you hate turnips you'll love them," he predicts), and samplings from each pastry bin. But the bread specialties, *Zahter* (thyme-flecked loaf), white and whole wheat, *Simson* (sesame) breads are sold out. Come early or call in your orders. *Leban* (yogurt) is also available.

*183 Atlantic Avenue. 875-0016. 8-4:40, Tuesday to Saturday; 8-1:30, Sunday; closed Monday. Phone orders.*

SAHADI IMPORTING CO., INC. runs a flourishing retail shop and importing firm, now in its second generation. Bob Sahadi is the son of Zahlé Sahadi, a Lebanese immigrant, who opened the store in the 1930s. With his older brother, Charlie, Bob stocks delicacies from France and Poland alongside the Middle Eastern ingredients that draw varied ethnic shoppers. Within fifteen minutes, four languages (Arabic, Russian, Greek, German) mix with English. Conversing in Russian, Jeanna Isakoe and her sister, Seda, discuss teas; Mathias Spiegel and Harriet Yarmolovsky, local residents, buy food to send to their children; German Hans Shabe, with his blue-eyed youngster Martin perched on his shoulders, shops with his wife and a family visitor from Frankfurt; a Dodecanese-born woman, Sophie Lignos, travels weekly by bus across Brooklyn to buy huge quantities of *Kasseri* and feta, sausages, olives, *Stragalia* (toasted chick peas), salami, and coffee. With a cozy early twentieth-century ambiance, the shop stocks spices, legumes, grains, olives, pickles, and wheats in a four-tiered, monumental display case along the right hand wall ("It was a Chock-Full-O-Nuts coffee storage unit that came with the shop when my Dad bought it!") On the shelves, many cans and jars bear the Sahadi label (also available in Manhattan Middle Eastern shops).

*187 Atlantic Ave. 624-4550. 9-7, Monday to Saturday; closed Sunday. No phone or mail orders. Delivery, wholesale only, $350 minimum.*

DAMASCUS BAKERY is a thriving baker producing pita bread by the hundreds and Syrian Pizzas (recipe, page 348) among other popular breads. Brooklyn-born Dennis Halaby, third-generation owner with his brother Henry, Jr., said they continue the business begun by their grandfather Hassan Halaby and father, Henry. Dennis says that pita, the popular pocket bread used for *Gyro* sandwiches (a Middle Eastern creation popularized in New York by Hellenes) is the fastest growing segment of the family business.

*195 Atlantic Ave. 855-1456. 7-9, seven days.*

At SHAMMAS ORIENTAL AND DOMESTIC FOODS, the stunning colors of dried papaya (from the Philippines), Calamyrna California figs, orangy quince (from Australia), pineapple, and black figs greet shoppers at the entrance. The shop is owned by Syrian Severius Shammas, who stocks herbs for tisanes used by Europeans and Middle Easterners for ailments and colds, as well as all kinds of spices. (A customer said he grinds a whole nutmeg to eat for sexual stimulation!) Grains and legumes, canned sauces and oils for cuisines from Syria to Iran are also stocked.

*197 Atlantic Ave. 855-2455. 10-8, seven days.*

# BAY RIDGE
## Norwegian, Oriental, Danish, Swedish, Greek, Irish, German, Korean, French, Chinese

Vaer sö god *(Be so good . . . to come to table)*
NORWEGIAN SAYING

BAY RIDGE seems to defy the fast-moving jet age. Within sight of the Verrazano Bridge, opened in 1964, the wide boulevards stretch out from Shore Road. Elderly Brooklynites in pairs walk alongside young mothers pushing baby carriages. Oriental and European shopkeepers work side by side. The traditional shops that operated most of this century with a strongly Scandinavian flavor, have changed hands in many instances and gradually adapted their wares to suit newer residents. The Irish and German groups remain with Norwegian influences, blending with newer Greek, southern European tastes, and even newer oriental ones.

Fruits and vegetables glisten in sunny displays at GREEN MOUNTAIN FARM (8322 Fifth Avenue, *745-9254)* and ORCHARD GROVE (8124 Fifth Avenue, *748-0186)*, only two of the many attractive greengrocers providing not only seven days of service but also phone orders and free delivery. Ethnic shops pull in the locals, among them COTOGNO AND PATTEN (8410 Fifth Avenue, *748-9412)*, famous for its meats (closed Monday like many other Bay Ridge stores).

The residents must love the fresh and crisp sweets of Scandinavian and Hellenic flavors. Pastries can be found ready and waiting. Or, should you prefer to make them, there are Norwegian and other old-fashioned decorative irons on which to griddle the prized holiday cakes with tender, loving care—not in the fast-food category. Integrating specialties is increasingly popular here as at ROUGEN'S PASTRIES, INC. (8502 Fourth Avenue, *748-0177)* where Danish linzertortes, pastry horns, and cookies are sold near the French Napoleons and eclairs.

BAY RIDGE FARM AND GROCERY, the name printed in English and Korean on the awning, meshes ingredients of the Orient and Occident for "New York" stir-fry vegetable dishes from Korea to Japan with stopovers in China and Indonesia. Hung Yong Pae, the tall, slender manager stocks seasonal greens, mung and soy bean sprouts, fresh basil and cabbages, and among the dry foods, more soy and mung beans, lentils, dried anchovies, and sauces. The shop is owned by Dooim Ra.

*559 86 Street. 833-5325. 8:30-8:30, seven days. Phone orders. Delivers.*

At MIKE'S DELICATESSENs, Irish blends with Norwegian, German, and Greek. John Michaelis, the German owner, runs two Bay Ridge shops catering to area residents. Irish manager John Regan sells cold cuts and fresh salads, and notes a holiday interest in salt herring, fresh lingonberries, smoked chubbs, *Rullepolse* (seasoned meat roll), *Sylte Flesh* (head cheese), and *Lutefisk* (salt fish)—Norwegian traditional favorites. Regular stocks abound with preserved lingonberries and cloudberries, cans of *Fiskeboller* (fish balls) and reindeer meat balls in gravy. Here, too, are jars of *Attiksprit* (white vinegar), and near the entrance, those inimitable, heavy *Kromkakejern* irons to griddle the delightful holiday Norwegian *Krumkake* (recipe, page 312).

*524 86 Street. 680-2555. 9510 Fourth Avenue. 238-5200. 8-10, seven days. Phone orders. Delivers.*

FREDERICKSEN & JOHANNESEN, a gem of a Norwegian specialty shop, stocks meat all year for a particular clientele and for holidays very, very special foods. Scandinavian shoppers haunt the shop for their cold cuts and sausages (made from beef, pork, veal, or lamb), and the *Korv Pølse (Pölse)*—knockwursts and wieners—to be simmered for 20 minutes and teamed with *Sürkal* (Norwegian sauerkraut) and boiled potatoes. In the refrigerator and on shelves are all manner of cheeses—*Graddost* and *Gjetost* (goat's milk or mixed with cow's milk) and Norwegian breads; in fact, anything and everything to serve a complete Norwegian dinner from *Suppe* to *Kjod Kager* (meat balls) and *Lefse* (potato pancakes), *Labskaus* (braised steak and potatoes) to *Peppernodder* (cookies). At holiday time, meat specialties made by owners Lloyd Fredericksen and Kristian Johannesen attract Norwegians from far and wide: *Fenalaar (Fenalor)* (dry cured leg of lamb); cured and dried mutton side—"The same meat that kept Leif Ericsson alive on his explorations," says Kristian Johannesen, a kind gentleman with a Norwegian accent who explains uses for many foods he carries. He and his partner have run the shop since 1957. For holidays, these experts also prepare *Spekshinke*, a Westphalian ham with or without bone. *Mange Tak!*

*7719 Fifth Ave. 745-5980. 8-6, Monday to Saturday; closed Sunday. Mail, phone, and airmail orders at holiday time (dry meats and groceries); minimum order, $75.*

HELLAS-AMERICAN IMPORTS, INC., owned by Cretan Manny Tzitzikalakis since 1962, includes well-stocked grocery, cheese, and olive departments. Meats include *Lokanico*—Greek-style sausage with spices and chopped orange rind. The cheese counter delights Greek cheese lovers: there are ten types here, including *Kefalotyri*, *Kasseri*, and *Graviera* among the three kinds of feta. There are green and black olives, spices, preserves in cans and jars, sauces, oils and vinegars galore, as well as noodles, including tiny square *Hilopites* as made in Greek villages, and *Trahana* (sour-milk pasta that resembles barley). Zoe Livadiotakis, the owner's niece, shares her *Pastitsio* recipe (page 290).

*8704 Fourth Ave. 748-2554. 8-10, seven days. No phone orders.*

SEVEN STARS GREEK BAKERY has, since 1976, brightened up the neighborhood with Greek pastries such as *Floyeres* (rolled filo around nuts in syrup, *Kataifi* (syrupy pastry of shredded filo called by the same name). Diamond-cut *Baklava* and *Melomakarona* or *Finikia* (hand-rolled spicy cakes sprinkled with nuts) are sold in 5 × 7-inch aluminum containers. Also frozen homemade *Spanakopita* (spinach pie) and *Tyropita* (cheese pies) are available, as are the bread specialties, baked in the other Bay Ridge shop. For New Year's Day, *Vasilopita* (New Year's sweet bread) is made with *Mahlepi* (spice); for Easter, there is *Tsoureki* (holiday bread).

*8103 Fifth Ave. 238-1679.*

*127 Bay Ridge Ave. 836-4223. 9-8, seven days. Phone orders.*

LUND'S is a long Danish bakery shop with hexagonal tile floor and two seats where the weary can rest before poring over the pastries. A traditional bakery originally run by the now retired Lund family. New owner Salvatore Peratore keeps stocks fresh and appealing. Stop in for the *Limpa* (orange-flavored rye bread) and *Jule Kakae* (Christmas bread sold all year round because "it is so popular!"), Swedish almond and cardamom-tinged ring (also available plain), and the Danish butter coffee cake called Seven Sisters.

*8122 Fifth Ave. 745-7590. 5:30-7, Tuesday to Saturday; 5:30-4, Sunday; closed Monday.*

# BENSONHURST
## Italian, Jewish, Greek, Chinese, Korean

*It is not well for a man to pray cream
and live skim milk.*

AMERICAN PROVERB

BENSONHURST, with its neat gardens dotted with rose bushes and edged with clipped hedges, blends European flavors into the American mainstream. A neighborhood where you will hear English spoken for the most part, shoppers are obviously avid about their food shopping. Many small Mom–Pop and family shops continue to flourish.

Eighteenth Avenue—a very lively artery—astounds you with food varieties. There are bakeries among the fish and meat markets, vividly hued produce markets, and zesty pork shops, *salumerias*, and coffee shops. MAPLETON FRUIT MARKET (1777 62nd Street at the corner of Eighteenth Avenue and 62nd Street, 232-3896), features free delivery. On its upper outdoor display, thirteen baskets are invitingly spilled onto tables to reveal seasonal peppers, cucumbers, eggplants, potatoes, and beans, and on the lower displays, the staple oranges, apples, and other fruits are shown for quick service.

Not to be overlooked in Bensonhurst is the live poultry market where you can almost imagine Brooklyn as a green farmland. Farm chickens and eggs are yours to pick, fresh from the farm, or you may call and have them delivered to you.

At the SANITARY LIVE POULTRY MARKET you'll see nonstop activity and hear nonstop clucking. Run at this location since 1975 by John Barile, a smiling young man born in Abruzzi, Italy, for fifty years before that the company was called Mapleton Live Poultry Market at 62nd and 17th Avenues and was relocated following a fire. "It's long hours and a lotta work," Barile exclaims, deftly holding two live "bullets" (gray and white or white oven stuffers weighing between 5½ and 6½ pounds). After weighing them for a Chinese man shopping with his son, John Barile takes the bullets to the back room. The throats are swiftly cut; then the slaughtered poultry is plucked (immersed in hot water for a minute to open the pores, then dropped into a mechanical plucker that spins for two minutes) and emerges featherless. Nephews Masimo and Claudio Barile help around the shop in summer, adding a family touch to the business that looks almost like a miniature farm. In the small garden behind the shop there are cages full of chickens and several lambs ("for one day only") ordered by farmers. Cages at the entrance hold pigeons ("Chinese people like them"), rabbits (4- to 8-pounders, sought mostly by Italians and some Hellenes), large soup chickens and oven stuffers ("Italians, Chinese, and Greek shoppers buy them"), cornish hens (2-2½ pounds) and broilers (3-3½ pounds). Fresh eggs are always available here.

*1465 61st Street. 851-6875, 4720, 7075, 6910. 5-5, Tuesday to Saturday; closed Sunday and Monday. Phone orders.*

At HENRY'S FISH MARKET you will hear lively banter between shoppers and salesmen. The sign over the entrance announces: "IF IT SWIMS, WE HAVE IT." No longer swimming, a lavish display of yellow pike, whitefish, clams, mussels, snails, crabs, and more pull in the Italian, Jewish, Greek, Chinese, and Korean customers. "I've been selling fish since I could see over the counter," says Mike, who graduated from college in 1974 and decided to follow in the footsteps of his father, Henry Stein, who is as active today as he was in 1952 when he opened the store. Their own favorites? Henry: "Gefilte Fish"; Mike: "Carp, from my heritage, cleaned with the head on, poached . . . It's the one fish you *must* eat with your fingers because there are so many bones."

*6014 Eighteenth Ave. 256-5013. 8-6, Monday to Friday; 8-4, Saturday; closed Sunday; closed Saturday in July and August, January and February. Phone orders. Delivers to restaurants.*

INTERNATIONAL BAKERY AND PASTRY is a cozy shop where you'll find Italian breads and all kinds of Italian cookies and biscuits. Along with the staple breads, you'll find semolina bread (long, small, large round), delicately yellow with incredible moistness and the expected crustiness. Brothers Mario and Anthony Savarese run this shop and also SAVARESE ITALIAN PASTRY SHOPPE, INC. a large corner Utrecht Avenue bakery (wedding cakes the specialty) where there is also a sidewalk counter selling their homemade Italian ices and ice creams in eight flavors including *Piña Colada.*

*6104 Eighteenth Ave., 837-6431. 5922 New Utrecht Ave. 438-7770. 8-9, seven days. Phone orders.*

At ANGELO'S SALUMERIA, on a busy day, the entire Landino family may be behind the counter. Papa Angelo, a black-haired, smiling man in his thirties, makes the mozzarella (salted or unsalted), five or six kinds of Italian sausages, roast beef, and basket cheese (soft white cheese made from whole or skim milk); Mama Anna serves the shoppers and, when not in school, Frances and Joseph help out in the bright shop where, since 1970, shoppers' thoughts have quickly run to antipasto. And the family's thoughts? "Breaded veal cutlets, served with a green salad, antipasto (olives, provolone, and ricotta salata cheeses), red wine and fresh watermelon for dessert."

*6110 Eighteenth Ave. 232-4465. 9-7, Monday to Saturday; closed Sunday. No phone orders.*

At ALBA ITALIAN PASTRY SHOPPE, a fourth-generation business, shoppers huddle around the counter for their orders. Currently managed by Sal Alba, the back room bakery turns out best sellers *Cannoli* and *Sfogliatella* pastries as well as dozens of Italian cookies and biscuits; also Sicilian *Cassata* and strawberry cakes (on order) and some French profiteroles and croissants. Versatile specialists help shoppers and then run to the back room to pipe filling into the *Cannoli* shells.

*7001 Eighteenth Ave. 232-2122. 9-9, Tuesday to Friday; 8:30-9, Saturday; 8:30-6, Sunday; closed Monday. Phone orders. Delivers. Mail orders, UPS and airmail.*

BARI PORK STORE windows are brilliantly spotted with cutouts of hot pink pigs, yellow and orange cows. Printed on the cutouts: "SCAMORZA" (a dry cheese), "SAUSAGE," "BRACIOLE" (fresh pork shoulder seasoned with cheese, prosciutto, parsley, and pepper and rolled up), "PEPATO PEPPER CHEESE" (a peppery dry cheese)—specialties you'll find inside. Spicy smells greet you as soon as you enter. *Latticini* (milk products) include fresh mozzarella and ricotta made by BARI; and the firm's sausages include the coiled *Cervellata* (parsley or plain) and links of *Bocconcini* (plain, smoked, or mozzarella). Boar's Head cold cuts are also stocked in four Brooklyn pork shops. Nick Tancredi, the manager, shares a recipe for his favorite Hero sandwich; "Slash a half loaf Italian bread, fill with sliced prosciutto, mozzarella, canned red pepper, lettuce, tomatoes and eat!"

*6319 Eighteenth Ave. 837-9773. 8-7, Monday to Saturday; 8-2, Sunday.*

*7119 Eighteenth Ave. 837-1257. 8-7, Monday to Saturday; 8-2, Sunday.*

*2351 86 Street. 449-5763. 8-7, Monday to Saturday; closed Sunday.*

*1981 86 Street. 266-9300. 8-7, Monday to Saturday; closed Sunday.*

PESCHERIA ITALIANA over the shop awning announces the large and small fish inside including *Trillia* (red mullet known as *Rouget* to the French and *Barbouni* to Hellenes)—excellent broiled. Joe Mondello, who calls himself *"Piccolo"* (he's small in stature) and his tall father Frank run the shop. Finfish and shellfish are always in stock, because shrimp is Joe's favorite (see page 259).

*6824 Eighteenth Ave. 331 50871 8-4, Monday to Friday; closed Saturday and Sunday.*

# BOROUGH PARK
Jewish, Israeli, Korean, Hungarian, Romanian,
Russian, Polish, Greek, Italian, Syrian, Asian-Indian,
Black, Spanish

*The stomach carries the feet.*
HEBREW PROVERB

WHEN YOU HEAR Yiddish, Hebrew, Hungarian, Romanian, Russian, and Polish and observe shop signs in Hebrew and English touting *"Falafel,"* and *"Knishes,"* and *"Kosher,"* you'll undoubtedly be in Borough Park. There is a heavy Jewish flavor to the neighborhood, reflected strongly in food habits and the distinctive quality that is "Kosher" or sometimes written "Kasher," meaning clean or fit to eat according to Laws of Kashrut or Jewish dietary laws. Kosher foods are available in Kosher markets throughout the five boroughs, but Kosher shops predominate in Borough Park and Jewish religious life is reflected in their customs. For example, Kosher shops always close for the Sabbath (Saturday), although some bakeries may reopen after sundown. Shopping excitement peaks before Holy Days, particularly Rosh Hoshana and Yom Kippur (autumn), Hannukah (December), and Pesach or Passover (spring). In Borough Park, these distinct characteristics are dominant in the food shops of the business sections, especially lively Thirteenth Avenue.

WEISS KOSHER BAKERY exudes an Old World feeling. Shoppers and saleswomen speak several languages including Yiddish. On the shelves are breads, cakes, and pastries—rolled, filled, layered, and stuffed—baked by experts. There are *Eier Kichel* (egg cake), strudels with various fruit fillings, "Kosher" Danish (the familiar Danish sweet coffee cakes made to Kosher specifications), a delicious seven-layer cake filled and topped with chocolate, ring coffee cake (sold in bulk or whole) rolled with cinnamon-raisin filling. Breads—pumpernickel, ryes (caraway seeded, or plain) and challahs—are stocked in profusion.

*5011 Thirteenth Ave. 436-3882, 3864. 6-10, Sunday to Friday; closed Saturday.*

OSSIE'S KOSHER FISH MARKET has old-style sawdust sprinkled on a really old tile inlaid floor and a long bench where shoppers can rest. Two women sell fish along with Irish, Puerto Rican, and Jewish salesmen. Operated by Josef Schonfeld, the market stocks live and salt-water fish for making gefilte fish, baked, boiled, pickled, broiled dishes, Romanian and Russian specialties.

*4905 Thirteenth Avenue. 436-1151, 4100. 10-6, Monday to Thursday; 9-11 A.M., Friday; closed Saturday and Sunday.*

At ISRAEL GLATT KOSHER MEATS, INC. meats and poultry are prepackaged, but you can see a half dozen butchers in the back room (large as the large shop) cutting beef, veal, and chickens and conversing in various dialects. Murray Hochhauser, store operator since 1952, between telephone orders will take a special order and tell you his customers are Jewish, Italian, Greek, and other nationalities. Here, activity peaks in early afternoon when meat deliveries go to local old age homes about 2 P.M.

*4907 Thirteenth Ave. 436-2948. 8-7, Monday and Tuesday; 8-8, Wednesday; 8-9, Thursday; 8-3, Friday; 8-7, Sunday; closed Saturday. Phone orders. Delivers. Will pack meats for air travel.*

DAVE'S FAMOUS FRUITS AND VEGETABLE STORE stocks kohlrabi, turnips, potatoes, cabbages, herbs, red beets, everything you'll need to make curries, apple and carrot puddings and *Borscht*—you name it! All these things provide a brilliant touch of color both indoors and on the sidewalk.

*4806 Thirteenth Ave. 438-2759. 7-7, Sunday to Friday; closed Saturday.*

13TH AVENUE BAGEL BAKERY, as the name implies, sells mostly bagels. David Turek, the owner, makes six kinds and "mini bagels for kids who can't eat a whole bagel." He also makes bialy bagels which come out of the oven flattened on top with a mixture of onions, poppyseed, and more spice.

*4807 Thirteenth Ave. 633-4009. 7-8:30, Sunday to Thursday; 7-3, Friday; closed Saturday until after sundown.*

THE THIRTEENTH AVENUE FARMERS' MARKET, of all the public markets operating on city property, seems the most neglected, almost deserted, with many stalls unrented. A rusty metal plaque at the entrance marking the 1939 opening clues the visitor to its condition, while, at the same time, local retailers hope for a revival of the once colorful market. "I used to get my favorite pickles there," recalls Mel Kafka, a local resident since 1950.

In 1981, a feasibility study was done by the New York Department of Ports and Terminals (under whose auspices the public markets function) in conjunction with the Southern Brooklyn Community Council and the decision was to keep the market open. Like the Manhattan, Spanish Harlem, and Bronx public markets, this and the other one in Brooklyn (page 143) were administered by the city until it became too expensive a function. Leased to individuals, stall owners pay rent to the lessee who pays the city an annual fee. Community changes and poor management are blamed for the decline.

In the large market, about the size of the Williamsburg, Brooklyn, market, a wide produce stand is run by BOB FERRANTE, who has been a retailer here since opening day. "I've been here more than forty years," he says from his post, built a foot above the floor level. "This used to be Jewish and Italian trade only. Now it is very mixed—about 40 percent Jewish, the rest Koreans, Syrians, Italians, Mid-Easterners, Indians, Spanish, blacks . . ." As for ethnic produce preferences, Bob Ferrante rattles them off rhythmically: "Swiss chard—Italians love that and Jews buy it now and the Syrians, too; dandelions—mostly Italians; okra—black people, Syrians, Indians, and some Jews, Italians don't know what it is!; flat greenbeans—mostly Italians and Jewish; hot peppers—Italians, Jews, Syrians . . ." A tall, portly man who chews on a cigar, the stall owner, with one helper, fills bags with spinach, beans, lettuce, and tomatoes as shoppers visit the long stall, hoping for bargains.

In addition to a small florist's stall and novelty corner, there is only one more food department: a Kosher meat market, opened in 1982, run by MARK SILVERBERG. Specializing primarily in chickens, the retailer expects to increase meat supplies.

Plans include opening a coffee stand. This public market is in a transitional stage, adjusting to changes in the neighborhood.

*7020 Thirteenth Ave. 438-8979. 8-7, Monday to Saturday. Kosher meat stall closed Saturday; open Sunday.*

BURDO'S, owned by Al Burdo, promotes itself as "The Poor People's Friend" on its awning. On a Saturday afternoon, dozens of shoppers pore over the fruit-filled baskets and vegetables heaped on stands along the sidewalk outside the store. "Dente di leone . . . lupini . . . melone . . . spinaci . . . cantaloupes now three for a dollar" call the hawkers as customers buy dandelions, beans, and grapefruit for their Sunday dinners at bargain prices. On Fridays, the Jewish customers rally around the stands. "You can go crazy here when it's busy," remarks the man at the cash register, ringing up sales.

*1281 39 Street. 438-9575. 7:30-6, Monday to Friday; 7-1:30, Saturday; closed Sunday.*

# WILLIAMSBURG
## Hispanic, Chinese, Black, Puerto Rican, Syrian, Italian, Middle Eastern, Jewish, Asian-Indian

*Love is like soup; the first mouthful is very hot,
and the ones that follow become gradually cooler.*

SPANISH PROVERB

HIGH DECIBEL dance music and foreign languages—mostly Spanish—besiege the ears in Williamsburg. As you walk toward the MOORE STREET RETAIL MARKET at Moore and Humboldt streets (see below), loudspeakers blare riotous Samba and Conga sounds. Salesmen bark for customers to buy their wares and call to each other across the streets. Trucks and busses, in heavy traffic, roar by, blocking their conversations, so they call louder. The unsuspecting visitor can feel almost crushed by the wild sounds.

And there are so many competing colors among the foods that eyes, too, are quickly overstimulated. Ubiquitous tropical vegetables and fruits lure you to pause and look; yellow, white, pink-flecked, brown, orange, red, spinach-green, chartreuse, collard green, okra green put an artist's palette to shame. You may have seen these same varieties on the Lower East Side, Ninth Avenue, or Spanish Harlem, but here in Williamsburg they seem more plentiful, more in demand, more foreign.

Foreignness is the intense feeling here: many racial groups mingling together, many dress styles and hues. Even though the endless shops in three-story buildings echo the architecture of other boroughs, reminding you that you are definitely in New York, in Williamsburg the ethnic effect is startlingly electric.

## Moore Street Retail Market

**MOORE STREET RETAIL MARKET,** like the other public markets built by the city to house the many pushcart vendors, has survived many community changes. When speaking to retailers—old-timers and newcomers—you wonder if the fluctuations ever will settle down. When the market opened, the neighborhood was Jewish, Italian, and Polish, they observe. The Polish moved to Greenpoint, Brooklyn; other original settlers have gradually been replaced by primarily Hispanic populations.

Meanwhile, twenty-six stall owners formed a corporation in 1968 and became self-managed when the city no longer could administer the public market. Georgie Miller, a bilingual Panamanian man, was hired as store manager, the only public market to employ a non-stall owner to handle these responsibilities. He trains new stall owners, collects rents, and pays the city.

Currently, Moore Street Retail Market, similar in size to the Arthur Avenue Poultry Market (page 118) includes twenty-two stall owners. While most stalls specialize in tropical foods, there are also stands selling flowers, toys, drugs, and a luncheonette where you can refresh yourself with a snack. Most stall owners are Hispanic, catering primarily to a Hispanic clientele. Overhead skylights are darkened ("The summer sun shines down to destroy our produce," points out Georgie Miller during a tour of the market.) And each stall is fluorescently illuminated, a distinctive touch. Few of the small stalls are identified by signs or names. As in La Marqueta (page 106) you are constantly looking around, getting lost in the curving aisles around the stalls.

Among the stalls, ABIERTO MARTES PESCADO, a fish stall, is equipped with a long counter full of fresh fish and shellfish. A few yards away, CARMELO CRUZ and his wife MARQUITA run the grocery/dairy stall stocking staple cheeses and legumes, canned and bottled sauces and soups.

At a nearby produce stand, ROBBIE GROSSMAN is the only old-timer remaining in the market. He works at a modestly stocked stall. "I've been here since 1952 . . . took over from my father. . . . He was a pushcart vendor," he explains. Then, suddenly, he turns to his neighbor at the adjoining stall.

"Carlo!" he calls and CARLO NIMES, operator of the tropical stand, joins him behind the counter. Colorful bags of *Ajicitos* (peppers) hang all around the Nimes stand, ready to be picked by shoppers who cook *Sofrito* (recipes, pages 180 and 181). A woman walks up to the stand and chooses tannion roots. She plans to cook them in salted water, after peeling them, as an accompaniment to her fish dinner. Carlo and Robbie talk about the changes in the market.

The largest stand is SAMMY GUZMAN'S tropical *bodega* in the central aisle. Carrying both domestic and imported fruits and vegetables, the highest part of the stand is three feet above floor level where pendent bunches of plantains and bananas hang as if from trees. There are mounds of avocados lolling under the sign bearing the Spanish name for them: *Aquacate.* Sellers stand up high, their heads appearing among the curling banana stalks. At lower levels are hundreds of roots and tubers, cut open to reveal *amarillo* (yellow), *blanco* (white), and flecked or star-studded cross sections: *Patata Blanca* (Puerto Rican sweet potatoes); *Yautia,* the root enjoyed in its many varieties by Caribbeans, blacks, and Chinese and *Yuca* (cassava). There are bushels and bushels of orange-flecked *Gandules Verdes* (fresh pigeon peas) to cook and mash with *Sofrito* seasonings (recipe, page 180, 181); fresh ginger, larger than hand size with pudgy fingers, and tons of *Ajicitos* (peppers)—subtly colored in coral, cream, and pale green tints, of tiny globe and lantern shapes.

Suddenly, the scale groans under the weight of forty pounds of green plantains bought by an ample-sized woman; then she buys fifteen pounds of *Yautia* roots and seven pounds of *Calabaza* pumpkin. "*Pasteles* [see recipe, page 291] for the holidays," she says, describing how the vegetables are rolled and cooked. Stall operator Sammy Guzman maintains a low profile as he refills his piles of potatoes and yuca from storage bins underneath the stands. "Thousands of tropicals, but the green bananas outsell all others," he says. "During peak holiday time, I can sell 500 cases of green bananas (40 pounds per case)!" Introducing his helpers, he states, "We all family. My uncle, my wife, my aunt." His clientele travels from other neighborhoods and suburbs "to find what they want," he adds.

At a small stall, Pepe, an old-timer planning to retire (like others, he prefers to speak Spanish), prepares to cut a five-foot sugar cane. He unsheathes his machete and swings, slicing a diagonal section, and begins sucking it.

*110 Moore Street (Moore & Humboldt streets) 384-8297. 7:30-6, Monday to Thursday; 7:30-7, Friday and Saturday; closed Sunday.*

# QUEENS

# ASTORIA
Greek, Italian, French, Hispanic,
Polish, Romanian, Ukrainian, Yugoslavian,
Cypriot, Asian-Indian, Pakistani, Jewish, Oriental,
Arabian, Turkish, Black, Lithuanian, Czechoslovakian,
German, Russian

*When do you have good food?*
*When I have a good appetite!*
GREEK PROVERB

IN ASTORIA you will hear more Greek on the street than Italian, but the synergism between the Italians and Hellenes is clear nevertheless. Joint ventures have produced prosperous shops and, as a result of these two groups who enjoy many Mediterranean foods, new recipes. Some are described in these pages (I haven't heard of any Italian people trying okra yet, however!).

But there are more than the dominant Greek and Italian foods available here. There are the French pastry shops, Hispanic tropicals, foods for cuisines of the Orient, foods of the Polish, Northern European, Middle Eastern, Romanian, Ukrainian, Yugoslavian peoples—and more.

HILTON PASTRY SHOP, sparkling and new, jazzes up an age-old Greek custom—the pastry/coffee shop. For its success, the clientele must love sweets and socializing, evident here. Greek style, this tradition peaks in the "afternoon" running between 5 P.M. and 10 P.M. (then the "evening" begins)! Rich sweets dazzle you at the entrance where Greek pastries and cookies bemuse the eyes near the *Cannolis* beloved by the Italians. At the counter, Rita Poulakis, a Sicilian married to a Hellene, is fluent in English, Greek, and Italian. Philip, the Italian owner, supervises Greek pastry chefs who whip up *Kourambiedes* (small sugared cakes), *Troufes* (candies), *Koulourakia* (cookie-biscuits), among the dozens of varieties. Upstairs, overlooking bustling Ditmars Boulevard, guests nibble and drink at the picture window.

*22-06 31st Street. 274-6399. 7-2 A.M., Sunday to Thursday; 24 hours, Friday and Saturday.*

LUCKY BOY MARKET is a woman's world. Two Greek women shopped in the rain and planned to cook *Koukia* (fava beans or long bean pods), and an Asian-Indian woman picked radishes as owner Hae Pak and helpers feverishly unloaded fruits and arranged brilliant displays with seasonal varieties.

*22-56 Ditmars Blvd. 24 hours, seven days. No phone.*

LA GULI, with its bounty of Italian pastry varieties, is a relentlessly busy shop, run by Virgil Cannatella since the 1930s. On the rear table, a seller wraps a party cookie array (four pounds) in cellophane, another apron-clad woman sells at the counter. A shopper orders a birthday cake for a party of thirty to be picked up the next day. Barbara Nasser, a lifelong Astoria resident of Italian descent, buys ricotta- and chocolate-filled *Cannolis* for a party dessert. John Ruskin's saying "There is hardly anything in the world that some man cannot make a little worse and sell a little cheaper—and the people that consider price only are this man's lawful prey" hangs over the door to the back bakery. Staggering cookie and biscuit specialties: *Pignoli* (pine nuts), *Anisette* (anise), *Saviardi* (toasts), *Taralli* (sugar-iced rounds), *Osi di Morti* (golden cookies), *Pipatelli* (whole wheat biscuits), *Marherita* (4-inch cookies), *Fior di Mandore* (iced rectangles), *Quaresimale* (cinnamon-almond hard biscuits)—each with a distinctiveness.

*29-15 Ditmars Blvd. 728-5612. 8:30-9, Monday to Friday; 8-9, Saturday, 8-8, Sunday.*

SMILING FRUIT, a perfect name for the fruits and vegetables spilling diagonally onto the sidewalk displays of this corner market where flowers and herbs decorate the pavement in summer. Owned by the Thallathina Trading Corp., the large market stocks seasonal vegetables and fruits along with Hellenic, Turkish, and California dried figs, honey, and preserves from Greece since 1972. Athina Tembelis, Samos-born part owner (whose name was chosen for part of the firm name), shares an eggplant recipe from her native island (see note, page 294). Oriental shoppers stop in for the peppers and zucchini to stir-fry, Italians and Hellenes for beans and spinach for their stews and casseroles, as herbs, pears, and bananas are replenished.

*31-01 Ditmars Blvd. 932-8006. 7-11, seven days.*

J&T GREEK-ITALIAN DELI may sound impersonal, but the shoppers (Hellenes, Italians, Arabians, Middle Easterners, and Anglo-Saxons) and a variety of ethnic foods brighten the shop. Jimmy Istavrof and brother Tommy have created a personal atmosphere since 1970, selling *Kasseri* (cheese), including spicy and aged *Kasseri Piperato*. (Fry it in butter until golden and serve with a squeeze of lemon juice.) Jimmy speaks Turkish, Bulgarian, German, Spanish, Armenian, Yugoslavian, Greek, and English. For a zesty treat, he suggests the following Turkish menu (everything available at his shop except the liquor): *Pasturma* (cured spiced beef); Stuffed Grapevine Leaves; Russian Salad, *Kasseri Piperato*, Feta, Eggplant Salad or Babaganoush, *Borek* (stuffed pastries) served with Raki or Ouzo (liquors) and *Shish Kebab* or *Souvlakia* (recipe, page 346).

*31-12 Ditmars Blvd. 545-7920. 8-9:30, Monday to Saturday; 8-7:30, Sunday.*

HUNTER OF THE SEA's (F&S, INC.) window is a still-life mosaic embedded in cracked ice with giant tile fish curved around octopus, red snappers, mackerels, calamari, whiting, and porgies. The long counter inside swarms with shellfish, whole fin fish, and filets. The sign, "GROPE A FRIENDLY GROUPER. PRIDE OF THE SOUTH," hangs over the case. Brothers Otto and Matthew Bardianos have sold fish here since 1974 and brim over with recipe ideas. House specialties are porgies (the "trapped" variety) and fish from southern U.S. waters ("local waters are too polluted") and tile fish (tender in soup, stews, or as barbecued steaks, but too soft for *Souvlakia*). Octopus, a great favorite here, is tenderized before being sold. Otto explains that Hellenes and Italians are avid fish consumers. Asian-Indians prefer the carp and Anglo-Saxons choose filets. "Real a-fish-ionados select the whole fish and ask the fishmonger to filet them," he adds. A gray-haired woman buys plump whiting to bake with butter; a Yugoslavian shopper picks a few pounds of calamari to slice into rings and fry in vegetable oil. Otto's dream dish? "Brush olive oil on tile fish steaks, barbecue over charcoal 5 to 6 minutes on each side. Set on a warm platter. Whisk a marinade of olive oil, lemon juice, salt, pepper, parsley, oregano, and paprika and pour over the barbecued steaks."

*22-78 31st Street. 726-6390. 9-6:30, Monday to Thursday; 8-7, Friday; 8-6:30, Saturday; closed Sunday.*

K & T is a great Greek-Italian partnership. Frank Biancanello has run the large meat shop at Broadway and 37th Street since 1962; partner Jerry Haritos runs this meat market where a red sign accents the entrance and specialties fill the cases. Whole ribs of beef, chickens, legs of lamb, veal cuts, veal feet, and tripe fill the window case. Livers, tripe, sweetbreads, brains, tongue, kidneys, and lamb heads (Greek and Italian traditional dishes) are also on hand. In the back there are several kinds of feta, olives, roe, cheeses, and a selection of cured meats. Best sellers are fresh young lamb cuts (especially legs and chops) and ribs of beef. Jerry Haritos, who collects money in an old-fashioned, glassed-in cashier's case equipped with a computerized cash register, has this sign displayed: "We give credit only to those 80 years or over, then only when accompanied by their parents."

*33-06 Ditmars Blvd. 728-3810. 8-6:30, Monday to Thursday; 8-8, Friday; 8-6, Saturday; closed Sunday.*

ST. HONORÉ PATISSERIE CONTINENTAL PASTRIES has a touch of Mt. Blanc, birthplace of owner-pastry specialist Flavius General. In Manhattan since 1962, he brought his shop *here* in 1979 to delight his new customers with his Napoleons, eclairs, cream puffs, *mille feuille*, and chocolate cream specialties. Best sellers are brioches and croissants. And for Italian tastes, *Cannolis.*

*33-18 Ditmars Blvd. 278-3558. 7-7, Tuesday to Saturday; 7-4, Sunday; closed Monday.*

JOE'S PORK STORE, a pork-chop sized shop, radiates warmth. There's a charming hexagon-tile floor and a 1905 antique cash register that still works. Gallons of vinegar and whole provolone cheeses hang on hooks in the window. Joe Livoti is tall and energetic and tells customers how to cook his fresh and smoked pork specialties. Homemade sausages—sweet, pepperoni, cheese, fennel—are perfect for breakfast or dinner casseroles. Joe told of his mother's recipe (see page 289).

*37-21 Ditmars Blvd. 721-1579. 8-5:30, Monday; 8-6, Tuesday to Saturday, except open until 7 on Friday; closed Sunday.*

KALAMATA FOOD IMPORTS, INC. is a high-ceilinged grocery store with Greek and Middle Eastern foods hanging from the rafters. Reminiscent of old-fashioned grocery stores, it is named for the Messenian capital famed for the smooth, purplish and sour

Kalamata olives stocked here in profusion. *Amphissa* (black, wrinkled, and bitter) and *Volos* (black, packed in brine rather than the usual olive oil), island varieties, and the house specialty *Nafplion* (green olives to season at home) are also stocked. There are more than five types of feta, as well as dried noodles, grape-vine leaves, and anything else you'd need to cook Middle Eastern and Greek specialties.

*38-01, 38-03 Ditmars Blvd. 626-1250. 8-10, Monday to Saturday; 9-8, Sunday.*

AKROPOLIS MEAT MARKET grinds out meat in a market that has been active all of this century. Run by Iannis Gatzonis, an enterprising man in his thirties, the store sells lamb, beef, veal, sausages, tripe, brains, sweetbreads, and tongue for the mostly Greek, Italian, Yugoslavian, Asian-Indian, and Pakistani shoppers. The retailer's favorite dish is roast leg of lamb with *Kritharaki (orzo)*—rice-sized pasta.

*31-16 30th Avenue. 728-1760. 8-7, Monday to Saturday; closed Sunday.*

ORIENTAL FOOD AND GIFT SHOP brings the tastes of the Orient to a strongly Middle Eastern and Greek neighborhood. Hispanic favorites are chilies, *malanga, yuca, Sofrito* seasoning ingredients, fresh coriander, *cilantro,* and papaya. Oriental staples include tofu, ginger, groceries. All of these can be found among the fresh fruit and vegetable displays. Young Kim and her brother-in-law Chang Kim have run the shop since 1977.

*30th Avenue, corner 32nd Street. 728-8584. 8-8, Monday to Saturday; closed Sunday.*

ELLINIKI AGORA (Hellenic Market) displays fruit and vegetable colors in a bountiful, amazingly stocked store. Run by Ioannis Dotsikas, Mike Savides, and Christos Skarlatos, local vegetables are best sellers among Greek, Cypriot, and Italian customers who demand freshness. Six kinds of peppers (including hot bell peppers), fresh cranberry beans, fava beans, celery knobs, leeks, cauliflower, dandelions, and okra tempt the shoppers.

*32-12 30th Avenue. 728-9122. 6-10, seven days.*

KASSOS BROS., a popular store on Ninth Avenue in Manhattan since 1952 is now in this old-fashioned shop in Astoria. John Kassos specializes in Greek, Cypriot, and Italian foods—fragrant cheeses, and juicy olives and oils from Mediterranean trees. He offers homemade *Tzatziki* (seasoned yogurt), *Taramosalata* (roe salad) and that thick yogurt, *Yaourti Sakkoulas*.

*32-22 30th Avenue. 932-5479. 8:30-9, Monday to Saturday; 9-5, Sunday.*

OCEAN #1 FISH MARKET, among the unending array of shops, attracts the eyes with its voluptuous facade. The walls are studded with shells and sealife mosaics, arranged in decorative curves. Shoppers at the counter watch their fish being cleaned. Tommy, the manager, discusses the fish varieties and the locals' preferences: "Asian-Indians buy carp, shad, and butterfish; Greeks—porgies, calamari, shrimp; Italians—crabs, mussels, dry salt cod, whiting, clams, lobsters; Jews—filets, shellfish (yes!); blacks—porgies, croakers, Virginia spots." As for his own favorite, see his recipe, page 177).

*35-08 30th Avenue. 721-2391. 7-6, Monday to Saturday; closed Sunday.*

MARINO & SONS GRAND FISH MARKET has offered fresh fin fish and shellfish for three generations to Italian, Jewish, and other ethnic shoppers. Ben Marino now runs the shop his grandfather started and he stocks everything for the local clientele.

*36-10 30th Avenue. 728-6160. 8-6, Monday to Saturday; closed Sunday.*

NIEBYLSKI BAKERY is famous for its wonderful breads stocked in many Manhattan stores, including Yorkville pork stores. The Niebylskis do their baking near the Astoria Boulevard entrance to the Triborough Bridge. Shopping here is like a family visit. Anthony Niebylski runs the business begun by grandfather Anthony, who emigrated from Poland. In the summer, his young son, Michael, carries trays, refilling the bread supplies in the shop. The store has a sense of history, of America's ethnic diversity and progress, of hard work and good food. For Polish, Lithuanian,

Czech, German, and Russian customers, there's pumpernickel, seeded and plain rye, whole wheat (regular and salt-free), Russian black, "corn" (sprinkled on the bottom with cornmeal), and six varieties of rolls. In fall and winter, babka (small, medium, large, and cheese-filled).

*23-64 Steinway Street. 721-5152. 8-6, Tuesday to Saturday; closed Sunday and Monday.*

MUNCAN FOOD CORP. is a Yugoslavian food center with meats—fresh and smoked—the specialties. John Muncan has run the shop since the late 1960s and is highly recommended by Yugoslavian people. Here you'll find fresh beef, pork, veal, smoked spareribs, and other smoked meats to make *Sarma* (stuffed cabbage rolls—see note on page 296). As a convenience to Yugoslavian shoppers who miss the taste of their native foods, John Muncan also stocks assorted cookies, chocolates, juices, and mineral water. But the homemade sauerkraut and sour cabbage (used in *Sarma*) may be the most popular foods, along with Yugoslavian paprika.

*43-09 Broadway. 278-8847. 7:30-6:30, Monday to Friday; 7:30-6, Saturday; closed Sunday. Phone orders.*

# SUNNYSIDE
## Romanian, Arabian, Armenian, Hispanic, Bulgarian, Yugoslavian, Egyptian, Israeli, Greek, Iranian

Better an egg today than an ox tomorrow.

ROMANIAN PROVERB

STANDING ON Queens Boulevard, dwarfed by the enormous train bridge with trains passing by overhead, you can look toward Manhattan and see the Empire State and the Chrysler buildings. Then, take a few steps into one of the delightful "ethnic" shops and you are transported, not to a metropolis, but rather to a hamlet or village atmosphere where English is a second language, spoken infrequently.

Stocking fascinating ingredients for many Middle Easterners, Balkan, and Greek shoppers, the shops are fun to visit. One important difference to be noted, however, is in the use of the word "oriental." Also true in Israel and other Middle Eastern countries, "oriental" is *not* perceived as defined by *Webster's Dictionary*: "of the Orient [the East; Asia], its people or their culture." Many Middle Eastern shops refer to themselves as "oriental." In this book, however, I have used the *Webster's Dictionary* meaning unless otherwise indicated.

While there are other clusters of shops in Sunnyside, the two shops described below are especially conveniently located to visit during the same trip.

SARKIS APROZAR, run by Sarkis Sarkisian, is a large corner store with fruits and vegetables on the left side and groceries, baked goods, and candies on the right. The shop caters to Romanian, Arabian, Egyptian, Armenian, Hispanic, Greek, Bulgarian, and Yugoslavian shoppers who seek their grains, herbs, coffee beans, and dried fish (herring and cod). Here they also find olives, nuts and fruits, baked goods in the Hellenic styles, *Loukoum (Liban)*—wonderful Middle Eastern jellied candy flavored with rose water or mastic. Among the beans, you'll see the special beans for making *Ful Madamis* (Egyptian breakfast dish). Among the world's most intriguing beans, *Ful* are clay-colored, as though shaped into creased oval shapes from Egyptian soil, touched with black specks at the top. (Soak overnight, cook with chopped onion and season with olive oil, lemon juice, salt, pepper, a little oregano and parsley for a superb, centuries-old favorite.) At the coffee counter: a Spanish-speaking shopper picks Venezuela beans; a Romanian the Turkish beans; Armenians prize mocha coffee and Hellenes buy imported Loumides coffee. Take your foreign language dictionaries because little English is spoken here. But the staff knows much about food and its preparation (for a sampling, see recipe page 311, for a filo dessert, *Saraïli*).

*39-52 Queens Blvd. 937-4682. 6-9, seven days. No phone orders.*

BARUIR's ORIENTAL-AMERICAN GROCERY, * a Middle Easterner's world, is almost hidden away under the tracks on Queens Boulevard. Before you step inside, the window delights you: Turkish coffee brewers called *Briki* are placed near a large growing plant; a sign reads, "REALLY! THIS IS A COFFEE TREE!" and another sign declares, "HERE IS GRINDING POPPY SEEDS AND NUTS." Within a minute, an Israeli (from Forest Hills) drives up to seek his coffee beans, fresh pita bread, and feta ("I always stop by here when I'm in the neighborhood," he explains. "It's a great shop.") Then a Bulgarian woman dropped by for cheese, a Greek shopper eagerly sought her favorite olives (black crinkly type from Amphissa). Owned by Baruir Nercessian, the shop is like a Middle Eastern bazaar, full of ingredients for Arabic, Armenian, Iranian dishes, from the oil to the zesty spices.

*40-07 Queens Blvd. 784-0842. 8:30-8, Monday to Saturday; closed Sunday.*

* "Oriental" here means "Middle Eastern" and "Arabic"; see page 156.

# ELMHURST
Hispanic, Puerto Rican, Mexican,
Dominican, Chinese, Argentinian, Colombian,
Italian, Asian-Indian, Cuban, Thai, Korean, Oriental

In an old allotment there is
never any lack of sweet potatoes.
MEXICAN PROVERB

ELMHURST, where it rubs elbows with Jackson Heights, is so ethnically diverse you can expect any dozen people stepping off the trains, walking, or shopping, to speak a dozen different languages (frequently no English) and possess individualistic food preferences. The diversity is obvious at the Elmhurst Avenue station of the "7" train, for instance. At Elmhurst Avenue, where it intersects with 90th Street, Roosevelt Avenue, and Case Street, you can find a fish market, meat market, bakery, Thai-Chinese grocery, and *Bodega*, among other small shops with highly specialized stock, each catering to specific groups. And though the elevated trains, traffic, and accompanying noises are never out of hearing range, the atmosphere—small shops, mothers, youngsters, and family groups, neighbors interpreting for shopowners who cannot understand English—is reassuring for those who enjoy cultural diversity in action. The unusual food ingredients available in such an ethnic neighborhood will amaze you and make a shopping trip to Elmhurst stimulating.

At CHARLIE'S MARKET, Hispanics are the most frequent shoppers. Fruits are abundantly arranged around the store's sides and in pavement displays. Lustrous vegetables are set around a high, central aisle of the ample shop. "Shoppers are 90 percent Dominicans, Cubans, and Argentinians with a small percentage of Asian-Indians, Italians, and Jewish customers . . . but no Puerto Ricans," says Hae Nam, the shop owner since 1980. For his varied clientele, the energetic Korean-born retailer and two helpers keep refilling bins with all kinds of tropical roots, leafy greens, herbs and seasonings from *Ajicitos* (peppers) to ginger root, and fruits including mangos and persimmons. Many staples are easy to spot in this friendly shop where English and Korean are spoken along with the Spanish dialects of customers and one salesman.

*37-61 90th Street, Jackson Heights (Elmhurst). 426-7800. 8:30-8:30, Monday to Saturday; closed Sunday. No phone orders.*

PIER 90 FISH MARKET, is Korean owned but the *"Pescado Fresco y Frito, Sopas, Ceviche"* (Fresh and Fried Fish, Soup, Ceviche") signs tell the story. Deliciously aromatic soup cooked

in the back room (recipe page 203) and the conversations in Spanish give you the Spanish flavor of the shop. "Our customers are mostly Hispanic," remarks Edward Jough, owner, standing near the long fish case displaying orderly rows of fin fish, whole and fileted. A New York resident since 1968, the owner took over the existing fish market in 1981 and keeps the fish shoppers happy.
*90-12 Roosevelt Avenue, Jackson Heights (Elmhurst). 426-5655. 10:30-10:30, seven days. (Spanish-speaking salesman for interpreting phone orders). No deliveries.*

BODEGA HISPANA will not disappoint you should you seek Dominican, Puerto Rican, Mexican, Argentinian, or other Latin American foods. Daniel Canela, the young owner since 1979, describes his own Dominican favorites such as *Longaniza* pork sausage, sold in a yard-long segment ("Boil it, cut it up, and fry with garlic and onions; then add rice and seasonings to make it yellow") and *Salchichon*, zesty sausage ("Slice and fry it for breakfast"), and tropical roots ("I like yellow *Yautia* cooked with pigs' feet"). You will find the popular Colombian precooked, refined corn flour *(Areparina)*, Mexican *Masa de Harina* (cornmeal) and tortillas in the freezer. There are frozen fruits including *Guanabana* (sour soup), ready-to-cook dough circles for Mexican *Empanadas* (page 350) and many varieties of *Queso* (cheese), sausages *(Chorizo)* and *Morcillas* (blood sausage) if they happen to be in stock.
*88-17 Roosevelt Avenue. 446-2772. 7-11, seven days. No phone orders.*

THAI GROCERY, L&T IMPORT CO. has a large CHINESE GROCERY sign over the door and ingredients are abundant for both cuisines. When you need questions answered in English, owner Chom Pon runs out of the shop for neighbor Samarn Sil, a Thai woman who also shared a recipe for the green-striped Thai eggplants (page 287). Every centimeter of this narrow shop, arranged like many oriental shops in Chinatown, is packed with cans, bottles, utensils rippling off the ceiling hooks, in the window (where the Thai stone mortar and pestle is stocked) and in the cases. The produce case, undoubtedly the most intriguing and popular, contains unusual vegetables, beans, seasonings, chilies, and leaves. On the counter you may find bananas preserved in honey and, on a top shelf, a three-tiered Thai aluminum steamer large enough for all your family extensions. Nucharee Coumsawang, a Thai woman, is partner in this shop which opened in 1979.

*37-60 90th Street, Jackson Heights (Elmhurst). 672-2183. (Call after 5 if you don't speak Thai). 9-9:30, seven days, except closes 8 p.m. on Tuesdays and Sundays.*

BUZZANCA BAKERY, has long Italian bread so crisp that the crust crackles when you cut it, but the inside is soft and moist. Philip Buzzanca, curly-haired son of the originator, Basil Buzzanca, sells bread—Italian and French-style—five kinds of biscuits, and twelve varieties of cookies, and proudly exclaims, "We've been here since 1957; I was born in Elmhurst." Like many bakeries in New York, the shop portion is small—its counter, window, and shelves lined with breads, while the large back room is the bakery.

*37-49 90th Street, Jackson Heights (Elmhurst). 429-9238. 6-7, Monday to Saturday; closed Sunday.*

# RICHMOND

# STATEN ISLAND

Italian, Jewish, Korean, Japanese, Chinese,
Vietnamese, Spanish, Puerto Rican, French,
German, Asian-Indian, Thai, Filipino, Danish, Viennese

*No corn without chaff.*
DUTCH PROVERB

A FERRY RIDE to Staten Island is one of New York's most enchanting trips. And what a surprising array of ethnic food shops can be found in its quiet hilly atmosphere.

On the other hand, not really surprising! Staten Island has always had a mixed ethnic history. It was discovered by an Italian, Giovanni da Verrazano (on a French ship) in 1524, and English Henry Hudson (for the Dutch East India Company) eighty-five years later when Algonquins lived in peace with each other. In 1660, both Dutch and French built houses and a small wooden blockhouse at South Beach (earlier Dutch settlements had problems with the Algonquins). Four years later, the British took over from the Dutch. Within forty years the population of Staten Island doubled and included an English, French, and Dutch mix, mostly farmers and fishermen.

Today, you can't travel far without spotting an Italian deli or pasta shop, a Kosher butcher or bakery, an Oriental shop catering to Koreans, Chinese, Japanese, Filipinos, Thai, and Vietnamese, and a tropical *Bodega*. Hellenes, who have no shop, can buy some ingredients at Italian delis and celebrate their ethnicity through an annual September festival in the Greek Orthodox Church of the Holy Trinity.

Local shoppers told me they also travel to Brooklyn to shop on Atlantic Avenue, or if Kosher, to Borough Park. Others said they are the second and third generation of families who have lived all their lives in Staten Island and have never needed to go elsewhere.

OH BOK ORIENTAL MART, INC. carries foods as varied as the East for seven Oriental (in the Middle Eastern sense) ethnic groups. The shop, here since 1975, and owned since 1978 by Tae Sung Park (also known as Edward) and his son, Samuel Park, stocks foods, utensils, and gifts for local shoppers. For Korean and Japanese cuisine there are three types of seaweed or *Laver* including *Nori* (Japanese) and *Kim* (Korean); *Kombu* (Japanese) and *Tashine* (Korean); *Kimchi* (three types) for Koreans and two kinds of soy sauce; for Japanese *Kantonmen Yakimba* (noodles) and three kinds of soy sauce. Chinese culinary treats include dried mushrooms, bean threads, and three soy sauces. For Filipinos, there are *Pansit Bihon* (rice noodles) and *Pansit Lug-Lug* (heavier rice noodles), numerous sauces including banana (red color). Fish sauce is available for Thai, Filipino, and Vietnamese shoppers. Brown and white rice are stocked along with raw peanuts and spices for Asian-Indians. The produce department carries eggplants, bitter melons, fresh ginger, asparagus beans. Among the utensils are *Pulgogi Pan* (a plate) and woks, charming lanterns, and many different saki and teacups in the densely packed grocery department.

*1772 Forest Avenue. 698-2669. 9-9, Monday to Saturday; closed Sunday. Phone orders. Delivers.*

D & S PORK SHOP/CATERERS makes pork products, mozzarella cheese, and Italian breads. In the long shop, the seven kinds of sausages are plump and appealing, with a pink-coral glow, full of herb and cheese flecks. D&S makes long, round, and twisted breads, as well as rolls and brings in popular semolina bread from a Brooklyn bakery. Nicholas Stottlemyer, the owner, also stocks fresh pork, veal, and poultry and enough antipasto to feed a regiment.

*1789 Forest Avenue. 448-8234. 8-6, Monday to Saturday; 9-2, Sunday. Phone orders. Delivers.*

LUI'S Spanish-American grocery has been run since 1977 by Lui Rodriguez. This is a center where shoppers can find their fresh avocados, plantains, and green bananas, dried codfish and beans, *Yautia* and *Yami* (Spanish yams) near the frozen *Yuca* (cassava). Here you'll hear Spanish and English, see customers who enjoy popsicles-on-the stick as much as *Pasteles* (see recipe, page 291), in a pleasant environment.

*199 Richmond Avenue. 442-9823. 8:30-9:30, Monday to Saturday; closed Sunday.*

HORST'S MEIERS CORNER BAKERY is truly a family bakery turning out a spectacular variety of German, Danish, Jewish, Viennese, Italian, and French breads and pastries to appeal to the Staten Islanders' sweet tooth. Walk into the cozy shop and you'll see glass cases and shelves full of Viennese and French breads, pumpernickel, rye, whole wheat and raisin. Trudy Roeck (pronounced "Roke") helps shoppers buy strudels, crumb cakes, cheese cake (baker's cheese, cream, and butter), Danish rings, *Hamantaschen* (Purim cakes) are always available; honey cakes and challahs usually on weekends. Horst Roeck, a Stuttgart-born and trained baker, makes rich apple turnovers and buttery, crisp cookies. Sons Michael and George help out on weekends during the rush hours.

*957 Jewett Avenue. 448-1290. 5-9, Tuesday to Sunday; closed Monday. Phone orders. No deliveries.*

DAVID'S KOSHER BUTCHER is a pleasant center for meats and Jewish specialties, including potato kugel (pudding) and noodle pudding (sweet). Here one finds beef, veal, and lamb, all in Kosher cuts, turkeys, ducks, and other poultry. Run since 1964 by Neil Gelenter, son-in-law David Medina is now associated in the business (his wife, Candy, shares her favorite family *Couscous* recipe, page 282). In addition to Kosher meats, shoppers can pick up old-fashioned toasted *Farfel* (barley-sized noodles) to make their specialties at home. The shop also caters for parties.

*1989 Victory Blvd. 442-3920. 9-7, Monday to Thursday; 9-sundown, Friday; closed Saturday; 10-4, Sunday. Phone orders. Delivers, $20 minimum.*

FAMOUS KOSHER BAKERY, run by Joseph Grossman since 1975, offers baked goods (from Brooklyn Kosher bakeries), and Kosher groceries. Marble cake, sponge cake, *Rugelach* (miniature Danish with chocolate, raspberry, nuts, cinnamon fillings and seasonings), bialys, rye and corn breads are popular but, of course, challahs are the best sellers.

*2208 Victory Blvd. 494-1411. 8-7, Sunday to Friday; closed Saturday. No phone orders.*

ALFONSO'S PASTRY SHOPPE is so famous on Staten Island, even Jewish residents told me "That's where I buy my pastries!" Here you'll find classic Italian cheesecakes and other cakes, pies and tarts. Among the best sellers are *cannoli*, Napoleons, and *Baba au Rhum*. Alphonso and Diane Carpatello, who run the shop in a neat brick building with a bright yellow store sign, also produce an unceasing array of cookies, *Biscotti* (biscuits) and "dunkers."

*1899 Victory Blvd. 273-8802. 7-9, Tuesday to Saturday; 7-8, Sunday; closed Monday. Phone orders. Delivers.*

# PART 2
# RECIPES

*What you like—eat.*
SLOVAKIAN PROVERB

# APPETIZERS,
# SEASONINGS & CONDIMENTS

*In eating and scratching,*
*everything is in the beginning.*
COLOMBIAN AND CUBAN PROVERB

## AUSHAK
### Afghan Herb Filo Pastries

The delicious Afghan fried triangular *Aushak* inspired me to adapt the filling idea to the Greek appetizers called *Tyropitakia* (savory cheese-filled filo pastries). It worked—a good ethnic adaptation! Freeze them for an instant party when guests surprise you.

*½ tablespoon olive oil*
*½ cup fresh scallions, finely minced*
*¼ cup fresh parsley, minced*
*¼ cup fresh mint, minced*
*12 leaves filo pastry (also called filo/strudel pastry leaves)*
  *12" × 18"*
*½ cup unsalted butter, melted and warm*

In a small pan, heat the oil and saute the scallions only enough to soften them; do not brown. Stir in the parsley and mint and turn off the heat. There should be about 1 cup of filling. Using a sharp knife, with filo stacked, cut the filo lengthwise into long strips (they will be 18" long and 3" wide); stack and cover them with plastic wrap or wax paper covered with a damp towel to avoid drying. Working with one or two filo strips at a time: Butter the strips with the narrow end near you. Scoop less than a teaspoon filling onto the filo near you; turn filo back over the filling to enclose it and fold back at right angles all the way to the end to make neat triangles. Butter lightly and cover * until all *Aushak* are stuffed.

TO BAKE: arrange on a baking sheet, preferably without touching, and bake in moderate oven (350°F) for 15 minutes until golden and crispy.

SERVE piping hot.

**Makes 48 servings (you can count on 4 to 5 per person)**

---

* If planning to freeze either spread them in a gift box between layers of wax paper, or set them upright (if making dozens and dozens) with wax paper between them to avoid sticking. Bake frozen but allow 20 minutes.

## SHARK, BERMUDA STYLE

Seafood retailers say that shark is increasingly popular in New York homes. Chinese, Italians, Hellenes, and Caribbean people are only a few of the groups who enjoy this fish. A Bermudian woman shares an interesting recipe for shark which I tried with sand shark, * a younger type that cooks very quickly—soft, crumbly, and with a delicate flavor. Prepare it and ask your guests what it is—they'll never believe it is a shark!

> 1 pound sand shark, sliced into 8 to 9 ¾-inch slices
> 1 small stalk celery, chopped
> 1 bay leaf
> 3 sprigs fresh parsley
> ¾ teaspoon dried thyme or 4 sprigs fresh thyme
> 3 tablespoons unsalted butter or oil
> 1 small onion or 2 shallots, finely minced
> 1 chili or 6 Ajicitos (peppers), seeded and chopped
> Salt
> Freshly ground pepper
> Toast points (optional)
> 1 large or 2 small avocados, peeled, pitted, and sliced
>    (optional)
> Lemon or lime wedges (optional)

Wash the sand shark and put into a pot with the celery, bay leaf, 1 sprig parsley, and a pinch of dried thyme or 1 fresh sprig. Bring to the boil and simmer 20 minutes until shark is fork tender. Drain and discard the liquid. When shark is cool enough to handle, remove and discard all bones. Squeeze out and save any liquid remaining in the fish; there should be a full 1½ cups.

TO SEASON: Heat butter or oil and saute the onion or shallots with chili or *Ajicitos* until soft, about 5 minutes. Stir in the shark. Chop remaining parsley and thyme and add them with enough salt and pepper to flavor the shark to your taste.

SERVE warm, spread on toast points. Or serve chilled heaped on avocado slices with a squeeze or two of lemon or lime. **Serves 4**

---

* Shark may be used for this recipe; it will take longer to cook and more weight to

## RUSSIAN HERRING

*2 salted herring*
*1 small onion, cut into slender rings*
*Olive oil*
*Vinegar*

Soak herring in cold water overnight. Drain; cut off and discard head and clean out intestines. Remove and discard skin. Cut herring into bite-sized pieces and place in a bowl with the onion rings. Dribble lightly with oil and just a drop or two of vinegar. SERVE with black bread and vodka.                              **Serves 2**

## MOULES CHEVAL BLANC
### Mussels, Brittany Style

When you serve this simple mussels dish, you will be re-creating a recipe of a Bretagne (Brittany), France family. The family now lives in New York and runs the CHEVAL BLANC Restaurant (145 East 45 Street). *Merci!*

*4 dozen mussels*
*Homemade bread crumbs from French bread*
*3 to 4 cloves garlic, crushed*
*6 tablespoons butter, melted*

Scrub the mussels and put them in a pot with 4 cups water. Cover and steam over low heat 10 minutes or until the shells open (discard any that do not open). Lift the mussels when cool enough to handle; discard the half shell without the mussel. Arrange mussels on the half shell close together in a casserole. Fill your hand with bread crumbs and let them slip through your fingers over the mussels to give a light dusting. Sprinkle the garlic and butter over the mussels. Broil 2 minutes until golden. SERVE hot.                              **Serves 6**

---

yield enough for 4 guests, so buy 1½ pounds. (For another meal, try broiling shark steaks 7 minutes on each side.)

## SALMON APPETIZER, KOREAN STYLE

Jong S. Pak of PAK'S FISH MARKET (page 111), serves this simple appetizer with bourbon or Scotch! Double or triple for more guests.

*FOR ONE SERVING:*
*¼ pound salmon, sliced thinly in 1¼-inch long slices*
*1 to 2 teaspoons Japanese hot mustard*
*1 tablespoon Japanese soy sauce*

In a bowl, combine the salmon with mustard and soy sauce. Taste and adjust seasonings to your preference. Marinate in refrigerator. SERVE with *Kimchi* (page 184).

## SCANDINAVIAN GRAVLAX
### Salmon

This is a classic Scandinavian appetizer. It can be found marinating between blankets of dill and peppercorns at NYBORG-NELSON (page 67), where the salmon is spiked with brandy.

*1 pound salmon, split lengthwise and boned,*
*  with skin on*
*2 to 3 teaspoons coarse salt*
*1 to 2 teaspoons sugar*
*4 tablespoons peppercorns, crushed*
*½ cup brandy*
*1 large bunch dill, chopped coarsely*

Select a rectangular container, preferably glass or porcelain, that will comfortably hold the salmon filets. Combine the salt, sugar, and peppercorns. Layer salmon, skin side down, drizzling brandy and sprinkling dill and the spice seasonings generously between the layers. Cover and marinate two days in the refrigerator, spooning marinade (released by the salmon) over the filets occasionally.
SERVE with mustard sauce and lemon wedges.          **Serves 6 to 8**

## CALAMARI APPETIZER, ITALIAN STYLE
### Squid

Maria Abbatescianne, a young blond shopper born in Toritto, Italy, describes her favorite method for serving raw calamari—an unusual dish—while shopping in FRANK RANDAZZO'S SONS FISH MARKET (page 117).

*1 pound small calamari, cleaned and washed*
*Salt*
*3 tablespoons fine olive oil*
*Juice of 1 to 1½ lemons*
*Freshly ground black pepper*

Spread calamari in a flat tray or pan; salt slightly and let stand for 15 minutes. Wash. Layer calamari in a bowl and cover with cold water; soak 15 minutes. Rinse thoroughly; drain. Slip calamari into a plastic or paper bag and sprinkle lightly with salt; fold the bag and shake gently and continuously 10 minutes. Turn into bowl or strainer and wash thoroughly to remove all salt; drain. Slice calamari into bite-sized pieces and put into a serving bowl. Sprinkle with oil, lemon juice, and pepper.
SERVE with toast or unsalted crackers.                    **Serves 4 to 5**

## CLAMS A LA MARINARA

Tommy, manager of OCEAN #1 FISH MARKET, Astoria (page 153), born in Sicily, prefers this appetizer to any other, calls it *"Zuppa di Clams."* He suggests 2 dozen clams per person.

*⅓ cup olive oil*
*3 cloves garlic, crushed*
*4 to 5 ripe tomatoes, peeled and chopped*
*½ cup dry white wine*
*48 clams*
*3 sprigs parsley*
*Salt (optional)*
*Freshly ground pepper*

In a large pan, heat the olive oil and saute the garlic for 1 minute. Stir in the tomatoes and wine. Cover and cook over low heat 5 minutes. Meanwhile, scrub the clams and wash thoroughly to remove all sand. Set clams into the sauce, sprinkle with parsley, cover and steam 10 to 15 minutes until all clams have opened (discard any that remain closed). Taste and season to your taste. SERVE warm with "lots of Italian bread and wine," preferably chilled white *Corvo Salaporuta*. **Serves 2**

NOTE: Another classic Italian appetizer or pasta topping— *Scungilli a la Marinara*—is also cooked, sliced, in a seasoned tomato sauce (with oregano, bay leaf, and basil) after parboiling about 15 minutes. *Scungilli* are conches and have been considered aphrodisiacs by Italians since ancient times.

## RILLETTES

A New York or any other cookbook would not be complete without a French *paté*. This is a lovely one, classic, flexible for your own seasoning touches.

> 1 boneless pork shoulder, about 3 pounds, diced
> 3 to 4 shallots, chopped
> 2 to 3 cloves garlic, chopped
> 1 stalk celery, chopped
> 1 bay leaf
> 2 sprigs parsley
> 2 sprigs thyme
> 1 to 1½ cups dry white wine
> 2 tablespoons fine Cognac

Put the pork dice into a pot with the shallots, garlic, celery, and a bouquet garni of bay leaf, parsley, and thyme tied together. Add only enough water to just about cover (only enough to cook the pork without any remaining, so it is better to add as you progress). Simmer over low heat, stirring occasionally, until water has been absorbed and pork begins to fall apart. Add the wine and Cognac and continue cooking until thickened. When pork is tender and thickened and still appears lumpy, pound in mortar or put through a food chopper to make smooth. Pack in small crocks or paté mold. Cover and refrigerate.

SERVE with toast, bread, or crackers. **Serves 10 to 15**

## YUGOSLAVIAN YOGURT SALAD

The popularity of homemade yogurt—not the commercial type— has spread through the Balkans from Bulgaria to Greece (where yogurt is richly thick from sheep or goat's milk) to the U.S. with ethnic groups. My mother made it when I was little and I don't know where the "starter" came from—neighbors who had yogurt, probably. A Zagreb-born woman, who has lived in New York for several years, told me that her mother also made this tasty salad when she was a child and she now makes it with store-bought yogurt.

*2 cups yogurt, preferably thickened by draining* *
*2 to 4 slices spicy salami, minced*

Combine yogurt and salami in a small bowl.

SERVE cold as a salad, dip, or snack with celery and other raw vegetables. **Serves 4**

NOTE: See Note on page 182, should you like to make your own yogurt.

* Yogurt is especially delicious when thickened by draining through a dampened cheesecloth draped over a strainer (place over a bowl to save the whey for use in a soup or beverage). Tie the ends of the cheesecloth together and suspend from a hook or cabinet handle; yogurt will be thick as cream cheese in one hour. For this recipe drain about 20 minutes.

## SOFRITO, WEST INDIAN AND CARIBBEAN STYLE

*Sofrito* is a fabulous seasoning that seems to enhance a cook's creativity. It has traveled from Spain all the way to Greece and South America. For example, "*Sofrito* originated in Spain and spread into many areas, changing costumes like a spy. It is a mystery how the Corfiotes developed another dish—*Sofrito Korfiatiko* (Pungent Braised Veal, Corfu Style)—for it bears no resemblance to *Sofrito* in the Caribbean, Italy, or the Middle East. Was it possibly brought to Greece by the Venetians?"* The *Sofrito* described with ardor by West Indian, Central, and some South American cooks for recipes in this book is a delicate combination of the aromatic vegetables and herbs listed below. Notably, the *Ajicitos* (tiny peppers ranging from mild to peppery with intriguingly muted coral, cream, and green hues and various shapes) are available at West Indian and Caribbean stands and stalls. *Recau,* an herb, and *Cilantro* (fresh coriander) are sold along with it and the stall owner and shoppers offer suggestions for amounts.* *

 *2 tablespoons vegetable oil*
 *1 onion, minced*
 *3 cloves garlic, minced*
 *1 large handful* Ajicitos *(about ⅓ pound), chopped*
 Recau *(green herb), chopped*
 Cilantro or *fresh coriander, chopped*
 *1 large red or green sweet pepper, chopped finely*
 *Black pepper*

Heat oil and saute onion, garlic, *Ajicitos, Recau, Cilantro,* and pepper together until soft but not brown. Season with black pepper. Cool. Freeze in 1 tablespoon portions for easy addition to dishes. Utterly delicious with fresh pigeon peas.

---

* Chantiles, Vilma Liacouras. *The Food of Greece.* Atheneum, 1975; Avenel/ Crown Publishers, 1979, 1981, 1984.
* * When you are buying *Ajicitos, Recau,* and *Cilantro,* the seller can help suggest proportions for you, but look carefully to pick fresh peppers and herbs. *Ajicitos* are milder than chilis and you'll need quite a few to achieve a rich flavor.

## SOFRITO, BOLIVIAN STYLE

Yet another version of *Sofrito*, this is from Teresa Loaiza, a Queens resident born in Bolivia. Teresa suggests stirring this delicious combination into stew, soups, and casseroles as a seasoning and simmering about 15 minutes before serving; especially, she likes to serve this with beef that has been simmered with onion, celery, and turnip before adding the *Sofrito*.

1 to 2 tablespoons vegetable oil
1 small red or green pepper, chopped finely
2 onions or 4 scallions, minced
¾ cup fresh shelled peas
1 large (or preferably) 3 tiny carrots, * shredded or sliced
   thinly into rounds
1 chili (called Locotos), chopped * *
2 to 3 tablespoons fresh parsley, chopped
Salt
Freshly ground pepper

Heat a pan and drizzle in only enough oil to coat the bottom. Saute the red or green pepper, onions, peas, and carrots for 5 minutes. Stir in the chili and parsley. Season lightly with salt and generously with pepper. Add to the soup, stew, or casserole you are cooking.
SERVE warm.
**(This amount is suggested for about 8 cups of soup to serve 4 to 5;**
**increase or decrease to your needs)**

---

* Tiny carrots, used in Bolivia, are not always available at New York greengrocers.
* * Teresa uses Goya chilis available in jars; or substitute a fresh chili and sauté with the other vegetables.

## KEFIR
### Homemade Polish Cheese

Ingrid Bolski, born in Bydgoszcz, has lived in New York since the 1960s and still makes this cheese—served with *Zarzy* (bacon-onion-pickle-mushroom filled beef rolls) and *Czerwona Kapusta* (red cabbage).

*4 cups milk, boiled*
*3 tablespoons sour cream or yogurt*

Cool milk slightly and stir in the sour cream or yogurt; cover. Rest at room temperature two days until thickened. Refrigerate. To thicken even more, drain through a wet cheesecloth draped over a strainer set over a bowl about 45 minutes. (Save whey for a beverage or soup.)
SERVE as a cheese.                    **Makes about 2½ cups**

NOTE: Yogurt can be made at home in a similar way by stirring the yogurt starter into the boiled milk, cooled to 125°F. Cover and keep warm overnight. Thick in the morning, it may be drained through a dampened cheesecloth to thicken even more. It's important to wet the cheesecloth to prevent yogurt from sticking to it; yogurt will unmold in a lovely round when inverted over your serving platter.

## YOGURT CHAKA

Afghans use *Chaka* to spoon on vegetable dishes and it also makes a tasty appetizer dip for crudités or as a spread on black or rye bread. Armenians make a similar condiment.

*2 cups yogurt, drained for 30 minutes (see footnote, page 179.)*
*4 to 6 cloves garlic, minced*
*Pinch of salt (optional)*

Combine yogurt, garlic, and only enough salt to flavor the mixture. Store 2 to 3 days, covered, in refrigerator.    **Makes 2 cups**

# KADHI
## Asian-Indian Yogurt Relish

Yogentra Chokshi runs SHIV, a small grocery (41 Lexington Ave., Manhattan) buzzing with shoppers. He sells 100 imported beers from 25 countries. He and Raju Gohil, his brother-in-law, suggested that all vegetable curries and chutneys are fine accompaniments with *Kadhi*.

> 2 cups yogurt slightly thinned with water to consistency of
>   buttermilk, or substitute buttermilk
> ½ teaspoon ground turmeric
> 1 teaspoon ground coriander
> 1 teaspoon ground cumin
> 2 cloves garlic, crushed
> 2 to 3 tablespoons vegetable oil
> Pinch mustard seeds
> 5 to 6 hot red chilies including seeds, chopped
> Pinch chick pea flour

In a bowl, combine the diluted yogurt or buttermilk with turmeric, coriander, cumin, and garlic. Set aside to marinate 15 minutes. Heat the oil. When almost boiling, add the mustard seeds and chilies. Cook, stirring, over very low heat for 2 minutes; then add the buttermilk mixture and pinch of flour and cook until dissolved. Cool.

SERVE at room temperature with rice vegetable curries and salads.

**Makes about 2½ cups**

NOTE: Messrs Chokshi and Gohil use the same procedure to make most of their vegetable curries: Heat the oil and cook mustard seeds and chilies, then add the cooked vegetables and the *masala* (spice mixture).

## KIMCHI
### Korean Pickled Vegetables

Truly a condiment, an honored accompaniment to *every* edible for Koreans. Jong Sun Yoo helps out at KIM'S MARKET (page 76) and continues to make *Kimchi* after having lived in the U.S. since 1972. This is for Korean tastes, so go easy on the red pepper—you can always add!

Korean markets increasingly sell the *Napa* cabbage for *Kimchi* uncut, to cut at home. Also, other vegetables are used in *Kimchi* seasonally: cucumber—a favorite—turnip, celery, and combinations. *Kimchi* is not as easy to make as it sounds. Whenever I tried it for a Korean acquaintance, she tasted it and said "In my con-tree. . . ." Then I knew it wasn't hot enough! Good luck.

1 Napa *cabbage, washed, drained, and cut into ¼-inch by*
   *3-inch shreds*
*Salt*
*2 to 3 scallions, chopped*
*3 to 4 cloves garlic, crushed*
*1-inch piece fresh ginger, chopped or grated*
*3 to 5 tablespoons hot peppers or red powder*

Place the cabbage in a bowl and sprinkle lightly with salt. Rest at room temperature two hours until soft. Wash and drain in several waters to remove traces of salt. In a large jar (with cover) combine the cabbage, scallions, garlic, ginger, and 3 tablespoons of the hot pepper. Cover jar; rest in warm place at room temperature overnight or one day. Taste and add more pepper if you wish.

EAT with *Pulgogi* (page 266) and fish dishes.          **Serves 4 to 6**

## COCONUT MILK or CREAM *

Jamaican students taught me how to handle the wonderful, brown, fibrous coconut and many ways to preserve and use its food. See LOPEZ FRUIT STORE (page 70) for handling of water

* To make *Coconut Cream* substitute milk for the water.

(jelly) coconut—which has a smooth green skin and is very large compared to the familiar brown ones.

> 1 coconut (shake it to hear the liquid inside)
> 3 cups very hot water

Using tip of sharp knife or ice pick, pierce two of the coconut "eyes" and invert over a glass; pour out the liquid (sometimes called the "tail") and use as a beverage or thinner in cooking sauces. With a whack of a hammer (some students use their shoe!) break open the coconut. To make it easier to remove the coconut meat, heat coconut for half a minute over the burner or in a pan. Pry out with a knife and chop coarsely. (This may be frozen to use at a later time, if in a hurry.) Drop coconut in a blender with 2 cups of hot water. Blend 30 seconds. Add another cup of hot water and blend. Pour into a strainer placed over a bowl; squeeze out all the liquid and discard the coconut fibers in the strainer.

USE the coconut milk in soups, rice, and beans—anywhere coconut milk is needed.

## CORIANDER or MINT CHUTNEY

Made with fresh coriander or mint, this delightful chutney sings exuberantly with fish and poultry dishes.

> 10 sprigs fresh coriander or mint leaves, chopped
> 1 cup onion, coarsely chopped
> 1 clove garlic, chopped
> 3 green chilies, seeds removed and cut up
> 1 small tomato, peeled
> Juice of a lime or half a lemon
> Dash of cayenne pepper

Place all ingredients in blender and mix thoroughly. Keep tightly covered in refrigerator. **Makes 1 cup**

## PEANUT SAUCE

A favorite among Indonesians. Excellent lasting qualities; if you make a large quantity, store, covered, in the refrigerator.

1 pound 2 ounce jar crunchy peanut butter
1 to 2 cloves garlic, crushed
1/2 to 1 teaspoon sugar
Pinch of salt
Juice of 1 large lime

In a large saucepan, stir the peanut butter, garlic, sugar, salt, and lime juice with 2 to 3 10-ounce glasses of water to make a thick, not soupy sauce. Cook about 5 minutes. Store, covered, in the refrigerator.

SERVE in a small dish with Indonesian cooked vegetables called Gado Gado (recipe, page 230), rice, and other Indonesian dishes.

## HAITIAN HOT SAUCE

Keep this sauce in your refrigerator and it will heat up your meat and fish dinners no matter how cold they are.

1 large onion or 4 to 5 shallots, chopped
1/2 cup white vinegar or lime juice
1 to 2 tablespoons vegetable oil
2 cloves garlic, crushed
1 to 4 chilies, crushed, seeds discarded
Pinch salt
Cayenne pepper

Put onions or shallots in a small bowl, pour vinegar or lime juice over them; marinate one hour. Strain over a bowl and save the liquid. Heat oil and sauté onions without browning, about 10 minutes. Stir in the garlic and as much chili as you like. Cover and simmer 10 minutes. Stir in the reserved vinegar or lime juice liquid. Season with a pinch of salt and dash of cayenne.

SERVE hot.                                          **Makes ¾ cup**

## SAMBAL
### Hot Pepper Sauce

This is the essential fiery sauce used drop by drop with Indonesian dishes. It is preferred "on the side" rather than mixed into the food, so that guests can control the quantity.

*1 ripe fresh tomato, chpopped*
*1 teaspoon Trassi \* (shrimp paste)*
*1 onion, sliced*
*2 cloves garlic*
*½ to 1 teaspoon sugar*
*Pinch of salt*
*Generous squeeze from half lemon*
*Dried red pepper seeds (Thai, Chinese, or Filipino)*

In a blender or old-fashioned stone mortar, grind the tomato, *Trassi,* onion, garlic, sugar, salt, lemon juice, and stir in the amount of red pepper seeds for your taste.
SERVE with *Rendang* (page 233) and *Sate* (recipe, pages 231 and 232) dishes in the *Rames* (page 230).

\* *Trassi* is available in Indonesian and many Indian food shops.

## SEPHAN
### Tibetan Hot Pepper Sauce

Like a thick chili sauce in texture with green flecks and seeds, this is really *hot* and even the Tibetans use only a dab in the dish to "fire" their dumplings *Momo* (page 296).

*2 ripe tomatoes, peeled and chopped*
*2 cloves garlic, crushed or minced*
*1-inch fresh ginger, chopped finely*
*2 large fresh chilies, chopped*
*½ teaspoon hot pepper seeds (Chinese, Thai, or Filipino if Tibetan are not available)*
*½ tablespoon fresh coriander, finely minced*

This is best ground in a mortar. Grind together tomatoes, garlic, ginger, chilies and pepper seeds. Stir in the coriander.

SERVE on a small plate for each guest. **Serves 4 to 5**

NOTE: Sprinkled among the recipes are more dipping sauces including a Japanese dipping sauce (for fish), page 265 and *Goma* dipping sauce (for meat), page 266.

## NUOC MAM SAUCE
### Vietnamese Dipping Sauce

Served with meat, fish, rice dishes, and spring rolls; orange-colored and deliciously appetizing.

> 1 chili, seeded and chopped or 1 teaspoon red pepper, more or
>   less
> 1 clove garlic
> Pinch salt
> Pinch sugar
> Juice of ½ lemon or lime
> 1 to 3 tablespoons rice wine vinegar
> 1 teaspoon finely slivered carrot
> 5 tablespoons Vietnamese fish sauce, or substitute Thai
>   Tiparos fish sauce

In a mortar or blender, grind the chili, garlic, salt, sugar, lemon or lime juice, adding as much vinegar as you like. Stir in the carrot and gradually add the fish sauce and enough water (about ¼ cup) to make a thin, tasty sauce. Taste and adjust. Stores indefinitely. SERVE from an empty soy sauce bottle or cruet to make pouring easy.

# SOUPS

*Better no spoons than no broth.*

GERMAN PROVERB

## ERWTENSOEP
### Dutch Pea Soup

Ludi Kerman, assistant for press and cultural affairs in the Dutch Consulate General's Manhattan office, has lived in New York since 1975 and still considers this her favorite soup. Very thick and hearty, it should warm you on a cold, wintry day as it did the Dutch settlers in the early seventeenth century.

*1 pound green split peas*
*3 stalks celery including green parts, chopped*
*2 leeks, washed thoroughly and sliced*
*4 scallions, sliced across into small rings*
*2 smoked pigs' feet*
*½ pound smoked sausages, preferably Dutch, sliced into thin*
    *rings*
*Salt (optional)*
*Freshly ground pepper (optional)*
*Large handful of fresh parsley, chopped*

Wash the peas and cover with water; soak overnight. Cook, covered, 30 minutes. Then add celery, leeks, scallions, and smoked pigs' feet. Simmer until peas are almost tender. Meanwhile, brown the sausages in a small pan and add to the soup. Simmer until flavors have blended and taste for seasonings, adding a few grains salt and some pepper, if you like. Save some parsley for the top and stir in the rest.
SERVE *Erwtensoep* hot, garnished with parsley, with buttered pumpernickel bread on the side.          **Serves 4 to 5**


## NEW YEAR'S DAY BLACK-EYED PEA SOUP
### Soul Food Style

Mother instilled in us a sense of contentedness. Our farm was bountiful; we had all kinds of foods, pigs (so easy to breed), and chickens. Veal, baked or fried, was an important meat, although beef was Mama's favorite. Fish—carp and red snapper, trout, haddock, porgies, butterfish, catfish for Catfish

Stew—was plentiful. All the vegetables we ate—collards, turnips, turnip greens, okra, dandelions, cabbage, kale, and asparagus—flourished on our farm.

These childhood memories of the late Cordia Watson, a remarkable woman who grew up in Laurens, South Carolina, unlocked an entire world of menus for me where only a tightly lidded blank pot had existed. During the four years I knew her before she died, Cordia revealed a warm family culture and remarkable dishes. She shopped in Italian markets for chitterlings (chittlins), dandelions, and hot peppers during the many years she lived in New York. The following recipe is a tribute to her memory.

Enjoyed on New Year's Day, this version of black-eyed peas is served thick, "not soupy," sometimes with rice, and spicy. Ham hock liquid adds flavor but is not absolutely necessary. Happy New Year!

*1 pound black-eyed peas*
*3 to 4 cloves garlic, more if you like*
*1 stalk celery, cut into finger-sized lengths*
*1 large onion, chopped*
*1 small carrot*
*1 to 2 tomatoes (optional)*
*4 to 5 hot peppers or 1 tablespoon hot red pepper*
*¼ pound salt pork or smoked ham*
*4 cups ham hock liquid (optional)*
*Fresh parsley*
*Thyme*
*Salt to taste*
*Freshly ground pepper to taste*

Soak black-eyed peas overnight or bring to the boil with water to cover and soak one hour. Drain * and add 2 cloves garlic, cut in half, celery, onion, carrot, tomatoes, hot peppers (if you are using them), and salt pork or ham. Pour in the ham hock liquid if you are using it, and enough water to almost cover. Cover pot and simmer slowly 1½ hours until peas are tender, adding only

* Cordia did not suggest removing the "black eyes" from the peas as suggested in Akara (page 242). Either way, the dish is tasty.

enough water, if necessary, to make a thick dish. Remove the carrot and save for another dish. Chop the parsley and thyme, crush the remaining garlic (more if you like) and mix them together. Stir into the beans. Taste and season with a little salt, pepper, and more red pepper, if needed.

SERVE warm with buttermilk biscuits or cornbread, and collards, or just plain. **Serves 4 to 5**

## HOPPING JOHN, BERMUDA STYLE

Cynthia Wilkinson, a kind Bermudian living in New York, praised the delights of this hearty pea-rice dish. She uses the coconut milk and also the liquid inside the coconut as stock. Very subtle flavor, soft pinkish colors. You'll need a brown coconut.

*1 cup black-eyed peas* *
*2 to 3 slices bacon, chopped*
*1 large onion, chopped*
*2 garlic cloves, minced*
*1 celery stalk, chopped (with or without leaves)*
*1 tomato, peeled and chopped or 2 tablespoons ketchup*
*2 cups coconut milk (see recipe, page 184)*
*½ cup long-grain rice*
*4 to 5 sprigs fresh thyme, chopped, or 2 teaspoons dried*
*   thyme, crushed in your palm over the soup*

Wash black-eyed peas, add enough cold water to cover and allow to soak overnight. Next day, fry the chopped bacon, add the onion, garlic, and celery and cook until vegetables are soft, about 5 minutes. Stir in the soaked peas, tomato, and coconut milk and bring to the boil, stirring constantly. Lower heat and simmer, covered, until peas are tender, not mushy. Stir in the rice and thyme, adding coconut milk or liquid if necessary. Continue simmering until rice is tender, about 15 minutes. Remove from heat and drape with a towel.

SERVE hot. **Serves 4**

* Jamaicans make a similar soup with kidney beans.

## EGUSI SOUP
### Nigerian Melon Seed Soup

Ethel Bolokor, New York University graduate student born of the *Itshkiri* tribe, shares a remarkable Nigerian dish, with *Egusi* (melon seeds) in a starring role. Made with beef, poultry, or shrimp, the soup can be created anew each time, thick or soupy, but Ethel prefers it thick and hearty. Ethel deserves a "thank you" in her own language: *Mo Du Kpe!*

*1 to 1¼ pounds stewing beef, cut into chunks* ＊
*2 onions*
*1 sweet red pepper, stem and seeds discarded, cut into*
  *chunks*
*1 fresh or canned tomato, chopped*
*1 teaspoon ground red pepper (more if you like)*
*1 cup* Egusi *(melon seeds)*
*¼ cup palm oil*
*1 pound fresh spinach or collard greens, stems trimmed,*
  *chopped*
*Salt*
*Freshly ground pepper*

Drop beef chunks into a 2-quart pan, cover with 4 cups water, and add one of the onions. Cover and simmer 30 minutes until beef is half tender. While beef is cooking, whirl the pepper, tomato, ground red pepper, and remaining onion in a blender. Pour into a small bowl and reserve. In the blender, grind the *Egusi* and reserve in another bowl. Drain the beef and reserve the liquid. In a large casserole, heat the palm oil and saute the beef, stirring constantly, for 5 minutes. Add the reserved tomato-pepper sauce and cook 10 minutes, stirring frequently. Stir in the reserved meat liquid, cover and simmer 15 minutes. Sprinkle in the *Egusi* and add the spinach. Partially cover the casserole and continue cooking until beef and spinach are tender, about 15 minutes. Taste and season with salt, pepper, and more ground red pepper, if you like. SERVE warm.                                         **Serves 4**

＊ A segmented broiler or fryer chicken may be substituted for the beef; frequently, dried shrimp are used (see next recipe).

## EGUSI SOUP WITH DRIED SHRIMP

Esther Adeleye, a Nigerian of the Yoruba tribe discussed *Egusi Soup* as made at her home in my Cultural Foods class at Lehman College. Hers is a quick recipe, which may suggest methods of cooking West African sauces. Esther, *Ose!*

½ cup palm oil
1 onion, ground
¼ cup hot ground pepper
¼ cup ground dried shrimp
2 cups collard greens, boiled and chopped
Salt to taste
1 cup Egusi (melon seeds, ground)

Heat the oil in a pan and stir in the onion, pepper, and shrimp to form a paste. Set over low heat and add 2 cups water. Stirring constantly, cook the sauce 10 minutes. Drop in the collards and mix thoroughly. Season lightly with salt, then sprinkle the ground melon seeds into the vegetable. Give it two minutes to settle with the collards. Stir. "It is good when the melon seeds form lumps.
SERVE with any solid food, *Fufu*, rice and beans, okra, etc," says Esther.                                                                **Serves 2**

## ARMENIAN CHICK PEA, WHOLE WHEAT YOGURT SOUP

Hourig Messerlian, manager of the book store of the Armenian Church Diocese of America (34th St. at Second Ave.), a lovely blue-eyed Armenian lass who was born in Lebanon, likes to cook this Armenian soup "when I want to remember my grandmother and how she used to make it for me." She suggests cooking enough for two or three meals. Yogurt can be stirred in just before serving. *Shnorhagalutiun!*

1 cup husked (peeled) whole grain wheat *
1¾ cups chick peas
Salt
Freshly ground pepper
3 to 4 tablespoons unsalted butter or olive oil or mixed
3 large onions, slivered (about 3 cups)
¾ cup fresh mint leaves, chopped finely or ⅓ dried mint
   (more for garnish)
½ cup yogurt for each serving or 2 to 2½ cups for entire dish

Wash whole wheat, cover with cold water, and soak overnight in bowl or pan. Next day, if postponing cooking, refrigerate until ready to cook and it probably will not need any cooking but will triple its volume; reserve all liquid. Wash and soak the chick peas the night before as well in a separate pan. When ready to cook, drain over a bowl to reserve liquid (some people throw this away but nutrients are lost); rub chick peas under water to remove the skins; if too difficult, return to the liquid and continue cooking until tender, from 1½ to 2½ hours depending on the dryness of the peas, adding more water if necessary. Discard the skins as they rise to the surface. (The mixture should have considerable liquid since it thickens up when cooling.) Combine with the swollen wheat and its liquid. Heat to boiling and season lightly with salt and pepper. Beat hard with a wooden spoon (or dull blade of food processor) to crush the peas and wheat. Heat butter or oil in a frying pan and saute the onions until golden, about 10 minutes. Stir into the hot chick pea-wheat mixture and add the mint. Simmer a few minutes, adding water if too thick. If serving a large group, stir in the yogurt and heat without boiling. Or, divide into small quantities and cool; freeze. Thaw and reheat gently before serving and either stir in more mint and yogurt and heat, or stir in mint and yogurt at the table.          **Serves 6 to 8**

---

* Available husked or unhusked (peeled or unpeeled) at Greek, Italian, and Middle Eastern shops. The peeled is white and looks like barley.

## MAUSHAUWA
### Afghan Soup

After relishing every drop of this soup several times at *Little Afghan* restaurant (106 W. 43rd St.), I count it among the great ethnic soups. Flavored with mint, it takes its name from mung beans called *Maush* in Afghan. Special thanks to owner Mohammed Salim, Russian-born Afghan, who answered so many of my questions. *Tashakur!*

1 cup navy beans or red kidney beans or mixed
1 cup mung beans or substitute green split peas
Soup herbs: 1 leek or shallot, 1 stalk celery, 1 bay leaf, 2
    sprigs parsley, 2 sprigs fresh thyme or ½ teaspoon dried
    thyme or savory
½ cup white long-grained rice
1 pound ground lamb or beef*
Dash of ground cinnamon
1 to 2 teaspoons red pepper
Freshly ground black pepper
¼ cup fresh mint leaves, chopped or substitute dried mint
    (more for garnish)
2 tablespoons vegetable oil
3 to 4 scallions or 1 medium onion, chopped
2 fresh tomatoes, chopped or 3 canned plum tomatoes,
    chopped
1½ cups Chaka (page 182)

Wash navy and/or kidney beans in large soup pot; cover with cold water, and soak overnight. About an hour before cooking, in a bowl, cover mung beans with boiling water and let soak to expand for one to two hours. Add to the other beans in the soup pot and add water to an inch above them. Add the soup herbs and simmer until tender, about 1½ hours. Mash beans lightly with potato masher or wooden spoon. Add the rice and only enough water to cook the mixture (1½ cups liquid); simmer 20 minutes (soup should be thick). Meanwhile, in a bowl, mix the ground meat,

* The meat balls and sauce can be made a day in advance; the flavor improves.

cinnamon, red and black peppers, and mint. Knead; shape into ½-inch balls. In a medium-sized pan, heat the oil and saute the scallions or onion until soft, about 2 minutes; then add the meat balls. Saute, turning constantly, until meat balls lose the raw color, about 5 minutes. Stir in tomatoes and enough water to half cover the meat balls. Cook, uncovered until sauce thickens, about 15 minutes. To serve, spoon bean-rice mixture into the bowl and top with meat ball sauce.

SERVE warm, garnished with mint leaves, and a generous dollop of *Chaka*.                                                                    **Serves 6**


## GOULASCH SOUP, HUNGARIAN STYLE

Ed Weiss, of PAPRIKAS WEISS (page 99), an enthusiast of Hungarian food and a cookbook writer, shares his favorite *Goulasch*—"long" method, his father's concept of *any* soup. The dish, if made "short," or without liquid, is also paprika-spicy.

*3 tablespoons chicken fat*
*3 onions, chopped*
*1 medium green pepper, chopped (seeds discarded)*
*1 tablespoon tomato paste*
*2 pounds stewing beef, cut into chunks*
*1 tablespoon paprika*
*Salt*
*Freshly ground pepper*
*Yogurt or sour cream*

Heat the fat and sauté the onion 7 minutes without browning. Stir in the green pepper, tomato paste, and meat and continue cooking 10 minutes until meat is browned on all sides. Sprinkle with paprika and enough water to cover. Simmer 50 minutes until beef is fork-tender. Season with more paprika, salt, and pepper.

SERVE warm with yogurt or sour cream.                           **Serves 6**

## MULLIGATAWNY

I've never tasted a Mulligatawny that was like any other, nor any that was not deliciously spicy. Here's a good one.

*3 tablespoons* Ghee* *or vegetable oil*
*1 small onion, sliced finely*
*2 to 3 dried curry leaves*
*½ teaspoon chili powder or 2 green chilies, chopped*
*¼ teaspoon ground turmeric*
*Small knob of fresh ginger, sliced*
*12 cloves garlic, sliced*
*½ teaspoon cumin seeds*
*2 teaspoons ground coriander*
*Black pepper*
*1 pound lean stewing lamb, diced*
*Salt*
*1 cup coconut milk (recipe, page 184)*
*Juice of ½ lime*

Heat the ghee or oil and sauté the onion. Remove half the onions and reserve for garnish. To the onions in the pan, add the curry leaves, chili powder or chilies, and turmeric and fry several minutes to make a paste. Stir in the ginger, garlic, cumin, coriander, and a grinding or two of black pepper, and fry another minute. Slip the lamb dice into the curry and cook, stirring, for 6 minutes. Season lightly with salt, pour in the coconut milk and enough hot water to cover the meat. Cover pan and simmer until lamb is tender, about 25 minutes. Sprinkle lime juice over the Mulligatawny, and taste for seasonings.

SERVE hot, garnished with remaining onions, rice, and chutney.

**Serves 4**

* *Ghee* is clarified butter. To make at home, melt butter (preferably unsalted) in a pan. Skim off and discard the floating foam. Gently pour the melted butter into a container; save the residue (milk solids) at bottom for another dish or discard. Store in refrigerator. Clarified butter will not burn or brown as quickly as unclarified butter.

## WONTON and NOODLE SOUP

At WONTON KING, INC. (page 31), Thomas Ju cooks wontons in the window on a long-handled mesh spoon. He generously shared his recipe for delectable Hong Kong style soup, a rich pick-me-up anytime, anywhere. Thomas Ju indicated that seasonings are "personal" and may be varied for your own pleasure. You may like more soy sauce in the mixture and may pass more at the table.

*½ pound lean ground pork*
*¼ pound shrimp, cleaned and minced*
*Seasonings: 1 clove garlic, crushed; ½ to 1 teaspoon ginger*
    *root, minced; 1 tablespoon thin soy sauce; 4 tablespoons*
    *vegetables (spinach, water leek, dried and soaked*
    *mushrooms, cress, celery leaves, bok choy), chopped*
*3 scallions, sliced into very slender circles*
*1 pound wonton wrappers*
*½ pound Chinese fresh egg noodles, cooked 3 minutes,*
    *drained*
*6 cups chicken broth*

In a large bowl, combine the pork, shrimp, seasonings, and about one-third of the scallions. Knead; divide into 25 to 30 balls depending on how large you like them. To stuff: set a ball in center of wonton. Wet around the edge with cold water and lift all edges, squeeze tightly together to enclose the stuffing, and twist the top to seal the tips. (Another method, not used by Thomas Ju, but popular among wonton cooks: after setting the ball on the wonton, wet edges with water and fold diagonally to form a triangle. Wet the long tips and squeeze together, then bend the top tip back in the opposite direction.) Continue stuffing until all the mixture is used. (Wrap and freeze any remaining wontons.) To cook: fill a soup pot three quarters full of water and bring to the boil. Place 4 to 5 wontons on a bamboo-handled strainer or large slotted spoon and immerse in boiling water, while holding the strainer, 3 to 4 minutes until cooked. Slide into bowl and continue cooking wontons until all are ready. *

TO SERVE: divide the cooked noodles among 6 bowls (preferably

Chinese), drop 3 to 4 wontons over the noodles (depending on how large the bowl is), fill with hot chicken broth and garnish with reserved scallion slivers. Serve hot. **Serves 6**

* TO FREEZE: Pack 3 to 5 stuffed, cooked, and cooled wontons in freezer wrap. When ready to serve drop into boiling broth, then lower heat and cook until thawed, about 7 minutes.

## CHINESE CHICKEN NOODLE SOUP

Rita Lam and Jennie Low, of WEST LAKE NOODLE CO. (page 33) suggest their delicious soup, whipped up quickly, as part of a meal with other dishes, or with a few helpings, a substantial lunch. Other types of noodles may be substituted, but they use the handy long spaghetti-like dried noodles. *Sie Sie!*

*Salt*
*¼ to ½ pound dried noodles (¼ pound, cooked, increases to 1¾ cups)*
*½ pound chicken breast, sliced into 1¼-inch julienne-type strips*
*½ pound* Gau Tsoi, *sliced thinly* *
*10 cups rich chicken broth*
*2 tablespoons scallions, slivered into rings (optional)*
*Soy sauce*

Bring a large quantity of water to boil in a soup pot and add 1 teaspoon salt per quart of water. When briskly boiling, stir in the noodles and cook 10 minutes or until tender. Drain. Meanwhile, simmer the chicken and *Gau Tsoi* in the chicken broth until chicken is tender, about 7 minutes.
TO SERVE: half fill the bowls with noodles and ladle in the broth, chicken, and *Gau Tsoi*. Garnish with scallions, if you like (they look and taste good) and pass the soy sauce. **Serves 4 to 5**

* *Gau Tsoi*, or Chinese chives, are available in bunches in Chinese markets. With bright-green, flat leaves that look like long grass, the flavor is distinctive—like garlic and onion combined, very much like wild spring onions, mild and fresh. *Gau Tsoi* is also delicious chopped into meat and shrimp fillings for dumplings.

## CHORBA PESCHTE
### Romanian Fish Soup

In Romania, *Chorba* (soup) is seasoned with a homemade liquid called *Borscht* (*not* the famed soup from Russia or the delicious vegetable soup called *Borscht Paysan* served us in Hangzhou, China). Romanian *Borscht* is made from fermented grain and sours the soup; in New York, Romanians substitute lemon juice, but they prefer the *Borscht*. * This wholesome soup recipe is shared by Ileana Popa, born in southern Romania on the Danube River, who has lived in New York since 1980. *Multsumesh!*

> 1 onion, chopped
> 2 stalks celery, chopped
> 3 to 4 carrots, chopped
> ½ green pepper, chopped (optional)
> 1 potato, chopped
> 50 to 100 grains white, long-grained rice
> 4-ounce glass of tomato juice
> 1 fresh carp, cleaned, cut into 3-inch slices
> 1 egg
> Juice of 1 large lemon (more to taste)
> Salt
> Freshly ground pepper
> Handful fresh parsley, chopped

Put the onion, celery, carrots, pepper, potato, and rice in large soup pot. Cover with cold water to 2 inches above the top of the vegetables. Cook until potato and rice are tender, about 20 minutes. Stir in the tomato juice and add the carp with enough additional water if necessary, to cover the carp. Poach until carp is tender, about 15 minutes. In a small bowl, beat the egg with 2 tablespoons lemon juice; stir into the soup. Season with lemon juice, salt, and pepper to your taste.

SERVE hot, sprinkled with parsley. **Serves 4**

---

* *Borscht* liquid is available in some Romanian shops, but I was unable to find any. I was told that a shop in Sunnyside, Queens, near the post office, has it. Let me know if you find it, by writing to me in care of the publisher.

## SINEGANG
### Filipino Soup

Distinguished by its use of the third rinse water of rice, * this *Sinegang* has a tamarind tartness (sometimes with *Calamansi*— Filipino limes) and flavored with the fish sauce, *Batis.* * * Delicious.

2 tablespoons vegetable oil
1 large onion, slivered
2 carrots, diced
1 clove garlic, chopped
2 tomatoes, peeled and chopped or ½ cup tomato sauce
4 cups of the third rinse water from long-grain or short-grain
    rice (cook the rice and serve with the main course)
1 teaspoon tamarind, dissolved in ¼ cup water or ½ teaspoon
    of tamarind concentrate
1 tablespoon Batis, or more to taste
4 large shrimp, cleaned

Heat the oil in a saucepan, and sauté the onion, carrots, and garlic until onion is translucent. Stir in the tomatoes and cook 2 minutes; then add the rice water and simmer 10 minutes. Season with tamarind and *Batis* and add the shrimp. Simmer 7 minutes longer until shrimp is tender. Taste and add more *Batis*, if you like.

SERVE warm, with 1 shrimp and vegetables in each bowl. **Serves 4**

* When rinsing rice (that needs to be rinsed) strain over a bowl to save the water.
* * *Batis* is available in Filipino grocery stores.

## SPANISH FISH SOUP, KOREAN STYLE

Did you ever step into a sparkling fish market that smells like delicious Spanish soup? You'll find one in Elmhurst at PIER 90 FISH MARKET (page 159). Edward Jough and his family simmer the soup in the back kitchen and serve it to hungry shoppers willing to pay $1 for an aromatic cupful as they shop. Here's the Jough family recipe. *Kamsamnida!*

¼ cup olive oil
2 onions, chopped
1 large green pepper, seeded and chopped
3 cloves garlic, chopped
4 to 5 plum tomatoes and juice to make 3 cups
1 bay leaf
Salt
Freshly ground pepper
1 pound cod steaks
1 pound pollock
1 pound hake

In a soup kettle, heat the oil and sauté the onions, pepper, and garlic until the onions soften. Stir in the tomatoes and juice, bay leaf, and enough water to cover the fish when you add them. Simmer soup 15 minutes and season lightly with salt and pepper. Gently lower the cod, pollock, and hake into the soup and simmer over low heat until fish is flaky, about 15 minutes. Cut the fish into bite-sized pieces, discard any bones, and stir into the soup.

SERVE hot.                                              **Serves 8 to 10**

## CALDEIRADA A PESCADORA
### Portuguese Fish Soup

P. Elias Adam, owner of the Portuguese Pavilion (140 W. 13th St., Manhattan), was born in southern Portugal and raised in Lisbon. He has lived in New York since 1947 and still raves about Portuguese seafood dishes. For this Portuguese seafood specialty, he suggests: "Be sure to pick 'hard' fish (cod, snapper, etc.) that won't fall apart when cooking." This lifelong restauranteur urges mixing Portuguese olive oil ("very heavy") with a light vegetable oil for a delightful flavor balance. When shopping for his favorite dishes, he frequently buys *Chorizo* (Spanish sausages) and *Morcillas* (blood sausages), and enjoys kale, red beans with salt pork, and winy pork and chicken dishes more than the "hot" Brazilian dishes. And he serves rice in tomatoes with clams rather than the Spanish saffron rice. *Obrigado!*

   4 tablespoons mixed Portuguese olive oil and light vegetable
      oil, or, substitute light olive oil
   3 cloves garlic
   5 plum or 4 tomatoes, chopped
   ½ tablespoon tomato paste
   1 cup dry white wine (more if desired for stock)
   1½ pounds cod, snapper, or other filets, cut into 4-inch slices
   Salt
   Freshly ground pepper
   2 tablespoons butter
   4 to 6 slices Italian bread, toasted
   4 to 6 cups fish stock

To make the sauce, heat the oil, slice 2 of the garlic cloves into the oil, and sauté without browning, about 1 minute. Stir in the tomatoes, tomato paste, and enough wine to make a nice sauce. Simmer 5 minutes, then slip in the fish filets. Continue simmering until filets are tender, about 15 minutes, spooning sauce over the fish after 10 minutes. Taste sauce and season lightly. (This much can be done well in advance.) When ready to serve, gently reheat the fish, crush the remaining garlic clove and mix with the butter and spread on the toast. Heat stock to boiling point. Set a piece of buttered toast into the bottom of each soup bowl. Divide the fish and sauce on the toast. Pour stock into each bowl to cover the fish, adding a dribble or two of white wine for more flavor, if you like.
SERVE hot.                                          **Serves 4 to 6**

## JAPANESE MISO SOUP WITH BEAN CURD

To cook this delightful soup, first make the *Dashi* broth; it may be stored in the refrigerator for a quick soup pick-me-up and varied infinitely.

*4 cups* Dashi *broth (recipe below)*
*4 tablespoons red* Miso *paste (soybean paste)*
*1 cake tofu or bean curd (Preferably Japanese type), finely slivered*
*4 teaspoons scallions, sliced into very fine rings*

Pour *Dashi* broth into a pan and heat to lukewarm. Measure the *Miso* in a cup and gradually stir a tablespoon of the broth into the *Miso*, repeating until the *Miso* is dissolved in almost a full cup of broth. Stir the dissolved *Miso* into the remaining *Dashi*, add the slivered tofu, and heat to boiling point without boiling. Remove the tofu and divide into 4 cups. Ladle hot broth over the tofu, and garnish with sliced scallions.

SERVE hot. **Serves 4**


## DASHI BROTH

*1 sheet* Dashi Kombu *seaweed*
*½ cup* Dashi No Moto *(Bonito shavings) or* Hanakatsuo *(fish flakes)*

Cut the *Dashi Kombu* into 4 pieces; slash around the sides of each piece, about 1½ inches. Put in bottom of a 2-quart pan. Add 4 cups of water; gradually bring to the boil, keeping tongs handy to lift out the *Dashi Kombu before* water boils. Then add the *Dashi No Moto* or *Hanakatsuo* (whichever you choose), and bring to the boil again. Strain over a bowl and discard the flakes. Use the *Dashi* broth for soup.

NOTE: When you see Japanese shoppers buying the instant *Miso* soups *(Yu-Ge Misoshiru)*, you may prefer to follow their example and try one. Invigorating with *Miso* and seaweed laced with onion.

# ROOTS
# & OTHER VEGETABLES

*The one who constantly eats*
*vegetable roots can do anything.*
CHINESE PROVERB

## ARTICHOKES AND FAVA BEANS

In Astoria, Maria Spetsieri, born on the island of Keffalinia, and Demetra Petses, from Cyprus, shopped with their youngsters and divulged their recipe for a flavorful dish when both vegetables are in season (spring) or any time you can get them.

*8 globe artichokes*
*1 lemon*
*¼ cup olive oil*
*1 large onion, chopped*
*2 pounds fava beans (Hellenes call them* Koukia*), shelled*
*3 to 4 fresh or canned plum tomatoes with juice*
*Small handful fresh dill, chopped*
*Salt*
*Freshly ground pepper*

Clean the artichokes and remove the chokes; rub with cut lemon to prevent darkening. In 2-quart pan, heat the oil and sauté the onion until translucent. Add the artichokes, shelled beans, tomatoes, and enough water to almost cover. Cover the pan and simmer 30 minutes. Stir in the dill and season with salt and pepper to your taste.
SERVE warm or cold. **Serves 4 to 6**

## GREEN BANANAS, JAMAICAN STYLE

The adored green bananas are used as vegetables. Boiled, they are a warm accompaniment to steamed fish and meat dishes, especially for Sunday breakfast, Jamaican folks suggest.

*6 green bananas*
*¾ teaspoon salt*

Slash banana skins lengthwise; cut off tips at both ends and discard tips. Half fill a large pot with water, add salt and bring to the boil; drop bananas in water, cover and cook over medium heat 30 minutes until tender. Drain. Peel skins off with a fork.
SERVE with steamed fish and other dishes (recipe, page 249).
**Serves 4 to 6**

333

## ASPARAGUS OR YARDLONG BEAN

Wonderful displayed tied at one end and spraying its green points at the other, it is most abundant in oriental markets, but also popular in Italian and other ethnic markets. It does taste a bit like asparagus. The Chinese call it *Dao Kok* and horn bean but many retailers just call it the "yard" bean (really only half a yard long—I sketched them about 18 inches). You can't miss it in summer. Once tied together, retailers like to sell the whole bunch.

TO COOK: Wash beans and pinch off the ends; cut into bite-sized pieces and stir-fry in a tablespoon or two of oil. Cover and cook 10 to 15 minutes. Or cut into thirds and steam for 15 minutes and season as you would green beans. Delicious cooked with meat or poultry in the same pot. One bunch can be used in several dishes over several days.                                        **Serves 2 to 3**

## HARICOTS VERTS

At the opposite end of the size scale, a delicacy for the French and others, these tender green beans respond to stir-frying and steaming. Cooking in butter or a bit of fine olive oil may be more European, so try all the different ways. Available in specialty greengrocers.

*1 pound* Haricots Verts
*1 to 2 tablespoons butter or olive oil, more for dribbling*
*½ cup chicken stock*
*Juice of ½ lemon or cider or rice vinegar*
*3 tablespoons walnuts or hazelnuts, chopped*

Trim the *Haricots Verts* and wash; drain. Heat the butter or oil in pan and sauté the beans, stirring until coated and the color brightens. Add the chicken stock or water and simmer, uncovered, only long enough to suit your taste, 10 to 15 minutes. Dribble with olive oil and lemon juice or vinegar.

SERVE warm garnished with walnuts or hazelnuts. **Serves 4 to 6.**

## BREADFRUIT

You'll see them in tropical markets, bobbing in water, like green baseballs and basketballs but with a leathery surface and tiny dark dots. Caribbean people like breadfruit, but Haitians seem the most excited about them, especially when cooked and mashed with codfish and fried in balls. (Breadfruit are stored in water to retard ripening; at room temperature, they will turn yellow and ripen.)

TO COOK BREADFRUIT: With a knife, slash all around the circumference once. Peel. If too hard to peel, immerse in lightly salted water and parboil like a potato. Peel, then cut into segments and cook until tender. Use like a potato. Delicious with smoked fish. **A small breadfruit * serves 4 to 6**

* 1½ to 2-pound breadfruits are small; they are usually much larger.

## SWEET AND SOUR RED CABBAGE

A very popular dish among Northern Europeans—Poles, Germans, Norwegians, and other Scandinavians (to name a few).

*2 tablespoons flour*
*Pinch salt*
*1½ teaspoons caraway seeds (optional)*
*1 tablespoon butter*
*2 cups warm chicken stock or water*
*1 small head red cabbage, sliced fine*
*¼ cup cider vinegar*
*¼ cup sugar (begin with 2 tablespoons)*

In a small bowl, combine the flour, salt, and caraway if using caraway. Melt the butter in a heavy saucepan and when bubbly, mix in the flour mixture. Lower heat and cook a minute or two without browning. Remove from heat and gradually add the stock, stirring constantly; return to heat and stir until the sauce comes to the boil. Drop the cabbage into the sauce and mix well. Cover and simmer until tender. Add the vinegar and sugar, stir until dissolved and taste for seasonings.

SERVE hot or cold. **Serves 4**

NOTE: Green cabbage may be substituted.

## STIR-FRIED TSOI SUM
### Flowering White Cabbage

Sold in bunches, this delicious leafy vegetable with bright yellow flowers may be steamed or stir-fried. May Wo, a Thailand-born resident of Brooklyn, when shopping with her mother in Chinatown, described her method of serving *Tsoi Sum*.

*1 bunch* Tsoi Sum, *washed and trimmed*
*1 to 1½ tablespoons vegetable oil*
*Black bean sauce*

Cut the stems and leaves of *Tsoi Sum* into bite-sized pieces. Heat oil in wok or frying pan and stir-fry the *Tsoi Sum* until bright green.

SERVE with black bean sauce and beef or chicken. **Serves 4**

## STEAMED KAI LAN TSOI
### Chinese Kale

With succulent and crispy yellow flowers, the large-leaf *Kai Lan Tsoi* is a delicious and easy to cook vegetable, high in flavor.

TO COOK: after cutting into bite-sized lengths, steam over boiling water and steep in a mild oyster sauce. *Kai Lan Tsoi* can also be stir-fried or boiled in a soup.

## CALABAZA
### West Indian Pumpkin

Delicious and always available, to use as you like. Cooked in lightly salted water, after peeling, *Calabaza* with butter makes a rich side dish; or with brown sugar and butter and baked, Haitian style, a hearty dessert. Drop cubes into soups and stews. You'll find many more dishes it can be added to. Since they are so large, you'll often see them sold in sections in tropical markets.

## CHAYOTE SALAD

Pear-shaped and creamy green to deeper green, the *Chayote* is called *Fa Chon Kwa* or "Buddha's palm melon" by the Chinese and is indigenous to Central America. West Indian or Caribbean and Oriental markets carry two kinds: larger ones, like a medium-sized avocado; and tiny ones, lime-size, but pear-shaped. Bland in flavor, it mixes well with other vegetables and aromatic seasonings.

*1 pound* Chayotes, *washed*
*2 shallots, minced (or substitute an onion and 1 clove garlic)*
*½ stalk celery, chopped*
*Fresh tarragon or basil, chopped*
*Favorite dressing or mayonnaise*
*Lettuce leaves*

Wash and arrange *Chayotes* in bottom of a pan; cover with cold water and bring to the boil. Boil until tender, from 5 to 20 minutes, depending on the size. Drain. Chill. Quarter the small *Chayotes* or chop large ones, including the edible seeds. In bowl, mix with the shallots and celery. Season with tarragon or basil and dressing and heap onto lettuce leaves. **Serves 4 to 5**

## CASSAVA or MANIOC

You'll see them in tropical markets, with barky skins ranging from orange-brown to dark brown, the sweet potato shapes tapering into a graceful point. Also called *Yuca*, cassava is such an important staple in South America and Africa that it seems to have an emotional appeal. When made into tapioca, its starch has a worldwide appeal to cooks for its thickening powers. Although its bark color and the sizes vary, the inside is white and, like a potato, it can be peeled and cooked in water or a stew.

A native of Brazil, where it apparently was a prized starch before the Portuguese arrived in 1500, the explorers adopted it as an important crop, cultivated it, and carried it to the African coastal regions and the Congo River during the last half of the sixteenth century. Easily cultivated in the tropics, cassava spread to Indian Ocean countries and then to Madagascar, India, and Indonesia, then on to East Africa. Finally it reached New York.

There are two major varieties: sweet and bitter. The sweet cassava is cooked into soups, stews, and casseroles, and pounded into pastes. Its infinite variety of forms include Ghana's *Fufu* and Nigeria's *Gari*, which is used by many West Africans living in New York. Breads, porridges, dumplings, and fried balls are also created from this tuber. The bitter cassava is treated to remove the poisonous prussic acid. Cassava roots are boiled to extract the poison and squeezed to obtain the juice called *Cassareep*, used in West Indian pepper pot.

## CASSAVA "BREAD"

To the utter confusion of many, *Cassava Bread*, made from the cassava root, has to be classified with vegetables, just as a potato bread would be. Cassava Bread looks like a 10 by 10-inch hard, dry piece of rippled toast. It is called *Cassave* or *Mamba* by Haitians. Gerard Bonny, a Brooklynite, suggests a delicious treat he has invented since living in New York: Spread cassava bread with peanut butter. *Merci*, Gerard. Cassava Bread is available in Cuban and Caribbean food shops.

# GARI
## Ground Cassava

*Gari* can be soaked, cooked, made into balls, and used with flexibility like mashed potatoes. *Gari* is light beige and finer than a fine couscous.

TO SOAK *Gari:* Pour 1 cup *Gari* into a small bowl and cover with 2 cups cold water. Allow to absorb water for 10 minutes.
SERVE with a zesty, savory sauce. (To serve as a dessert, just add sugar.) **Serves 3 to 4**

# GARI DOUGH BALLS
## Cassava Balls

Spread ½ cup *Gari* in a flat pan. Sprinkle 1 cup boiling water on the *Gari* and knead to make a dough. Work for 5 minutes. Form into balls. Dip the balls in hot sauce like Ghanaian Hot Shrimp Sauce (page 258) or other favorite sauces.

# COLLARD GREENS, BRAZILIAN STYLE

Delicious, may also be used for a Soul Food supper. Collards are prized among U.S. Southerners and Africans as well. A Brazilian woman suggested this recipe as a side dish for *Feijoada* (page 239) or any bean dish. Try to cook the ham hocks a day in advance.

*3 ham hocks, cracked*
*4 pounds collard greens, washed and trimmed of heavy stems*
  *(or substitute kale)*
*2 slices bacon, sliced*
*Salt (optional)*
*Freshly ground pepper*

In a large pot, cover the ham hocks with cold water. Cook two hours until tender, adding only enough water to end up with 4 cups. Drain and reserve the liquid. If refrigerating overnight, next day, discard the fat on the top of the liquid. When ready to cook, shred collards or cut *very* finely. In a pan large enough to hold the collards, fry the bacon until crisp, pour into the reserved ham hock liquid and when it boils add the collards. Cook, uncovered, 20 minutes, then tuck in the cooked ham hocks and continue simmering until collards are tender and ham hocks warm, about 20 minutes. You may not need much salt, but don't forget to add pepper generously.

SERVE collards with the meat, cut into small pieces.      **Serves 6**

NOTE: Collards are also delicious cooked without meat, as you would cook escarole or kale, drained; chop finely and season as you like (fried, crisp bacon is especially tasty on top, Soul style).

## SUNCHOKE or "JERUSALEM ARTICHOKE"

Native of North America around Indiana, this root is best called Sunchoke to avoid the name confusion. Delicious raw, the root has a thin coat, thinner than a new potato, and if scrubbed well, the skin, like a new potato's, is edible. Also good steamed and served with butter, but too much cooking demolishes the sunchoke.

## JICAMA or MEXICAN POTATO

More abundant in Midwestern and Western markets, the reddish, top-shaped *Jicama* is hard to pass by, and once tasted, difficult to forget. Crisper than a potato, it can be cooked like one, and its crispness lends texture similar to a water chestnut's.

## BAUNJAUN BURAUNEE
### Afghan Eggplant with Yogurt Chaka

Excellent flavor with *Yogurt Chaka* (recipe, page 182). Make *Chaka* in advance. The following recipe may be used with long green squash, zucchini, pumpkin, and other mild vegetables. I tried this recipe with plain yogurt as well, and it was superb.

*1 pound eggplants, preferably slim purple ones*
*Salt*
*Oil for frying, preferably fine olive oil*
*2 scallions, minced*
*1 green pepper, seeded and chopped*
*½-¾ cup tomato sauce*
*¼ teaspoon chili powder or tip of a green chili, minced*
*4 tablespoons mint leaves, very finely minced*
*1 to 1½ cups Yogurt Chaka or substitute plain yogurt,*
    *drained 30 minutes in wet cheesecloth draped over bowl*

Peel the eggplants and cut off the stem ends. Slice lengthwise into ¼-inch slices. Salt very lightly and set on rack for 15 minutes to drain. Wipe off eggplant slices with kitchen towel. In fry pan, heat 3 tablespoons oil, slip in eggplant slices and sauté on both sides. Drain on paper towels and continue until all are sauteed. In oil left in pan, sauté the scallions 2 minutes without browning. Stir in the green pepper, tomato sauce, and eggplant slices. Season with chili powder or chili. Add enough water to half cover the eggplant. Simmer gently until eggplant is cooked and liquid thickened. Cool. (This much may be done a day in advance.)
TO SERVE: spread half the *Yogurt Chaka* or plain yogurt on a platter and sprinkle with half the mint leaves. Cover with the eggplant slices and spoon yogurt on top. Garnish with remaining mint. Serve at room temperature. **Serves 2 to 3**

## OKRA OR BEANS COOKED WITH KAUN

Femi, a Nigerian graduate student who lives in Brooklyn, shops at WEST AFRICAN IMPORTS CO. (page 77) for ingredients for cooking his family dishes. He recommends a fascinating ingredient available in jars—a hard ingredient called *Kaun*, that adds both flavor and tenderizing qualities to okra, beans, and other dishes. Grate a few grains into the simmering food. *Ose* (pronounced O-sheh)—thank you in the Yoruba language.

## FRIED OKRA, SOUTH CAROLINA STYLE

Remembering her grandmother's delicious okra recipe from South Carolina, a college student said she cooks it the same way, but substitutes oil for the lard. A native of Africa, okra graces the table of many ethnic groups, but the Hellenes, who adore it, are the only people I know of who soak the okra first in vinegar before cooking (to avoid the vegetable's secreting its gummy gumbo, which others seem to like). And the West African combination of chicken and okra in a peanut sauce repeats the Greek combination of chicken and okra in a tomato sauce. Orientals like okra fried, too.

*1 pound okra, trimmed and cut across into ½-inch pieces*
*Corn meal seasoned with salt and pepper, for dipping*
*Deep fat or vegetable oil for frying*

Dip the okra in corn meal until covered. Heat the fat or oil to depth of 4 inches to 360°F, drop in the okra a few pieces at a time and fry until browned lightly. Taste for doneness and continue until all are fried.

SERVE hot with chicken and fresh corn on the cob with sweet potato pie for dessert. **Serves 4**

## PAWPAW
### Papaya

Versatile yellow or green (green for cooking; yellow, raw), the pear-shaped papaya could be included in any chapter, its uses are so varied. "Squeeze the juice of green papaya and drink for high blood pressure," Caribbean people say or grate into *Pasteles* (page 291). The Philippine people cook papaya in chunks with chicken, a delicious dish; and both the flesh and skins have been used as meat tenderizers for ages. Here are more ideas for papaya:

BAKED: cut lengthwise into halves or thirds, remove the seeds. Sprinkle with lemon or lime juice, a pinch of salt and dot with butter or margarine; bake 30 minutes in moderate oven; serve hot with any foods.

DESSERT: Ripe, yellow papaya, delicious with a squeeze of lime or combined in a fruit salad; see Bolivian Fruit Salad (page 323).

BEVERAGE: see page 336.

## MOFONGO
### Plantains

Some Puerto Rican folks top off the cooked plantains with a spicy meat sauce; others cry "No, plain." Whichever way, just "mash and eat." Everyone agrees about that.

Plantains may be baked or boiled and need 30 minutes either way; baking is the preferred method. Cut off the tip of the stem end and peel the plantains.

TO BAKE: place snugly in a baking dish and bake in moderate oven (350°) until soft.

TO BOIL: cover the plantains with cold water and a pinch of salt. Boil until plantains are fork-tender; check after 20 minutes. Drain.

SERVE hot.                              **Four plantains will serve 4 to 5**

## JAMAICAN PLANTAINS

Here's yet another method.

*3 ripe plantains, sliced into rounds about ¾-inch thick*
*1 tablespoon peanut oil, more for frying*
*Juice of 1 lemon*
*Salt*
*Freshly ground pepper*
*¾ cup flour*
*½ teaspoon baking powder*
*½ cup milk*
*1 egg, lightly beaten*

Peel the plantains. In a bowl large enough to hold the plantains, whisk the oil, lemon juice, and a pinch of salt and pepper. Dip the plantains in the marinade and soak for 30 minutes. Meanwhile, mix a batter. In a large bowl, combine the flour, ¼ teaspoon salt, and baking powder. Make a well in the center and pour in the milk and egg. Mix quickly to make a medium thick batter. Dip plantains in batter. Heat oil to depth of 4 inches and when very hot (360°F), fry plantains until golden brown.
SERVE hot. **Serves 4 to 5**


## MASHED RUTABAGAS

Rutabagas can be found in Jewish, German, Scandinavian, and Chinese markets. Cook this root like potatoes, but expect a sharper flavor.

TO COOK: peel and cut into small segments and add a teaspoon of sugar to the cooking water. Drain, mash with butter and cream, a pinch of salt and pepper.
SERVE warm.

## STUFFED AND CURRIED LONG GREEN SQUASH

Many Asian-Indian men and women have told me their favorite way of cooking the phallic long green squash (sometimes called "snake" squash), which I've seen most frequently at the Asian-Indian, Chinese, and Italian markets. This recipe epitomizes the best of all. Leftover roast meats or poultry may be added to the stuffing mixture.

> 2 long green squash
> Salt
> 2 cups leftover roast, minced, or substitute cooked ground
>    lamb
> 6 onions—3 minced, 3 sliced into rings
> 5 dry chilies, ground
> 1 teaspoon black pepper
> ½ teaspoon ground cinnamon
> 1 teaspoon powdered turmeric
> Salt
> 1 tablespoon ghee or vegetable oil
> 2 tablespoons coriander, ground
> ¼ teaspoon mustard seeds
> ½ teaspoon cumin seeds
> Milk (page 184) and shredded coconut of 1 coconut
> 1 clove garlic, crushed
> Juice of 2 limes

Lightly scrape the squash and cut across to make finger length rounds. Using an apple corer, remove and discard seed. Drop squash into salted boiling water; boil 5 minutes and drain. Meanwhile, combine in a bowl the lamb, minced onions, half of the chilies, black pepper and cinnamon, half of the turmeric and a grain or two of salt. Mix thoroughly. Using a spoon, stuff the squash cavities, dividing the filling equally among the pieces. To prepare the spices, heat the *ghee* or oil and sauté the sliced onions. When onions are translucent, stir in the remaining turmeric and chilies, coriander, mustard, and cumin. Cook briefly (1 to 2 minutes) after adding each spice. Stir in the coconut milk and

garlic. Season with salt only if necessary and adjust the spices to your taste. Set the stuffed squash into the coconut milk curry. Cover pan and simmer gently until tender, about 15 minutes. Sprinkle the shredded coconut on top and stir carefully. Remove from heat. Add the lime juice.
SERVE warm.                                                        **Serves 4 to 6**

NOTE: Like many beloved foods served as "vegetables" long green squash is also found on the dessert tables (see page 320).

## SALSIFY or "OYSTER" ROOT

A long, white, tubular root, salsify is also known as "oyster" plant, goatsbeard (from the Greek *Tragopogon*—the root end does resemble a goat), and vegetable oyster, because when cooked it does taste oyster-like. But unlike the oyster, which has always been prized as an aphrodisiac by many ethnic groups, the salsify is known by few, perhaps because it has less than half the amount of phosphorus (which seems to be the mineral contained in many foods considered aphrodisiacs). Native to areas southeast of Europe and Algeria, salsify is preferred by Europeans.

TO COOK: scrape lightly, cut up, and steam or boil in lightly salted water. Season with butter.
SERVE with main dishes as you would any other vegetable.

## TARO ROOT

Taro is *Wu Tau* (black head) to the Chinese, a mysterious root-like potato with rough, hairy texture. And taro is also *Yautia* to Puerto Ricans, *Malanga* to Cubans, *Dasheen* to British West Indians, *Eddo* to some Caribbean people, *Kolokassi* to Cypriots, and *Poi* (the ingredient in *Poi*) to Hawaiians. A major food among Pacific Islanders and Far Easterners, it is grown in the south, east, and central areas of the United States. The barky skin ranges from beige to browns to violet-black and awaits you at Oriental, Hispanic, many Asian-Indian and specialty markets. Taro is usually large lemon-size, but in its brown forms (lighter colors from Plains regions) it grows longer and pointed, like a sweet potato.

## KOLOKASSI
### Meat, Celery and Malanga or Taro, Cyprus Style

Cypriots use a derivation of the botanical name—*Colocasia Esculenta*—and love the root as many Caribbean people do. This is a delicious combination; cooked in a tomato sauce, *Malanga* or *Taro* looks like potato and absorbs the red tomato color. It's tasty, sweet, soft, and starchy.

> *1 large or 2 medium* Malangas (Yautia, Taro, Eddo, Tannion)
> *Oil for frying vegetables*
> *1 pound lean pork or chicken, cut into serving pieces*
> *1 bunch celery (about 8 stalks, sliced diagonally into half-*
>     *finger lengths)*
> *2 to 3 tomatoes, peeled and chopped*
> *Salt*
> *Freshly ground pepper*

Peel the *Malanga* and cut into chunks. In a casserole that will hold all the foods, heat 3 inches of the oil and drop the *Malanga* chunks into the hot oil. Using tongs, fry quickly until reddened and remove from oil to drain. Pour off all but a light film of the oil and fry the pork or chicken pieces, turning on all sides; combine it with the *Malanga* (there should be a few tablespoons of oil remaining in the casserole). Stir the celery and tomatoes into the casserole and saute a few minutes. Then tuck the sauteed pork or chicken and *Malanga* into the celery-tomato sauce, cover, and simmer until all are tender and juices have been released. Uncover after 40 minutes to allow the sauce to thicken, season lightly with salt and pepper and test for doneness. Continue simmering, uncovered, until cooked, about 10 minutes.
SERVE warm. **Serves 6.**

NOTE: Should you be wild about scallions and onions, you can add them with the celery, but it is delectable with the celery dominating and the blend is curiously delightful.

## STEAMED TARO

As preferred by a salesman at WING FAT CO. (page 32), easy, and a good way to vary the diet.

 4 to 5 taro roots
 1 tablespoon peanut oil (optional)
 1 to 2 tablespoons black bean paste*

Wash and peel the taro corms; avoid wetting the white flesh to inhibit the slimy liquid. Cut into strips or dice. Steam until crisp but tender, about 10 minutes.
SERVE with a drizzle of peanut oil, or just the black bean paste.

**Serves 2 to 4.**


## CURRIED MIXED SALAD, ASIAN-INDIAN STYLE

A ravishing salad, delicious with grilled fish.

 1 tablespoon ghee (clarified butter)
 ½ teaspoon mustard seeds
 6 curry leaves
 4 green chilies, seeds discarded, crushed
 1 inch fresh ginger, ground
 1 tablespoon lime juice, more to taste
 2 tablespoons coriander leaves, chopped
 1 cup Chinese or other cabbage, shredded
 2 carrots, shredded
 4 green tomatoes, chopped**
 1 cucumber, seeds discarded, shredded
 Pinches of sugar and salt, to taste
 2 to 3 tablespoons fresh coconut, shredded

* Also good in soup, mixed with other stir-fried vegetables after steaming. Available in Oriental markets, especially Chinese.
** Substitute a cup of any green vegetable (or leftover). Also a cup or two of cooked lentils add a delicious touch to this curry.

In a saucepan, heat the *ghee* and fry the mustard seeds, curry leaves, and chilies, stirring constantly for 3 minutes. Add the ginger, lime juice, and coriander to make a paste, cooking and stirring over low heat for 5 minutes. Combine the cabbage, carrots, green tomatoes, and cucumber in a bowl. Pour the fried spices over the vegetables and stir to mix thoroughly. Taste and season with salt and sugar, if you like. Chill.

JUST BEFORE SERVING, shower vegetables with the coconut.

**Serves 4**

## FOGLIA MISTA DI NATALE
### Mixed Greens for Christmas

Maria Balducci, wife of Louis Balducci, founder of BALDUCCI'S (page 45), is matriarch, "Mama," to her enterprising four-generation family. Still active in her eighties, she continues to invent new dishes in the store's kitchen. *Foglia Mista di Natale*, which she graciously shares, is "Mama" Balducci's holiday favorite, a traditional dish from her native Corato, in the Bari region of Italy. *Nine* green vegetables, cooked separately, are layered with slivered beef and grated cheese in a "very rich stock." The result? An irresistibly hearty *Manestra*—a celebration of vegetable flavors—with crusty bread and crisp salad, as she suggests, a lovely menu. "Make the stock in advance, using turkey carcasses, if you have them," "Mama" Balducci suggests. *Grazie!*

*10 cups turkey or chicken stock*
*1¼ to 1½ pounds stewing beef*
*2 large onions, sliced*
*2 stalks celery, sliced*
*3 to 4 ripe tomatoes or substitute 4 to 5 Italian plum canned tomatoes, chopped*
*1 carrot, sliced*
*Herbs: 1 bay leaf, 2 sprigs parsley, 1 to 2 sprigs fresh thyme (tied in cheesecloth or with string)*
*Salt*
*Mixed Greens (recipe on next page)*
*1 cup Romano Locatelli, grated*
*Freshly ground pepper*

In a soup pot bring the stock to the boil, add the beef, onions, celery, tomatoes, carrot, and herbs. Lower heat, season with salt, and simmer until beef is tender, about 1½ hours. Using slotted spoon, remove the beef. Cool slightly; tear into shreds and stir beef shreds into the stock. Discard herbs. To assemble: Ladle broth (with some beef and stock vegetables) into a large, heatproof tureen or casserole. Spread a layer of the Mixed Greens (recipe below). Sprinkle with some of the grated cheese and several grindings pepper. Continue layering and ladling broth and beef until all have been assembled. Top with cheese and more pepper. Heat *Foglia Mista di Natale* to the boiling point.
SERVE immediately.                                    **Serves 8 to 10**

## MIXED GREENS FOR FOGLIA MISTA DI NATALE

*1 bunch fennel*
*1 bunch celery*
*1 bunch cardoons*
*1 bunch escarole*
*1 small head cauliflower*
*1 bunch chicory (curly-leafed endive)*
*1 small Savoy cabbage*
*2 to 3 white turnips*
*3 to 4 parsnips*
*Salt*

Work with each vegetable separately to wash, scraping stalks and roots, discarding tough leaves and heavy cores. Slice each into bite-sized pieces (break cauliflower into "flowers"). Cook each separately in slightly salted water, cooking until tender with vegetables still holding their shape and not mushy. Drain (liquid may be saved*). Combine all vegetables in a large bowl and layer as instructed above.

* Combined with tomato juice, seasoned with lemon juice, crushed dried or fresh thyme or oregano, the vegetable liquid is appetizing and delicious chilled (add your favorite herbs). Store in refrigerator and serve within several days.

# GRAINS (including Pasta)
# LEGUMES (Pulses)

*Eat pulse and keep your health.*
HINDUSTANI PROVERB

## CHINESE MAY 5 FESTIVAL RICE CAKE

In Chinatown, when I asked about the May 5 Festival Rice Cake, Chinese shop owners urged me to visit "Nai Nai" at 8 Pell Street. "Nai Nai" I found, is Margaret Tong, owner with her husband Tong Kui Choy, of the JUNG KU BOOK & STATIONERY CO. Margaret Tong told me the legend of Chung, for whom the rich rice bamboo-wrapped cake is named. It seems, the legend says, that a king had a servant, well liked and respected by everyone. When Chung died, his body was thrown into the lake (no one knows why) and the people were upset that he might be eaten by fish. So the Chinese people threw in rice cakes to feed the fish so they would not be hungry enough to eat Chung's remains. Every year, to honor his memory, Chinese eat the rice cakes. (We were told the same legend in 1982 in June when visiting Peking, China, where the rice cake is still eaten on May 5.) Margaret Tong also shared the recipe.* *Sie Sie! Do Je!*

You will need ½ cup filling for each cake, so plan for the number of cakes you wish to make.

> *Bamboo leaves (dried), soaked 2 to 3 days in water to hydrate*
>   *and soften*
> *Glutinous rice (marked "sweet rice")*
> *Pork sausage, cooked and sliced thinly or chopped*
> *Dry shrimp, swollen in water, cooked and drained*
> *Dry mushrooms, soaked*
> *Salt*
> *String to tie the cakes*

When bamboo leaves are softened, in a bowl, mix 2 parts rice for each part sausage, shrimp, and mushrooms and knead. Season. To stuff: lay the bamboo leaves flat, using two for each cake. At one end, place a good half cup of the filling. Fold up the bamboo leaves to enfold, at the end. Working away from yourself with enfolded end near you, continue folding cake into the bamboo leaf, slowly working it into a pyramid; work as tightly as possible moving from left to right until a small portion of bamboo is left. Wrap it

---

* Should you prefer to buy rice cakes ready-made, they are stocked in Chinese stores in the freezer.

tightly and tie around the middle of the cake with string. Size does not matter as much as tightness (commercial rice cakes are 3 inches at the pyramid base and 4 inches high). Freeze.

TO COOK: immerse in water and cook over low heat at least 3 hours to be sure heat has penetrated. Unwrap and serve warm.

## INDONESIAN RAMES
### Small Rice Table

Rice is the central food of Indonesians, a part of each meal. Around the rice are many dishes, varied in flavor and method of preparation, but the staple is *rice*, which belongs on the world's most significant grain menus. Hari Martini Soedarmasto, a young Java-born woman who is an excellent cook and runs the canteen at the Indonesian Consulate (5 East 68 Street), shared her expertise and helped plan a menu with five dishes.\* For a more elaborate dinner, twelve to twenty dishes could surround the rice. Appetizers are not served and soup is not important in the meal. *Trimakasi!*

TO BE served with cooked white long-grain rice, *Sate Ayem, Sate Kambing,* and *Gado Gado* (recipes follow), *Peanut Sauce* (page 186) and *Sambal* (page 187)

---

\* Hari uses *Aji-No-Moto* (MSG type seasoning) in most of her mixtures; the same seasoning is used by many Philippine and Thai cooks.

## GADO GADO
### Cooked Vegetables, Indonesia Style

A famous dish—a must for the *Rames* and delightful with Peanut Sauce (page 186).

*2 cups Chinese cabbage, shredded*
*½ pound bean sprouts, washed*
*1 bunch watercress, stems removed (optional)*
*½ bunch asparagus beans or ½ pound green beans, sliced into*
*  1-inch pieces*

Steam the cabbage, sprouts, cress, and asparagus beans until crisp but not soft.

SERVE hot or cold with Peanut Sauce and *Rames* dishes.

**Serves 4 as a side dish**


## SATE AYEM
### Yellow Barbecued Marinated Chicken

*Sate* is barbecued over charcoal after marinating. The chicken is light-yellow from the turmeric.

> *2 to 3 tablespoons vegetable oil*
> *½ small onion*
> *1 teaspoon ground coriander*
> *1 slice lime*
> *½ teaspoon ground turmeric*
> *½ teaspoon sugar*
> *Pinch of salt*
> *2 cups chicken breast, cut into chunks*

Grind the oil, onion, coriander, lime, turmeric, sugar, and salt together. Put the chicken in a bowl and rub the marinade into the chicken with your fingertips. Marinate ½ to 1 hour. Thread chicken on skewers. Barbecue over charcoal.

SERVE with *Rames* rice table and other accompaniments.

NOTE: The Dutch *Rijstafel*, an adaptation of the Indonesian Rice Table, is believed to have evolved from the ancient and still-practiced *Slamatan*, a rice blessing ceremony marking births, circumcision, new home building, weddings, and other significant cultural occasions. Following its blessing, the family shares *Slamatan*, the yellow rice, cooked with coconut milk and colored with ground turmeric. *Trimakasi* also to Mr. Soedarmasto, Hari's husband, of the Indonesian Consulate, who explained many Indonesian customs. **Serves 4 as a side dish**

## SATE KAMBING
### Barbecued Marinated Lamb

Lamb is popular among the Indonesians (it's considered an aphro-disiac), and like beef and pork is marinated with soy sauce which makes it dark in color. (Pork is avoided by Muslim Indonesians.) If you prefer the lamb, you won't need the *Sate Ayem* (page 231) for the menu.

> 2 to 3 tablespoons vegetable oil
> 1 onion
> 2 cloves garlic
> Juice of ½ to 1 lime
> 1 teaspoon ground coriander
> 2 to 4 tablespoons sweet soy sauce (Thai soy sauce is
>     substituted for the more expensive, but more flavorful
>     Indonesian)
> ½ to 1 teaspoon sugar
> Pinch salt
> 1½ pounds lean lamb, cut into chunks

In a blender or mortar, grind the oil, onion, garlic, lime juice, coriander, soy sauce, sugar, and salt. Rub into the lamb in a bowl and knead well with your finger tips. Marinate 1 to 2 hours. Skewer the chunks and barbecue over charcoal.

SERVE hot with rice, *Sambal* and Peanut Sauce (page 186) and other dishes. **Serves 5 to 6**

## RENDANG
### Indonesian Curried Beef

For the more festive *Rames*, this curried *Rendang* provides more variety, or could be the meat dish with rice and accompaniments for a simpler meal.

*1 large onion, chopped*
*2 cloves garlic, chopped*
*2 to 3 tablespoons vegetable oil, warm*
*¼ teaspoon ground cinnamon*
*2 teaspoons brown sugar*
*¼ teaspoon ground cloves*
*3 pieces lemon grass*
*2 teaspoons ground coriander*
*½ teaspoon ground cumin (optional)*
*Juice of 1 lime*
*1 to 2 tablespoons Thai sweet soy sauce*
*1½ cups coconut milk (recipe, page 184)*
*1½ pounds beef, preferably from the round, cut into ¾-inch*
  *cubes*

Sauté the onion and garlic in warm oil over medium heat without browning. Stir in the cinnamon, sugar, cloves, lemon grass, coriander, cumin (if using), lime juice, and soy sauce. Cook 5 minutes, stirring constantly to make a paste. Stir in the coconut milk and continue cooking until the sauce boils. Slip the beef cubes into the sauce, cover, and cook over low heat until tender, about 40 minutes.

SERVE warm with rice and other accompaniments.     **Serves 6**

## TAGLIATELLE AL PESTO
### Noodles with Pesto Sauce

Either green (spinach) or white *Tagliatelle* are delicious smothered in Pesto Sauce (when not smothered in Bolognese, Vongoli, or other). Recommended by Anna Macari, born in Conversano, Bari on the Adriatic, who has worked several years at PIEDMONTE HOMEMADE RAVIOLI CO., INC. (page 27). The amount of noodles depends on appetites and number of courses, but she warns: "We cooked four pounds of *Tagliatelle* last week for fifteen people and it was too much!"

*5 large cloves garlic*
*Pinch of salt*
*½ pound fresh basil leaves, washed and dried, chopped*
*¼ pound Parmesan cheese, grated*
*Small handful pine nuts ("just a taste")*
*6 to 7 tablespoons olive oil*
*1 to 1¼ pounds* Tagliatelle, preferably green

To make the Pesto Sauce: Pound the garlic with the salt in a mortar. Gradually add the basil leaves, cheese, and pine nuts. Pounding steadily (this can be done in a blender or processor), drop by drop add the oil, only enough to make a smooth sauce like churned butter. (This may be made in advance and frozen.)

When ready to cook, have the Pesto Sauce at room temperature and your serving platter warm. Cook the *Tagliatelle* according to the time needed for *al dente*. Drain, but reserve some of the liquid. Thoroughly mix the Pesto Sauce into the *Tagliatelle* with about ½ cup of the cooking liquid to make a nice consistency. SERVE immediately. **Serves 4 to 6**

## FETTUCINE A LA CARBONARA

Mario Borgatti of BORGATTI'S, (see page 119), delights in many Italian recipes learned from his parents, but this is his own eye-twinkling, mouth-watering favorite.

8 slices bacon
2 to 3 slices prosciutto, thickly sliced (6 ounces)
6 tablespoons unsalted butter
2 tablespoons onion, finely chopped
⅓ cup dry white wine
½ cup heavy cream
½ cup milk
1 pound fettuccine (⅛ inch wide)
Salt (¾ teaspoon per quart of water)
1 tablespoon finely chopped parsley
½ cup grated Parmesan cheese
1 egg yolk
Freshly ground pepper

Cook bacon in boiling water 5 minutes; drain thoroughly on paper towels. Slice bacon and prosciutto into half-inch squares. Heat butter in pan and sauté onion until translucent without browning. Stir in bacon and prosciutto and cook over low heat 4 minutes, stirring frequently. Pour in the wine, bring to the boil and simmer, stirring constantly, 5 minutes. Add cream and milk and continue cooking 5 minutes. Lower heat to minimum. Cook the fettuccine in a large pot filled with a large quantity of salted, boiling water. Drain fettuccine, shake out excess liquid and return to the pot. To the sauce in the other pan, add the parsley and half the cheese; stir and pour over the fettuccine. Drop in the yolk and toss until thoroughly mixed. Divide into warm serving dishes (or serving platter), grate pepper over the top, and pass the remaining cheese at the table.

SERVE warm.                                          **Serves 4 to 5**

## SHINNECOCK INDIAN FRIED BREAD

Round, golden and pliable, this bread is also used to make *Tacos* (recipe, page 355)—as made by the New York Indian Shinnecock tribe for generations. The recipe is shared by Sandra Lacy, a member of the tribe and an administrative assistant at the Indian Community House (842 Broadway, Manhattan).

*6 cups flour, more for kneading*
*Baking powder*
*Salt*
*Dash of sugar*
*About 3 cups lukewarm water*
*Lard*
*Confectioner's sugar for sprinkling*
*Grape jelly or raspberry preserves*

Measure the flour into a bowl. "Sprinkle the top with baking powder" (about a scant tablespoon), a little salt, and sugar. Add the water and work into a sticky dough. Work in more flour and turn onto a floured board and knead. Break off lemon-sized dough pieces and roll into balls. To make the breads, flatten out to make a round bread with diameter about 6 to 7 inches and about ⅛-inch thick. When all have been made, heat a griddle or large frying pan and grease with lard. When *hot*, drop in one bread and fry until golden brown, turn over, and fry on the other side, adjusting heat to avoid burning. Rub lard over the griddle as you progress, until all the breads are fried.

TRADITIONALLY, the bread is dusted with confectioner's sugar and spread with jelly when eating Succotash (see page 286), or eat plain.                                                                      **Serves 12**


## STUFFED CRACKED WHEAT, LENTILS, AND FRUITS

Combining dried fruits with cooked foods is popular among Iranians, Armenians, and many Middle Easterners, and raisins in the filling is not unusual among Northern Hellenes. But the combination of cracked wheat and lentils with the fruits is fantastic. Serve as a main dish or accompaniment to fish or poultry.

*1 cup lentils*
*½ cup cracked wheat or burghul or* Pligouri *

*2 tablespoons vegetable or olive oil*
*1 small onion, minced*
*1 cup raisins or currants*
*½ pound dried apricots (the harder variety), half chopped, half unchopped*
*2 tablespoons fresh mint, minced or 1 tablespoon dried mint, crushed*
*1 teaspoon ground coriander*
*Salt*
*Freshly ground pepper*
*1 jar grapevine leaves or 1 pound loose grapevine leaves, rinsed and drained (cooked 5 minutes and drained, if tough)*

Cover the lentils with water and cook 30 minutes. Drain and reserve liquid for a soup. Meanwhile, in a small bowl, pour boiling water over the cracked wheat to cover; soak 15 minutes. Heat the oil and sauté the onion, add the lentils, swollen cracked wheat, raisins, chopped apricots, mint, coriander, a little salt and pepper, and only enough water to make a runny, not soupy, mixture.

TO STUFF: spread the grapevine leaves shiny side down. Place a tablespoonful of the filling in the center near the stem end; enfold with sides toward the filling, then roll back tightly. Lay seam side down in a casserole (preferably spread at the bottom with a few coarse and torn grapevine leaves). Continue until all are rolled. Tuck remaining apricots around the sides. Invert a plate right over the rolls; add just enough water to reach but not cover the plate. Cover casserole and simmer over low heat 50 minutes. Unroll one roll and taste for doneness; continue simmering 10 minutes longer, if necessary.

SERVE cold.                                                **Serves 4 to 6**

* Available in Greek, Middle Eastern, and Arabic shops.

## POIS ET RIZ OR POIS AC DIRI
### Haitian Beans and Rice

The national Haitian dish—a spicier variation of beans and rice prized throughout the Caribbean, and Central and South America. This recipe is from Gerard and Simone Bonny, a Haitian couple who have lived in Brooklyn since the late 1960s who shared many, many Haitian food habits with me. *Merci bien!*

*½ pound kidney beans (or substitute pigeon, navy, or other beans)* \*
Bouquet garni: *Sprig parsley, fresh thyme, 1 bay leaf, onion studded with 2 cloves, 4 to 5 peppercorns*
*Pinch salt*
*3 cloves garlic*
*3 sprigs fresh thyme, chopped*
*1 tablespoon chives or scallions, minced, more for garnish*
*Vegetable oil or lard for frying*
*¼ pound salt pork, sausages, or smoked ham, diced*
*1¼ to 1½ cups white, long-grain rice.*

Soak beans in cold water overnight if very dry.\* Next day, bring to the boil, skim off and discard foam, add the bouquet garni, cover, and simmer until almost cooked but still firm. Drain and reserve liquid. Meanwhile, in a mortar or blender, grind together the salt with 2 cloves garlic, thyme, and chives or scallion. Heat 1 table-spoon oil and fry the blended paste about 3 minutes; add to the beans. In the same pan, fry the diced meat with remaining garlic, crushed. Add to the beans with rice and 3 cups of the reserved bean liquid. Simmer 20 minutes or until rice and beans are tender, adding more bean liquid or water, if necessary (the dish should be thick, not soupy).
GARNISH with chives or scallions. **Serves 4**

---

\* Beans, lentils, and peas are available for quicker cooking. Ask when you buy them or look at the package; navy beans need soaking.

## ARROZ CON GANDULES VERDES
### Rice and Fresh Pigeon Peas

Migdalia Reyes, born in Bayamon, Puerto Rico, is an expert cake garnisher at the VALENCIA BAKERY'S Harlem shop (page 110). For a main dish, she ranks this version of the national dish her favorite. *Gracias!*

> ¾ to 1 pound fresh * Gandules *(pigeon peas)*
> Salt
> Recau *leaf (fresh herb used in* Sofrito*)*
> Handful Ajicitos *(tiny bell peppers used in* Sofrito*)*
> 3 to 4 tablespoons Sofrito *(pages 180, 181)*
> ½ cup white, long-grain rice

Wash the *Gandules*. In a soup pot, lightly salt 4 cups of water (1 teaspoon per quart is a lot of salt if you're cutting down), add the gandules and a *Recau* leaf and the *Ajicitos*, chopped. Cook, covered, until *Gandules* are half cooked, about 15 minutes. Stir in the *Sofrito*. Measure liquid remaining in the *Gandules* and add enough water to make 1½ cups. Bring to the boil, stir in the rice, and simmer 15 minutes until rice is tender but not mushy. Taste and add more *Sofrito* and seasonings, if you like.
SERVE warm with a fresh salad such as tomato or cabbage.

**Serves 4**

* Gandules are also available dried. Soak 1 cup and then use this recipe.

## NEW YORK FEIJOADA
### Black Beans with Meats

I used Brazilian black beans, Portuguese, Italian, and Spanish sausages and my Greek-American taste and shared the results with my Polish-Ukrainian-American and Norwegian-American neighbors. These are very ethnic—not exactly the real Brazilian *Feijoada*—but close and good.

*1 pound black beans*
*1½ pounds smoked pork neck ***
*6 links* Chorizos *(Spanish sausages)*
*6 links or ½ pound hot Italian sausages*
*½ pound Portuguese sausages*
*4 scallions, sliced or chopped*
*1 large onion, chopped*
*3 stalks celery, chopped*
*4 to 5 cloves garlic, cut in half*
*2 bay leaves*
*5 plum tomatoes and juice (canned Italian) to equal 1½ cups*
*6 fresh chilies, crushed, or blended with ¼ cup water*
*Salt (optional)*
*Freshly ground black pepper*
*Ground red pepper (optional)*

Wash beans and soak overnight. After beans have soaked add the smoked pork neck and simmer, covered, one hour. Meanwhile, fry the sausages lightly until fat is released (cut into large chunks if not links), add to the beans, and simmer 30 minutes. In the remaining fat, sauté the scallions, onion, celery, and garlic and stir in the bay leaves, tomatoes, and chilies. Simmer 15 minutes and add to the soup. Continue cooking everything together 30 minutes. Taste for seasoning with salt, if needed, and much black pepper. If possible, cool the food, refrigerate overnight, and taste the next day for seasonings. Slice meats and sausages and return to the beans.

SERVE hot with rice, sliced oranges, collard greens, Brazilian or Soul style (page 215), and pass the hot pepper.

**Serves 10 (or freeze in smaller portions)**

---

* Smoked neck bones were recommended to cook with beans by Nick Parrotta of CALABRIA PORK STORE (page 117) and he was absolutely right; but any smoked pork, tongue, bacon, or spare ribs will do as well.

## MOUCHENTRA
### Cypriot Lentils and Rice with Crispy Onions

A mainstay in the Cyprus winter menu, and nutritious by combining grain and legume to improve the quality of vegetable proteins. Leftover *Mouchentra*, combined with chicken broth, becomes a lovely soup.

> 1 cup lentils
> 1/3 cup white long-grain or converted rice
> Salt
> Olive oil or vegetable oil
> 2 large onions, sliced into thin rings

Wash lentils and cover with water in a soup pot; bring to the boil and turn off heat; cover and let rest 40 to 50 minutes (to cut down cooking time). Cook until tender, about 50 minutes. Stir in the rice and a cup water if needed for the rice to cook. Simmer until rice is done but not mushy and season lightly with salt. Meanwhile, heat a thin layer of oil in a frying pan and saute the onions until crisp. Remove onions and drain, saving the oil. Pour 3 tablespoons of the oil over the *Mouchentra* and stir; taste and add more salt and oil, if you like.

TOP with the fried onions and serve warm with a green salad and olives. **Serves 4 to 6**

## BLACK GRAM CURRY
### Asian-Indian Chick Peas

Rubina Alam of SPICE AND SWEET MAHAL (page 58) describes a quick curry for working folks, using a packaged *Masala*. Black gram, which is darker and more irregular than the more common type, is very hard and must be soaked (preferably bring water to boil before soaking) overnight. They taste good with much hot curry. This makes a great dip or garnish for blander dishes.

*1 pound black gram or Asian-Indian chick peas*
*2 tablespoons Chat Masala (contains mango, black salt,*
*    cumin, black pepper, chili, pomegranate seed, coriander,*
*    mint leaves, ginger, cloves, asafoetida, salt)*
*1 tomato, peeled and chopped*
*1 onion, minced*
*3 to 7 hot green chilies\* or 3 to 4 teaspoons hot pepper*
*Small bunch fresh coriander, chopped*

Pick over black gram and remove any stones, wash and place in a
pot. Cover with cold water (Asian-Indians add a pinch of baking
soda, but I don't). Bring to the boil. Turn off heat, cover, and soak
overnight. Next day, drain and cover with water two inches above
black gram. Simmer until tender, 1½ to 2 hours. Drain and reserve the liquid. Black gram may be mashed or left whole. It is
especially good mashed in the blender, adding enough of the
cooking liquid to make a fairly thick paste. Add the remaining
ingredients, stir, taste for flavors, adding more chilies or hot pepper.
SERVE at room temperature.                              **Serves 6 to 8**

\* 6 or 7 chilies were recommended, but 3 are quite hot (add gradually to your
taste).

## AKARA
### Nigerian Pea Fritters

Esther Adeleye, a Yoruba tribe Nigerian student whom I taught at
Lehman College gave me this recipe, a favorite, and since I've lost
touch with her, I share it in her name. *Ose*, Esther! (Isn't it fascinating to observe the fondness for the African black-eyed peas
in African and Soul foods?)

*½ pound black-eyed peas*
*3 to 4 fresh chilies or ½ teaspoon red hot pepper*
*1 onion, slivered or 3 to 4 scallions (white parts), chopped*
*Salt*
*Freshly ground pepper*
*Vegetable oil for frying*
*Palm oil for frying (optional)*

Cover peas with cold water and soak overnight or, for quicker method, bring to the boil, turn heat off, cover, and soak an hour or two. Rub peas to loosen skins and keep discarding skins and the black eye until clean. Using mortar and pestle (the really old-fashioned way), blender, or processor, grind the peas with just enough water to make a paste, adding the chilies or pepper and onion. Season lightly with salt and pepper, beating until smooth. Heat oil to a level of five inches, adding some palm oil for flavor, if you have some. When oil is hot enough to fry potatoes (375°) drop tablespoonsful of the pea paste into the oil, turning until browned. Keep warm and continue until all are fried.

SERVE with hot pepper sauce and corn meal cereal, cassava porridge, or yam balls. **Serves 3 to 4**


## GARBANZOS SALTEADOS
### Spanish Chick Peas

Salvador Betancourt, United States-born, who traces his Spanish ancestry to the Canary Islands, works in the Embassy of Spain Commercial Office in Manhattan and enjoys many Spanish dishes, this version of *Garbanzos,* and shops for ingredients at CASA MONEO (page 49).

*3 tablespoons Spanish olive oil*
*1 medium onion, minced*
*1 to 2 cloves garlic, minced*
*1 pound can Garbanzos (chick peas), drained*
*1 tomato, peeled and chopped*
*¼ cup ham or Chorizo (Spanish sausage), chopped*
*Salt*
*2 tablespoons fresh parsley, minced*

Heat the oil in a pan and gently saute the onion and garlic until soft. Stir in the *Garbanzos,* tomato, and ham or Chorizo; cover pan and simmer 10 minutes. Season with salt to your taste and sprinkle the parsley into the *Garbanzos Salteados.*

SERVE warm or cold. **Serves 3 to 4**

# SEAFOOD
# & FRESH WATER FISH

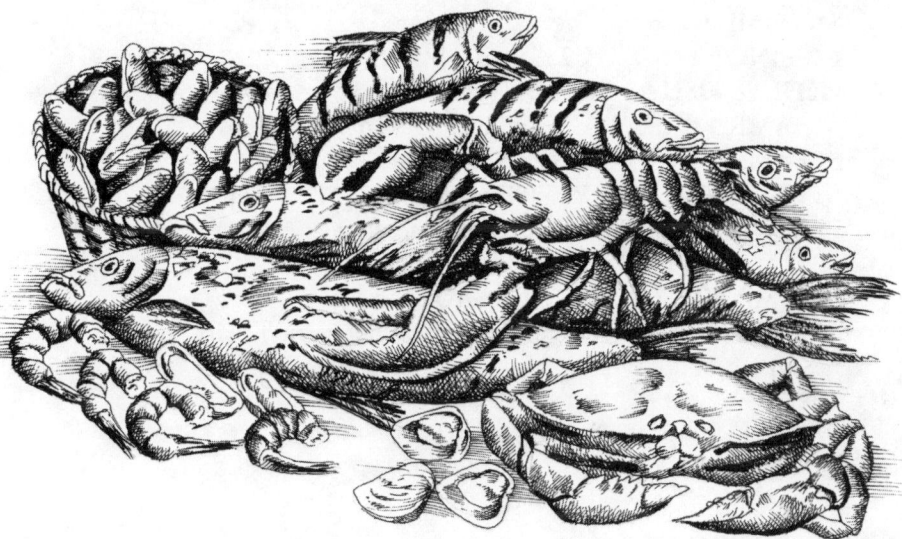

*The bigger the fish, the more butter he takes.*
JAMAICAN PROVERB

## STEAMED BAK SU KONG
### Moon Fish

Shining with smooth, silvery skin—flat and graceful with a pointed, almost smiling mouth—this fish is hard to resist in Chinatown fish stalls. Related to the butterfish, the Chinese call it Moon fish. It's not too meaty, is very tasty, and can be cooked quickly.

*2 to 4 Moon fish, cleaned*
*Sauce*

Wash and dry the fish and put on a steamer (this may be done over soup or vegetables cooking in the pot below). Steam 8 to 10 minutes until tender.
SERVE with your favorite sauce, rice, soup, or vegetables.

**Serves 2**

## SOUTH INDIAN FISH CURRY

Gray mullet was chosen for this recipe by a South Indian woman shopping in an Arthur Avenue fish market. With gentle motions and colorful language, she explained her favorite method of serving her curry.

*2 gray mullets, washed*
*3 tablespoons coconut oil*
*2 cloves garlic, crushed*
*1 large onion, chopped*
*½ teaspoon turmeric*
*1 to 2 chili peppers, seeds removed, sliced*
*½-inch piece fresh ginger, chopped*

Slice the mullet across into one-inch steaks. In a wide-bottomed pan, heat the oil and stir in the garlic, onion, turmeric, chili, and ginger. Cook slowly, stirring constantly, 5 minutes. Slip mullet slices into the curry paste and turn over to cover with the paste on the other side. Cover pan; steam very slowly over low heat for 20 to 25 minutes until fish flakes when pierced with a fork.
SERVE warm with rice, chutney, and nuts.

**Serves 4**

## RED SNAPPER, TANDOORI STYLE

Mike Malhotra, former operator of a Little India shop, predicts that after trying the tandoori mix "you'll go back for more." Containing ten spices, the mix simplifies a savory, aromatic recipe.

> *2 red snappers, cleaned with heads on (or substitute other fish)*
> *3 teaspoons tandoori mix* \**
> *1 cup plain yogurt*

Using tip of sharp knife, slash the snappers diagonally on both sides. Rub tandoori mix into all the slashes. Stir one teaspoon tandoori mix into the yogurt and spread on the fish. Marinate at room temperature 30 minutes. Slip long skewers through the fish lengthwise. Broil over charcoal, preferably, or 5 inches below broiler for 5 to 6 minutes on each side.

SERVE warm with rice, mango chutney, and vegetable curries.

**Serves 4**

---

\* If you find the ready-made mix too heavy with cinnamon, as I do, dust the 3 teaspoons lightly with ground cumin and red pepper with a dash of lemon or lime juice. Should you have time to mix your own curry, see Tandoori Spices, following.

## TANDOORI SPICES and CURRY

Tandoori fish, poultry, or other food is baked in a Tandoor clay oven fired by charcoal or wood or, without a Tandoor, over charcoal or wood fire. Yogurt and lime juice are preferred marinades (often with salt) rubbed into slashes or pricks around the flesh. Should you prefer to mix your own curry, grind together 2 green chilies (seeds removed), ¾ teaspoon ground cumin, 1-inch piece fresh ginger, ½ teaspoon ground turmeric, juice of 1 lemon, pinches of ground cinnamon, nutmeg, or mace, and black pepper. Mix spices with the yogurt or rub separately into the slashes or pricks.

## KOREAN STYLE BROILED RED SNAPPER

Try this favorite recipe of Ik Sang Kim, owner of PUSAN FISH MARKET (page 72).

*2 red snappers, skinned, left whole with head on*
*Salt*
*Freshly ground pepper*

Broil snappers over charcoal or under flame; carefully turn to broil on the other side as well. Season with salt and pepper.
SERVE with steaming rice, seaweed, and your favorite *Kimchi*.

**Serves 4**


## STEAMED FISH AND GREEN BANANAS

Nigerians and Jamaicans enjoy this delectable combination; or like the Haitians, use the hot sauce (page 186).

*2 pounds codfish, snappers, or porgies, cleaned with head on*
*Juice of lemon or lime*
*Vegetable oil for frying*
*1 medium onion, chopped*
*1 teaspoon West African red pepper*
*2 sprigs fresh thyme, chopped*
*Salt, if necessary*
*Green bananas (recipe, page 209)*

Wash and dry the fish, place in a bowl and sprinkle with lemon or lime juice; marinate 10 minutes. Dry fish with paper towels. Heat oil in large frying pan to level of ½ inch. When hot, slip fish into oil. Season with onion, pepper, thyme, and salt, if needed. Cover pan, lower heat to minimum. Cook 20 minutes, turning fish once, until tender.
SERVE hot with green bananas with or without the sauce.

**Serves 4 to 5**

## ZUPPA DI PESCE
### Sicilian Fish Stew

Giuseppe Vitale cooked this fabulous dish on a small burner in a simple pot in the back of his Ninth Avenue fruit market (see page 76) and you can do the same, with fresh ingredients, in less than 40 minutes. *Grazie!*

> ¼ cup olive oil, more to taste
> 3 onions, sliced
> 5 to 6 fresh tomatoes, sliced in eighths, or substitute canned
>     Italian plum tomatoes
> Salt
> Freshly ground pepper
> 3 large sprigs of fresh basil
> 3 pounds salmon, fileted with skin on
> Dry white wine
> 2 sprigs fresh parsley, chopped

Heat the oil in a soup pot and stir in the sliced onions and tomatoes; cook over medium heat until tomatoes collapse and onions are almost cooked, about 15 minutes, stirring constantly. Season lightly with salt and pepper. Drop in the basil and cook another few minutes, then add the salmon and enough wine or water to cover the fish. Lower heat and simmer until salmon is flaky, about 15 minutes.

SERVE warm strewn with parsley.                    **Serves 4 to 5**


## ESCABECHE DE BECADA
### Puerto Rican Pickled Fish

*Escaveche, Escovitch, Escovits,* no matter how you spell it, this is a favorite in the Caribbean. I tried it with bluefish. Made a day in advance, it is certainly tastier and delicious served cold. Great for a picnic or lunch.

*1½ pounds fish steaks or small whole fish (bluefish, etc.),
    washed and dried
Juice of 1 lemon or lime
½ cup olive or vegetable oil
½ cup red wine vinegar
2 bay leaves
5 to 6 peppercorns
3 cloves garlic, cut in half
2 to 3 fresh chilies, crushed, seeds discarded, or 1 teaspoon
    red pepper
Flour to roll fish
2 large onions, sliced into thin rings
½ cup green olives, pitted (optional)
2 pimentos, sliced (optional)*

In a flat dish, drizzle the fish with lemon or lime juice; let stand while preparing the marinade. In a small pan, whisk ¼ cup of the oil, the vinegar, bay leaves, peppercorns, 2 cloves garlic, and chilies or red pepper. Cook 15 minutes and keep warm. Meanwhile, roll fish in flour. Heat remaining ¼ cup oil in a large frying pan and saute the remaining garlic clove; brown and discard garlic. Slip fish into the hot oil, lower heat and fry on both sides until thoroughly cooked, about 15 minutes, tucking onions around the sides during last 5 minutes (if not overcooked the onions will retain a delightful crispness), turning constantly. If using olives and pimentos add them when fish is tender. Carefully arrange the fish on a deep platter with onions, olives, and pimentos. Pour the hot marinade over the fish. Cool. Cover tightly and refrigerate at least 24 hours.
SERVE cold. **Serves 4**

NOTE: In Haiti, *Escaveche* is made with fish or meat; carrots and celery, chopped, may be added to the marinade. And in Puerto Rico, green bananas are pickled the same way.

## SASHIMI

Beauty, flavor, simplicity, and freshness are all qualities of a superb *Sashimi*. The first time I tasted it with Akie Terai when she lived in New York will never be forgotten (in Japan when we met again, the box lunch we enjoyed together was another edible art form with dazzling surprises). The *Sashimi* can be served following warm *Sake*. The exquisitely cut fresh raw fish and shellfish on a 14 to 16-inch black lacquer tray, either flat or footed, creates a glorious contrast of white, green, reddish, orange colors. Once sampled as created by an expert, *Sashimi* is not difficult to present, and New York provides a remarkable array of fish departments from which you can select fresh seafood. Japanese and Korean food shops carry the other ingredients needed. *Domo Arigato!*

> *Raw, fresh fish (preferably 4 to 5 types): salmon, haddock, cod, tuna, sea bass, sea bream, octopus, kingfish, shrimps, tile, flounder, calamari, preferably sliced for you by the fish expert*
> *2 cakes tofu, sliced into bite-sized pieces*
> *Fresh ginger, ground*
> **Wasabi** *horseradish, shaped into walnut-sized balls*
> *Nori seaweed (edible seaweed also called* **Nori Suski** *or dried laver)*
> *Cooked rice*
> *Dipping Sauce (see recipe below)*
> *Garnishes: seaweed cut into points along one side, or other bright green garnish.*

Wash and cut the chosen fish into flat slices that can be rolled into ½-inch by 3-inch segments; small (3-inch) calamari are sliced in half lengthwise without cutting the pointed end, then opened lengthwise for serving; larger ones are sliced into 3- by ½-inch slices. Arrange seafood in rows across the serving tray, angled diagonally with each variety forming a row. Angle the tofu squares the same way with each 2 squares forming a diagonal. Fish and tofu should be parallel with about 1 inch between the rows. Arrange the ginger, horseradish, seaweed, and rice in separate serving saucers for each guest. Dainty, various colored dishes, cups, saucers, and pitchers lend considerable charm.

THE DIPPING SAUCE is served in a small pitcher with empty saucer for each guest in which to pour the sauce.

**1½ pounds fish serves 6**

## DIPPING SAUCE

*1 cup Japanese soy sauce*
*2 to 3 teaspoons Japanese horseradish* (Wasabi)
*6 tablespoons sake or dry sherry*
*2 teaspoons sugar*

Shake ingredients in a jar until mixed. Lasts indefinitely.

## GEFILTE FISH

Jewish people prize *Gefilte Fish* highly. Ingredient and methods of preparation vary widely. The following tips are a composite of suggestions for preparing *Gefilte Fish:* "Get the head, skin and bones;" "You have to *Meschit* and *Megist* [Yiddish for add and pour]"; "Put the head and bones in the stock"; "Use carp!" "Use three kinds of fish—and carp"; "Save the jelly"; "Just a little matzo"; . . . Most of these directions are from black-haired and pink-cheeked Vladimir Katz, born in Minsk, Russia, who works at EMPIRE COFFEE AND TEA COMPANY (page 71), who warmly shared several versions. You might like to mix the fish first and refrigerate while making the stock, but this recipe is simpler if you're cooking it all at once.

*Head, bones, and skin of fish (preferably carp)*
*1 stalk celery*
*2 onions*
*1 small carrot*
*1 to 2 sprigs parsley*
*Salt*
*Freshly ground pepper*
*2 pounds mixed white fish filets—3 kinds (preferably carp,*
*    yellow or blue pike, cod, or haddock)*
*1 large egg, lightly beaten*
*Matzo meal*

To make stock, combine head, bones, and skin of the fish with celery, 1 onion, carrot, and parsley in a pot with only enough water to cover the *Gefilte Fish* balls, about 3 cups (you can add water later). Simmer the stock while preparing the fish balls. Season lightly with salt and pepper.

Mince the fish filets and remaining onion and mix in a bowl with the egg, a little salt and pepper, and just enough matzo meal to bind. Roll mixture into balls about the size of lemons, but round, and drop into the boiling stock. Add water, if necessary, just to cover the fish balls. Bring to the boil, cover pot, and lower heat. Cook very slowly for 50 minutes or until fork-tender. Check occasionally and add water if necessary but keep water to a minimum. Carefully lift balls into a serving bowl using slotted spoon. Strain the stock (discard bones, etc.) and spoon some over the balls. Cool and refrigerate and save remaining stock to serve as a jelly with Gefilte fish.

SERVE cold. **Serves 4**

NOTE: Chopped parsley may be added to the fish mixture before making the balls. The above method is made in Minsk and Vilna. Another Minsk method is more complex: The fish is poached whole for a short time, carefully removed and sliced across into steaks; from each steak the large portion from side is removed without disturbing the skin, mixed with filling ingredients and carefully restuffed into the steak, then gently cooked. An even more complex method (old-fashioned and lovely): the fish filet is removed without disturbing the fish, mixed and restuffed, then cooked whole with vegetables!

## STEAMED LAPU-LAPU, FILIPINO STYLE *

*Lapu-Lapu* (spotted grouper), was named for the chieftain Lapu-Lapu who killed Magellan, and a favorite joke among Filipinos is: "Lapu-Lapu killed Magellan, and the cook killed *Lapu-Lapu.*" This version was inspired by a delectable dish at Tagaytay, the famed volcano near Manila, where you see enroute the pineapples, papayas, and bananas growing along the roadside. In New York, spotted grouper is available in season, or any white fish may be substituted.

*Banana leaf or substitute rinsed grapevine leaves*
*2 crabs, washed and immersed in boiling water, drained*
*1 spotted grouper or any white-meat fish, cut into segments*
*6 oysters, cleaned*
*6 mussels, cleaned*
*2 to 3 carrots, scraped and sliced diagonally*
*1 to 2 onions, sliced into rings*
*2 cloves garlic, sliced*
*Small piece fresh ginger, chopped*
*Batis (Filipino dipping sauce) or substitute Thai fish sauce*

On a steamer, preferably bamboo, spread with banana leaf or rinsed grapevine leaves (to remove excess salt), set the crabs, segments of fish, the oysters and mussels, with carrots, onions, garlic, and ginger tucked amid the fish and shellfish. Cover and steam 10 to 15 minutes until fish is flaky and shells have opened. SERVE in steamer (as a serving dish) with *Batis* and rice.

**Serves 3**

* This recipe first appeared in the author's article in *The Athenian Magazine,* (Athens, Greece), September, 1982.

## STEAMED HOI SAM
### Sea "Cucumber"

Ethnic groups all seem to have their phallic and sex foods, but Orientals seem to have the edge on the rest of the world—note the roots and *Hoi Sam*, for example. Stocked in water in tubs by the produce department, *Hoi Sam* is a dark melon color inside and blackish-gray on the skin. A woman shopper, eyeing it longingly, at KAM MAN FOOD PRODUCTS, INC. (page 28) asked the salesman the price (in Chinese), frowned at his answer, and may still be looking at it.

1 Hoi Sam, *sliced thinly*
*Oyster sauce*

Spread the *Hoi Sam* slices on a steamer; steam 10 to 15 minutes. SERVE warm with Oyster sauce, vegetables and rice. **Serve 3 to 4**

## STUFFED CALAMARI WITH SPAGHETTI

Otto Bardianos, Greek owner of HUNTER OF THE SEA (page 150) learned this wonderful dish from an Italian employee—ethnic assimilation at work! Otto Bardianos recommends the commercial Italian ragout sauce.

16, 6 to 7-inch calamari, cleaned and tentacles reserved
4 eggs, hard-cooked and chopped
8 slices salami, preferably various types—hot, sweet, etc.,
   chopped
½ onion, grated
1 to 2 cloves garlic, crushed
¼ cup grated Parmesan cheese (or substitute your favorite)
3 tablespoons bread crumbs
Few gratings black pepper
Pinch oregano, crushed
1 cup dry red wine
Ragout sauce
1 pound spaghetti, cooked Al Dente

For the stuffing, chop the tentacles and mix in a bowl with eggs, salami, onion, garlic, cheese, bread crumbs, pepper, and oregano. Using a small spoon, stuff the calamari cavities with the filling; skewer closed or sew tightly. Arrange stuffed calamari in an oiled casserole. Pour enough water into the pan to half cover the calamari. Cover and bake in moderate oven (350°F); uncover and pour wine over calamari. Continue baking, uncovered, 15 to 20 minutes longer until tender. Pour hot ragout sauce over the top of the food and allow flavors to permeate each other 5 minutes, shaking pan gently.

SERVE over hot spaghetti. **Serves 4 to 5**

## PERUVIAN CEBICHE
### Marinated Seafood

Leonore Paz was born in Lima, Peru and has lived in New York for many years. She enjoys the peppery tang of chilies on *Cebiche* as much now as she did in Peru. "Increase or decrease chilies to suit your taste," she says. The following proportion is hot but not *very* hot.

> *1 pound fresh calamari, shrimp, and fish filet or use all fish filets*
> *4 to 5 juicy limes*
> *2 cloves garlic, crushed*
> *Salt*
> *Freshly ground pepper*
> *2 chilies, seeds removed, pounded ("the long Italian chilies")*
> *1 large onion, cut into thin rings*
> *Lettuce for garnish*

Cut the seafood into small dice, about ½ inch, and place in a nonmetallic bowl. Rub limes across the table to soften and make them easier to squeeze. Squeeze limes and pour juice over the seafood dice. Stir in the garlic, a few grains of salt, and some pepper. Pound the chilies well and stir them into the seafood.

Cover and refrigerate 3 to 4 hours and allow to marinate.* Just before serving, arrange the *Cebiche* on a platter and top with the onion rings. Decorate platter with lettuce.

SERVE as an appetizer or main course. Sweet potatoes and fresh ears of corn are traditional garnishes and add rich colors as well.

**Serves 4**

* *Cebiche* may be marinated at room temperature in cold weather. Seafood must be strictly fresh.

## GHANAIAN HOT SHRIMP SAUCE

Robert Eshun, a graduate student born in Ghana, solves his home cooking needs for quick meals by making a hot shrimp sauce and heating portions to serve with cassava and other favorite dishes. He buys dried shrimp, West African red ground pepper, and other victuals at WEST AFRICAN IMPORTS CO. (page 77).

*½ cup dried shrimp*
*1 large onion, chopped*
*¼ teaspoon salt*
*1 to 2 cloves garlic, chopped*
*1 tablespoon ground red pepper (more to taste), or 5 to 6 fresh chilies, chopped, and seeds removed*
*2 to 3 tomatoes, peeled and chopped*
*2 to 3 tablespoons palm oil*
*Juice of 1 lemon or lime (optional)*

In a mortar or blender, grind the shrimp, onion, salt, garlic, red pepper together to make a smooth paste. Continue pounding or blending and add the tomatoes. Heat the palm oil in a pan and cook the sauce, adding lemon or lime juice or water to make a smooth consistency; liquid from a soup or cooked vegetables adds flavor. Cook only until thoroughly heated.

SERVE on cassava, rice, potatoes, okra, meats, and other dishes.

**Makes about 1½ cups**

## SHRIMP WITH PIZZAIOLA SAUCE

Although many Italians enjoy *Pizzaiola Sauce* on steak, Joe Mondello of PESCHERIA ITALIANA (page 136) creates his with shrimp! Sharing his quick and delicious recipe, he suggests serving it on "spaghetti, rice, or anything."

> 4 to 5 tablespoons olive oil or olive oil and unsalted butter,
>   mixed
> 3 cloves garlic, chopped
> 3 cups fresh or canned Italian plum tomatoes, peeled and
>   chopped
> ½ cup tomato sauce
> ½ cup dry white wine
> 5 to 6 generous grindings black pepper
> Pinch salt
> 2 pounds medium or large shrimp, cleaned and deveined
> Pinch dried oregano or rosemary (optional)
> Fresh parsley for garnish

Heat the olive oil or mixed oil and butter, if using, and gently saute the garlic for one minute or two without browning. Stir in the tomatoes, tomato sauce, wine, pepper, and salt. Simmer 5 minutes and add the shrimp. Simmer 15 minutes or until shrimp and tomatoes are just tender (large shrimp may need 20 minutes). Season with oregano or rosemary.

SERVE warm garnished with chopped parsley.          **Serves 5 to 6**

## CASSOLETTE
### Seafood in Cream Sauce, French Brittany Style

Suggested for a summer menu by a lovely French woman born in Brittany who has lived in New York twenty years and who still makes her own home-cooked French meals in the grand manner. She is married to a French chef!

    *1 lobster, cooked and removed from shell*
    *½ pound shrimp, cooked, shells removed, and deveined*
    *½ pound scallops, cooked*
    *7 tablespoons butter*
    *6 tablespoons flour*
    *2 cups fish fumet (seasoned with bay leaf, thyme, and*
      *parsley), hot*
    *Cooked rice*
    *Fresh parsley, chopped*

Cut lobster meat into bite-sized pieces and mix with shrimp in a bowl. Slice scallops (if using the large ones) and add to the other shellfish. To make a roux: melt the butter in a saucepan and cook 1 minute without browning; stir in the flour and cook over very low heat, stirring constantly, without browning. Remove from heat and cool slightly. Gradually add the fumet, stirring. Return to heat and bring to the boil, stirring diligently. Cook 2 minutes until thickened and pour over the seafood. Bake in moderate oven (350°F) until heated through, about 20 minutes.

SERVE warm over rice, tossed with parsley. **Serves 4**

# MEATS, POULTRY, & GAME

*When the food is fat the will is lean.*
PORTUGUESE PROVERB

## ROAST BEEF and YORKSHIRE PUDDING, ENGLISH STYLE

Sally McDermott, born near Devon in England, described her food habits and how she continued to cook her family dishes when living in New York. I've lost touch with her but she knew I was a food writer and enjoyed sharing these foodways: Sunday dinner is special with a roast beef and gravy,* roast potatoes garnished with peas, carrots, and other seasonal vegetables. Certainly Yorkshire Pudding is included, served like the recipe below in its baking pan, or as popovers, pancakes, "toad-in-the-hole" with sausages (all made from the same batter). She admitted the cuisine is a bland one, but likes to add nutmeg, thyme, bay leaf, and parsley when cooking. Thank you, Sally!

*1 cup flour, more if needed*
*Pinch of salt*
*Pinch of baking powder*
*½ teaspoon grated nutmeg*
*2 eggs, lightly beaten*
*½ cup milk or water*
*½ to ¾ cup beef drippings from your roast, very hot*

In a bowl mix the dry ingredients—flour, salt, baking powder, and nutmeg. Make a well in the center and add the eggs and milk or water. Beat until light and smooth. Choose a 2-quart baking-serving casserole or 9-inch pan and pour in the beef drippings. Spread the batter over the drippings. Bake in moderate oven (350°F) for 15 to 20 minutes until golden brown.

SERVE piping hot with roast beef, gravy, and seasonal fresh vegetables. **Serves 4 to 6**

* Make your favorite roast beef, preferably rare.

## SHABU SHABU
### Japanese Beef Dish Cooked at Table

With varied fresh vegetables, tofu, bean thread, and complex dipping sauces, *Shabu Shabu* centers on even more finely sliced beef than the famed *Sukiyaki*. As in other Japanese dishes, the incomparable presentation of textures, cutting,* colors, and table utensils are integral elements. As for the beef, Japanese, Korean, and some non-oriental meat departments can slice it (or have it ready and packaged), and incidentally, you'll find yourself serving less beef per person in more varied and nutritious style than in some typically Western menus. Sauces for dipping are available at KATAGIRI (page 92) and other oriental shops. Should you prefer to make your own, the recipes are below. *Itadakimasu (Bon appétit).*

Daikon *radish, grated*
Ponzu *Sauce (recipe on page 265)*
Goma *Sauce (recipe on page 266)*
*¾ pound finely sliced beef, preferably rib roast*
*1 cake tofu, sliced into eight pieces*
*White long-grain rice, cooked*
*Five of the following:**
  *Small cauliflower, steamed 10 minutes, rinsed in cold*
    *water and cut into bite-sized portions without crumbling*
  *3 green peppers, poached in boiling water 5 minutes, rinsed*
    *in cold water, cut into 2½-inch by ½-inch strips*
  *1 pound Chinese cabbage, cut into 1½-inch squares*
  *6 to 8 fresh mushrooms, stems removed (cap can be*
    *decorated with "star")*
  *½ pound fresh okra, salted, rinsed, then slashed in half*
    *lengthwise*
  *¼ pound bean thread, softened in boiling water 2 minutes,*
    *rinsed in cold water and cut into 6-inch lengths*

---

* Cutting vegetables needs more patience than art, but both help. Significant shapes: *Hyoshigi* (strips); *Kik Ka* (chrysanthemum circles); *Umegata* (plum flower shapes with 5 scallops made with cookie cutter); *Hangetu* (halfmoons); curls (for scallions, celery—sliver half the cut section and soak in ice water); *Namigata* (wavy lines across radish, carrot, turnips, etc. done with potato peeler). Invent more.

½ head broccoli, steamed 10 minutes, sliced into bite-sized
portions
3 taro roots, peeled, steamed until tender and sliced into
strips
Bamboo sprouts, in bite-sized pieces
Any fresh seasonal vegetable that you enjoy raw or quickly
steamed

Everything is done in advance but the cooking. Table is clear (no tablecloths) and a variety of lacquerware, china, bamboo mats, soup bowls, cups, saucers, sake cups, rice bowls, chopstick holders (Hashioka), tiny pitchers—these are ready to delight the eyes.

Prepare grated radish, Ponzu, and Goma sauces and arrange individually in small saucers on the table. Roll the beef into graceful curls and layer near the center of a large, preferably white, platter. Using color and shapes to create beauty and refined grace, cluster the vegetables, bean thread, and tofu around the beef (use your eye but try for an assymetric design with curves), as in an Utamaro painting). Save extras in serving bowls on a serving table to refill platter as food is cooked. Fill chafing dish with boiling water.

TO SERVE: using chopsticks, lift a slice of beef and dip it into the boiling water until the raw color disappears. Dip it into the dipping sauces and eat. Repeat with each vegetable, varying and seasoning to taste. Serve with rice and warm Saki or tea.

**Serves 6**


## PONZU SAUCE

This is best made at least a day before you need it.

1 Kombo dried seaweed (also called Dashi Kombo), about 1
ounce
1 bag dried shaved Bonito (dried Bonito fish), about 2 full
tablespoons
1 cup Shoyu (Japanese soy sauce)
1 cup bitter orange juice (or substitute a mixture of fresh
orange and lemon juice)

Wash the *Kombo*, cut into sections, and combine in a bowl with the *Bonito*. Cover with 4 cups cold water. Soak at least 6 hours; drain. Stir the soy sauce and bitter orange juice into the *Kombo-Bonito* liquid. Use *Ponzu* Sauce to make the *Goma* Sauce (recipe follows).

STORE in refrigerator. **Makes 4 cups**


## GOMA SAUCE

Your own taste is the best guide to flavoring the dipping sauce.

*1 cup Ponzu Sauce*
*½ cup Shoyu (Japanese soy sauce)*
*1 to 2 teaspoons hot mustard*
*2 tablespoons sherry or dry wine*
*1½ tablespoons sugar*
*2 to 3 tablespoons sesame seeds*
*Grated horseradish (optional)*

In a covered jar shake the *Ponzu* sauce, *Shoyu*, mustard, sherry, sugar, sesame seeds, and a pinch of horseradish. Taste for flavor. Pour into small pitcher. Store in refrigerator.

SERVE in individual saucers for dipping **Makes 1⅔ cups**


## PULGOGI or PULKOKI
### Korean National Beef Dish

Like most Koreans, Kim Chung Un of DAE WOO ORIENTAL FOOD MARKET (page 65), enjoys *Pulgogi* and he makes it like this:

*1 pound lean beef, cut into strips, ½ inch by 2 inches*
*4 cloves garlic, minced*
*1 large onion, chopped*
*1 tablespoon Korean sesame seeds*
*3 to 4 tablespoons Japanese soy sauce*
*Freshly ground pepper*
*2 tablespoons peanut or vegetable oil*

In a bowl whisk all ingredients except beef; slip beef into the marinade, and marinate beef one hour, turning frequently. Drain beef and reserve the marinade. Grill on a *Sinsulo* (Korean metal cooker with central stem for burning charcoal) or fry lightly on a griddle, brushing with marinade.
SERVE with *Kimchi* (Korean pickled vegetables, recipe, page 184), fresh vegetables and rice, and dipping sauce (recipe below).

**Serves 4**

NOTE: Fresh, sliced mushrooms, spinach, turnips, celery, and other vegetables may be sliced and cooked on the *Sinsulo* in broth that accumulates around the lower rim (a great party or "community" dish).


## KOREAN DIPPING SWEET & SOUR SOY SAUCE

Make in advance and keep handy as a salad dressing, marinade, or dipping sauce for fish, meat, and poultry.

*⅓ cup Japanese or light soy sauce*
*½ cup rice wine vinegar*
*2 tablespoons sugar*
*1½ tablespoons pine nuts, finely chopped (optional)*

In a covered jar, shake the ingredients except the pine nuts.
SERVE about 2 tablespoons in a small saucer for each guest and garnish with the pine nuts, if you like.  **Makes about ¾ cup**

## KJØD BOLLER
### Norwegian Meatballs

Joyce Peterson Kildahl, a Norwegian-American and a good friend, shared this recipe for our home economics classes which I taught at Scarsdale Junior High—one of her endless kindnesses. Joyce shared wonderful Norwegian books and anecdotes, offered delectable Norwegian dishes, learned from her Minnesota family, which she continues to make in New York. The breads and casseroles, the cakes and, oh the Christmas cookies! I wait 364 days just to have a crispy *Krumkake* disappear on my tongue (recipe, page 312). Better, if you can make the meat balls one day in advance.

*1½ pounds ground beef, preferably chuck or round*
*1 egg*
*1 cup very finely ground bread crumbs (hard leftover breads*
  *including whole wheat)*
*1 small onion, grated or very finely chopped*
*½ teaspoon grated nutmeg*
*Salt*
*Freshly ground pepper*
*Oil (optional)*
*1½ cups beef stock or consomme*
*½ cup light cream* \*
*Dash of Worcestershire or soy sauce (optional)*

In a bowl, knead the beef, egg, bread crumbs, onion, nutmeg, and a little salt and pepper with enough water to form a soft, but firm, mixture. Unless planning the *Kjød Boller* to serve as an appetizer (which can be much smaller), shape the balls in your palms to lime size. To fry: heat a heavy skillet and either sprinkle very lightly with salt or rub with a film of oil (fat will be released from meat, so a hot griddle is enough). Using a spatula, sauté the balls over medium heat until cooked but not tough. (This much can be done in advance; cool and store in refrigerator and skim off excess

---

\* Sour cream may be substituted, but should be added after simmering to avoid curdling; heat but do not boil.

fat that forms on the surface.) When ready to serve, mix the beef stock, cream, and dash of either sauce, if using, and have ready. Put meatballs and drippings (fat skimmed off) in a larger pan and stir in the sauce; heat gently 20 minutes.
SERVE warm. **Serves 6.**

## FRIKADELLER
### Danish Meatballs

Although many ethnic groups enjoy meatballs, the individuality of each is unmistakable. Anneliese Gaarde and Anneliese Heidelberg, with the Danish Mission to the United Nations in New York, share this national favorite, *Frikadeller*. When prepared for a *Smorgasbord*, the meatballs should be a much daintier size using the same ingredients. This version is for a wholesome dinner, served with whole boiled potatoes and pickled sweet and sour beets or red cabbage. *Tak!*

½ *pound ground veal*
½ *pound ground pork*
¼ *cup all purpose flour (more if making the gravy)*
*Salt*
*Freshly ground pepper*
*1 egg, lightly beaten*
*2 to 4 tablespoons milk (more if making the gravy)*
*1 large onion, grated, or chopped and sautéed in 1 to 2*
  *tablespoons butter or margarine*
*4 tablespoons butter or margarine*
*Kulør or Swedish Soya sauce\**

In a bowl, combine the veal, pork, ¼ cup flour, a little salt and pepper, egg and enough milk to make a mixture that can be rolled in the fingers. Mix in the onion or, if you prefer, saute the onion and knead with the meat. Scoop tablespoon-sized portions of the meat and roll into balls (for *Smorgasbord* or appetizers, use a

---

\* *Kulør* or Swedish Soya sauce is available at NYBORG-NELSON, page 67.

teaspoon). Heat 2 tablespoons of the butter or margarine in a large frying pan and sauté the meatballs gently, turning frequently until thoroughly cooked; add more butter or margarine if necessary. Turn heat up at the end to develop a nice crust on the balls. Drain on paper towels. If you like gravy (a traditional Danish custom), add 2 or 3 tablespoons flour into the pan drippings, depending on an equal amount of the remaining fat, to make a roux. Stir over low heat for 2 minutes. Heat 1½ cups milk and gradually add to the roux. Continue stirring until the sauce thickens. Add enough *Kulør* to color the gravy. Drop meatballs into the gravy and heat to boiling point.

SERVE hot. **Serves 4 to 5**

## ARGENTINIAN DRIED BEEF WITH SOFRITO

Filemina Miranda, a fine-featured woman, buys Argentinian beef to season with her favorite seasoning, Sofrito (which can be made in large batches and frozen in small portions). This popular beef has many names including *Tasajo* and *Asado de Tira*.

*1 pound Argentinian beef*
*Salt*
*Freshly ground pepper*
*1½ teaspoons Sofrito (recipe, page 180, 181)*
*1 to 2 green peppers*
*4 ripe tomatoes, or 5 canned plum tomatoes*

Cover beef with water and simmer until tender, about 40 minutes. Drain and cut into cubes. Season with salt and pepper. Combine in pan with *Sofrito* and saute until beef is well seasoned. Add the green peppers and tomatoes and simmer, covered, 30 minutes. Grate more pepper over the food.

SERVE warm with rice. **Serves 4**

## GROUND MEAT SAUCE WITH SAUSAGES

Tony Esposito of GIOVANNI ESPOSITO & SONS (page 72) likes meats and uses more than one kind in his pasta sauce. Divide and freeze into portions or plan a dinner party.

> 3 pounds ground pork and beef mixed
> 2 to 3 onions, chopped finely
> 3 cloves garlic, minced
> 4 links hot sausages (½ pound)
> 5 to 6 links sweet sausages (¾ pound)
> 2 large cans plum tomatoes, drained and liquid reserved
> ¾ cup tomato paste dissolved in ½ cup reserved tomato
>    liquid
> Salt
> Freshly ground pepper
> 3 to 4 sprigs fresh parsley, chopped
> 2 sprigs fresh basil, chopped, or 1 teaspoon dried basil,
>    crushed
> Linguine
> Romano pecorino cheese

In a heavy-bottomed large pan, over moderate heat, mash the ground meats with onions and garlic. Stir and continue to cook until the raw color disappears and meat grains are separated from each other. Tuck in the sausages and brown on all sides (or it may be simpler to brown the sausages in another fry pan, then add to the ground meat). Chop the tomatoes and add them to the meats with the tomato paste. Cover, lower heat to lowest and simmer 1½ to 2 hours, stirring in seasonings—salt, pepper, parsley, and basil—during the last 30 minutes. Remove sausages and serve separately.

SERVE meat sauce over linguine sprinkled liberally with *romano pecorino*, with crusty bread, and red Burgundy wine. **Serves 10**

## CARNE MECHADA
### Stuffed Roast Meat

A Puerto Rican favorite, cooked by Willy Velez from Ponce, who has lived in New York since 1957, and still enjoys the old-time flavors.

> Stuffing: 6 green olives, pitted; 1 onion, minced; 2 cloves
>     garlic, minced; 2 chilies, chopped; ½ green pepper,
>     chopped; ½ teaspoon capers; ½ cup smoked ham, chopped;
>     1 tablespoon fresh lime juice
> 4½- to 5-pound roast (pork from thigh or beef eye or rolled
>     sirloin)
> Salt
> Freshly ground pepper
> Paprika
> 15 new potatoes or 6 all-purpose potatoes

In a small bowl, combine the stuffing ingredients and mix well.

TO STUFF MEAT: slash meat all around and work 1 tablespoon stuffing into each slash, penetrating as deeply as possible. Dust meat lightly with salt, pepper, and paprika. Set roast in center of roasting pan. Add 1 cup water to the pan. Roast in moderate oven (350°F) for 60 minutes, turning once. Peel potatoes and halve them if large. Drop around the meat and add 2 cups water. Shake pan to mix meat drippings. Continue baking 45 minutes, turning potatoes every 15 minutes.* If roasting pork, the interior temperature must register 185°F to be thoroughly cooked; beef may be served rare.

SERVE warm.                                                  **Serves 6 to 8**

---

* If roast is finished before the potatoes are tender, remove roast to a warm platter; continue baking potatoes at 375°F, adding water to pan, if needed, for 15 minutes or until fork tender.

## IRISH STEW

A favorite of Irishman John Gilmartin, manager of B. ALTMAN food department (page 59). It is traditionally cooked in a pot on the burner but could be baked if the oven is on for another dish. Wholesome, easy, and rib-sticking.

*½ leg of lamb*
*Salt*
*Freshly ground pepper*
*3 to 4 onions, preferably the same size, whole or halved*
*4 to 5 carrots, cut into thirds*
*3 stalks celery, cut into chunks*
*6 potatoes, peeled, and covered with cold water to prevent*
  *discoloration*
*¼ cup barley*

Heat a heavy casserole and sear the lamb, beginning on the fat side to melt some fat; brown on all sides. Season with salt and pepper. Half cover with water, cover casserole, and simmer on burner or in moderate oven for 30 minutes. Uncover and add the onions, carrots, and celery; take 5 potatoes out of the water, cut in half, and add them to the stew with the barley. Cover casserole and continue baking. Dice the remaining potato, cover with water in a saucepan, and cook until mushy. Strain and add the liquid to the stew; mash the potato and stir into the gravy to thicken. Continue baking uncovered until lamb and vegetables are tender, about 15 more minutes. Season with additional salt and pepper.
SERVE warm with Irish brown bread, climaxed by Irish coffee (strong coffee, sweetened with brown sugar, and spiked with Irish whiskey topped off with whipped cream). **Serves 6**

NOTE: Many Irish cooks stew lamb in water without browning.

## ISCAS
### Portuguese Marinated Sautéed Liver

Delicious served with its sauce over steaming rice accompanied by delectable Portuguese red *Graovesceo* wine!

> *1 pound beef liver, preferably, or calves liver may be used*
> *⅓ cup mixed Portuguese olive oil and vegetable oil or all olive oil*
> *3 to 4 tablespoons vinegar*
> *¾ cup dry wine*
> *1 bay leaf, crushed*
> *2 cloves garlic, crushed*
> *Salt*
> *Freshly ground pepper*
> *1 onion, sliced into thin slivers*
> *Fresh parsley for garnish*

Slice the liver diagonally into slices ¼ inch thin and 3 inches wide. To make a marinade, whisk together half the oil, 3 or 4 tablespoons vinegar (depending on how sour you like it), wine, bay leaf, and garlic with a light sprinkling of salt and pepper. Dip liver slices into the marinade and saturate both sides. Cover; refrigerate 3 to 4 hours. To cook: drain the liver and reserve the marinade. Heat remaining oil and when hot, but not smoking, sauté the liver on both sides briefly if you like it pink or a few minutes on each side for well-done liver; arrange on a warm platter and keep warm. Sauté the onion slivers in the oil remaining in the pan. Stir in the reserved marinade and simmer a few minutes to blend flavors. Taste and season with more pepper, if you like. Strain directly over the liver. Garnish with parsley.
SERVE warm with rice.                                    **Serves 4**

## CHITTERLINGS or CHITLINS, SOUL STYLE

Chitterlings are intestines, available at Italian and German pork shops. They are quite different from the prized *Kokoretsi*, barbecued intestines and innards from a young lamb, beloved by Hellenes. For any dish, the intestines must be scrubbed, turned inside out as you would a belt (after stitching the seam) using a thin dowel or long pencil and working over a pan so you won't lose them down the drain! Suggested for Sunday dinner by a former student.

*1 pound chitterlings*
*2 stalks celery, cut diagonally into short lengths*
*2 onions, quartered*
*1 apple, peeled and quartered*
*½ cup vinegar*
*Salt*
*Freshly ground pepper*

Thoroughly wash the chitterlings inside and out and cut into 12-inch lengths. In a large soup pot combine the chitterlings with the celery, onions, apple, and vinegar. Cover pot and simmer 3 to 4 hours or longer until chitterlings are tender. Drain and discard broth and vegetables.

SERVE with rice, collards (page 215)* and hot corn bread with butter. **Serves 2 to 3**

* Collard Greens, Brazilian Style (with meats), or, for plain collards, see note following recipe.

## CURRIED GOAT, JAMAICA STYLE

Begin the evening before . . .

*2 pounds goat's meat, preferably from ribs, leg, or thigh*
*1 onion, diced*
*1 clove garlic pounded with ½ teaspoon salt*
*1 tablespoon freshly ground pepper*
*4 to 5 sprigs fresh thyme, chopped, or 2 teaspoons dried*
  *thyme, crushed*
*2 tablespoons curry powder*

Cut meat into serving portions and put in a large bowl. Sprinkle with the onion, pounded garlic, pepper, thyme, and curry powder. Mix thoroughly to saturate goat meat. Cover and refrigerate overnight. To cook: turn meat and seasonings into a casserole, rinse marinade bowl with 1 cup water and add to the meat. Cover; cook over lowest heat, turning frequently, adding water if more sauce is needed, about 1½ hours or until tender.

SERVE on a bed of rice with fresh pigeon peas, and mango chutney.

**Serves 5 to 6**

NOTE: Goat's meat is available in most specialty meat markets catering to Caribbean, Italian, South American, Hispanic, and many Mediterranean groups.

## STUFFED QUAILS, GREEK STYLE

Baked by Sotirios ("Sam") Karamouzis, meat expert and partner of INTERNATIONAL GROCERY STORE AND MEAT MARKET (page 75), this dish was utterly delectable at the Ninth Avenue Festival. He shares his recipe for this prized Greek dish *Ortikia Yemista* (Stuffed Quails) and suggests two quails per person for a main course. He recommends *Retsina* (resinated Greek wine) for that special pine flavor.

> *12 quails (about 24 ounces)*
> *Salt*
> *Freshly ground pepper*
> *1¼ cups feta, crumbled*
> *4 to 5 sprigs parsley, chopped finely (more for garnish)*
> *1 teaspoon dried oregano, crushed in your palm over the bowl*
> *4 to 6 tablespoons unsalted butter, melted*
> *¾ cup to 1 cup warm* Retsina *white wine*

Wash and dry the quails. Lightly salt and pepper them. In a small bowl, combine the feta, parsley, oregano, and a few grindings pepper. Using a spoon, stuff the quails and skewer opening tightly to close. Arrange quails in a baking pan where they fit loosely, and brush with melted butter; turn over and brush other side. Bake in moderate oven (350°F) until *kokkinisto* or reddish brown, about 50 minutes, turning once and basting with the juices. Pour the warm *Retsina* over the quails and bake 5 or 10 minutes longer.

SERVE warm.

**Serves 6**

## HOT CHICKEN CURRY, THAI STYLE

Shared by Chichi Paleewong of SIAM GROCERY (page 89) using her recommended *Prig Khing* (green curry paste).

2 cups coconut milk *(recipe, page 184)*
2 to 3 tablespoons Prig Khing *(green curry paste)*
2 cups cooked chicken breast, shredded
1 to 2 tablespoons Nampla*
*Pinch sugar*
1 to 2 green chilies, chopped (optional)

In heavy pan, bring coconut milk to the boil and stir in the green curry paste. Lower heat to minimum to avoid burning and cook, stirring constantly, until the oil of coconut shines on the surface, about 5 minutes. Add water or coconut "tail" (liquid from the coconut), if necessary. Mix in the chicken, *Nampla*, sugar, and chilies, if you like the dish hotter.
SERVE warm with rice. **Serves 4**

* *Nampla* is anchovy fish extract, the same sauce used in *Nuoc Mam* (page 188) in Vietnamese recipes. I have used the excellent Tiparos brand for years.

## STUFFED BONED CAPON

Joe Broder, of RAOUL'S BOUCHERIE (page 38), removes all bones from poultry including the wish bone (and he'll show you how to bone a chicken, if you wish). When ready to stuff, the bird will be flat. Prepare two cupfuls of your favorite dressing. Make sure it's a binding type that can be sliced like a paté after baking (Joe emphasizes that you should avoid wild rice or any rice stuffing because they cannot be sliced). Using your fingers, stuff the legs, wings and body cavity until the shape is plump and natural. Roast for one hour and 20 minutes to 1½ hours in moderate oven (350°F). Cover for five minutes with aluminum foil to allow the liquids to congeal. Slice across like an ice cream or jelly roll.
SERVE warm. **Serves 4 to 6**

# COMBINATION DISHES,
# CASSEROLES, &
# DUMPLINGS

*What's sweet in the mouth,*
*sometimes hot in the belly.*
AFRO-AMERICAN PROVERB

## SHA O POKKUM
### Korean Fried Rice with Shrimp and Pork

Minhee Jang, who works with her uncle, Captain Park, at CAP-TAIN PARK FISH MARKET (page 80), reveals her fried rice recipe (a terrific way to use leftover cooked rice in a simple dish).

*1 to 2 tablespoons vegetable oil*
*1 tablespoon toasted sesame seeds*
*2 cloves garlic, minced*
*2 scallions, cut into fine rings, including green parts*
*Freshly ground black pepper*
*3 to 4 tablespoons Kimchi\**
*1 tablespoon sugar*
*½ pound lean pork, cut into thin slices*
*½ pound baby shrimp or large shrimp, cleaned and chopped*
*2 to 3 cups cooked white rice*

In a wok or frying pan, combine the oil, toasted sesame seeds, garlic, scallions, a few grindings of black pepper, 3 tablespoons *Kimchi*, sugar, and pork. Stir-fry over high heat until pork changes color; lower heat and cook 5 minutes, stirring occasionally. Stir in shrimp and cook until shrimp turns bright orange. Then add the rice, cook until all flavors blend and the rice is hot (the pork must be cooked). Taste and add more *Kimchi* if you like. SERVE hot. **Serves 3 to 4**

* *Kimchi* is available in Korean, Japanese, and some Chinese shops. It is the favorite Korean seasoning; 2 tablespoons *Kimchi* would not be enough for this dish and 4 tablespoons would not be too much for a Korean taste, according to Minhee Jang. Should you like to try your own, turn to page 184.

## MOROCCAN CHICKEN COUSCOUS

Candy Gelenter Medina of Staten Island, whose father and husband are partners in DAVID'S KOSHER BUTCHER, (page 166), warmly shares this North African recipe learned from her Moroccan grandmother and mother. Named for the bead-like wheat product called couscous, steamed with the meat or poultry and vegetables, the dish is delightful, basically simple, and perfect to serve guests, Candy suggests. Particularly convenient to cook in a *Couscoussier*, a traditional double-cooker with smaller steamer on top for the couscous, and the large, rounded pot below for the stew, but you can easily adapt a colander over a soup pot. Chick peas have to be soaked overnight in advance; and the couscous should be prepared before beginning to cook the stew. *To Da, Merci!*

> 1 cup chick peas
> Prepared couscous (see recipe on page 283 before beginning)
> 1 fryer or broiler chicken (about 2½ pounds), cut into serving
>   portions
> 3 turnips, cut into thirds
> 4 carrots, halved across
> 2 onions, quartered
> 2 stalks celery, sliced into 1-inch slices
> 1 tomato, peeled and chopped
> 2 cups fresh pumpkin, cubed in ½-inch dice (calabaza always
>   available in Hispanic markets)
> 6 to 8 cups chicken stock or chicken bouillon cubes *
> 1 pound zucchini, cut into thirds
> 1½ to 2 teaspoons ground turmeric
> Salt
> Freshly ground pepper

In a bowl, cover chick peas with cold water and soak overnight. Next day, drain and rub under cold water to remove husks. Rinse and place in bottom of *Couscoussier* or soup pot. Prepare the couscous as directed in the recipe below and arrange in the top steamer of the *Couscoussier* or colander and set aside. In the bottom pot, add the chicken to the chick peas, turnips, carrots, onions, celery, tomato, pumpkin, and enough stock to come within two inches of the top. Slowly bring the soup to the boil, then set the couscous in the steamer over the soup. Sprinkle the remaining half bouillon cube over the couscous. Cover the *Couscoussier* or colander tightly; simmer until chicken and vegetables are tender, about 45 minutes, adding zucchini and seasonings during the last 15 minutes (begin with one teaspoon turmeric, salt and pepper, adding more turmeric for a brighter yellow color). Also sprinkle ½ teaspoon turmeric over the couscous in the steamer and stir to distribute the color evenly. Simmer 5 minutes longer.

SERVE warm with chicken and vegetables in soup bowls accompanied by the steamed couscous. **Serves 6**

* Candy Medina uses chicken bouillon cubes dissolved in water to make chicken stock (3 cubes per 4 cups water) and reserves ½ cube to sprinkle over the couscous balls for richer flavor.

## PREPARED COUSCOUS

*1½-pound box couscous (tiny bead-like grain product
available in Arabic and Middle Eastern shops)
⅓ cup vegetable or olive oil*

Spread couscous in a flat tray. In a smaller bowl or 4-cup measuring cup, whisk the oil with ½ cup water. Working the couscous with your palm, gradually drop the oil-water mixture into the couscous. Continue working to make small balls about the size of silver sprinkles used in cake decorating—smaller than ¼-inch diameter. Place prepared couscous in steamer.

## CHOLENT
### Jewish Bean and Meat Casserole

Edith Klein, wife of Murray Klein (co-owner of ZABAR's, page 86), shared her *Cholent* recipe. A fascinating dish inspired by the Orthodox Jewish traditions forbidding cooking on the Sabbath (Saturday), *Cholent* is set in the oven before sundown on Friday evening, cooks overnight, and is tender and appetizing for the Sabbath! Born in Hungary, Edith Klein, an excellent cook who has maintained her Kosher food habits, learned this dish from her mother. Like many ethnic cooks, she learned to adapt. In Hungary, smoked goose "is delicious in *Cholent*," she says, "but since Kosher smoked goose is not usually available in New York, I substitute Kosher pastrami."* Try it, Kosher or non-Kosher, you'll love it!

> *1 pound navy beans***
> *2 tablespoons chicken fat*
> *1 large onion, diced*
> *1 to 2 shallots, diced (optional)*
> *2 pounds short ribs of beef*
> *¾ to 1 pound smoked pastrami or smoked goose**
> *½ cup pearl barley, rinsed and drained*
> *½ cup white wine (optional)*
> *2 tablespoons Hungarian paprika*
> *Salt*
> *Freshly ground pepper*

Wash and drain beans. Set into electric bean pot or Dutch oven; cover with boiling water and let soak while preparing the remaining ingredients (this procedure begins tenderizing the beans). Heat the chicken fat in a large pan; saute the onion and shallots, if using, until translucent but not brown. Drop in the short ribs and saute on all sides until the beef loses its raw color. Tuck the beef into the beans with all the onion, shallots, and drippings. Stir in

---

* Smoked goose legs and breast are available at SCHALLER & WEBER (page 101) during the holiday season beginning about Thanksgiving time (for non-Kosher cooks). They are already cooked and need only about 30 minutes to heat through just before serving.

** Edith Klein uses Great Northern and Goya navy beans.

the pastrami, barley, wine, if using, and paprika. Add only enough water to cover the beans and meat. Cover pot and cook very slowly overnight (or six hours by electric pot), on burner or in a slow oven (250°F) until beans are tender and liquid has been absorbed. *Cholent* is a thick, not soupy, dish. Taste and season with a little salt, pepper and more paprika to make it flavorful. SERVE hot. **Serves 6**

## CALALOO
### Leafy Greens, Trinidad Style

Salt beef, pork, or fresh crabmeat may be simmered with the *Calaloo* (Caribbean leafy green, available in cans) and coconut milk, suggested by a young Trinidadian who works in a hospital.

*1 pound dried beef, pork, or crabmeat*
*Juice of 1 small lime*
*2 to 3 tablespoons vegetable oil*
*1 teaspoon sugar*
*1 large can Calaloo or substitute 1½ pounds fresh spinach or*
*  2 packages frozen spinach*
*2 cups coconut milk (page 184)*
*3 sprigs fresh thyme or 1 teaspoon dried thyme (more for*
*  garnish)*
*Salt*
*Freshly ground pepper*

In a bowl, sprinkle the beef, pork, or crabmeat with lime juice and marinate 30 minutes to 2 hours. When ready to cook, heat the oil in a large casserole and stir in the sugar. Stir constantly over medium heat until the sugar caramelizes (just beginning to turn brown), drop in the beef, pork, or crabmeat, and saute on all sides. If using the beef or pork, add 2 cups water, cover, and simmer 40 minutes until almost tender; if cooking the crabmeat, sauté lightly. Stir in the Calaloo or spinach, coconut milk, thyme, and a light sprinkling of salt and pepper. Stir and cook until tender, about 30 minutes. Taste and add more thyme for flavor. Cut the meat up into bite-sized pieces.
SERVE warm with rice or mashed potatoes. **Serves 4**

## SUCCOTASH, NEW YORK SHINNECOCK STYLE

Sandra Lacy, a New York-born Shinnecock Indian, whips up the same Succotash recipe she learned from her mother, Wanda Lacy, who learned it from her mother. When the family gets together for an *Askowala* (pow-wow), there are about fifteen guests including Sandra's mother, three sisters, two brothers, and their children. Hence the enormous quantity—which you might like to try for your own *Askowala*.

> *5 pounds kidney beans*
> *4 to 5 large onions*
> *Chili powder*
> *Salt*
> *Freshly ground pepper*
> *3½ to 4 pounds ground beef*
> *2 to 3 green peppers*
> *2 to 3 cloves garlic, chopped (optional)*
> *12 ears fresh sweet corn*
> *2 to 3 potatoes cooked and cut into eighths (optional)*
> *1 cup rice, cooked (optional)*

The beans and meat are cooked separately before combining, so you'll need two large pots. In a large soup pot, pick over beans, wash, and cover with cold water. Bring to the boil, cover, and simmer 30 minutes. Chop 2 to 3 onions and add to the kidney beans with a generous sprinkling of chili powder, a little salt, and lots of pepper. Continue cooking while you prepare the meat. In a large pan, mash the beef over medium heat, stirring steadily, until the meat begins to release liquid and loses its raw color. Chop 2 onions, remove stem and seeds from the green peppers, chop, and add them with the onions to the beef. Stir in the garlic, if using, cover, and simmer over low heat, adding water, if necessary. Check the beans and add water but avoid too much liquid since you want them to end up thick, not soupy. When beans are about tender, add the meat mixture. Using a sharp knife, cut kernels off the corn and add to the beans and meat with either potatoes or rice (Sandra prefers potatoes), if you like. "Taste and add more seasonings—especially chili powder—it should be peppery but not burning," Sandra says.

SERVE with Indian Fried Bread (page 236).        **Serves 15**

NOTE: If using the rice or potatoes, they may be added to the beans when half cooked, with enough water for them to absorb while cooking (about double the volume).

## THAI BEEF AND EGGPLANTS

Thai eggplants, resembling green figs in shape and size, are not as bitter as some of the large varieties. In suggesting this recipe, Samarn Sil, a neighbor interpreting at THAI GROCERY, L&T IMPORT CO. (page 160) predicted "You won't like it." She was wrong; it is not only delicious, but a quick meal.

*1 pound lean beef, sliced into 1¼-inch thin strips*
*2 teaspoons sugar*
*1 tablespoon heavy soy sauce (more for color)*
*1 to 2 tablespoons Thai anchovy fish sauce (Tiparos brand preferably) ***
*1 to 2 tablespoons vegetable oil*
*2 to 7 chilies to your taste (it should be hot), chopped*
*8 to 10 Thai eggplants, leaves cut off and discarded, quartered*
*2 to 3 sprigs fresh basil, chopped (more for garnish)*

In a bowl combine the beef with sugar, soy sauce, and fish sauce. Heat oil, preferably in a wok, and cook chilies until softened, about 2 minutes. Stir in the beef and seasonings; stir-fry until raw color disappears, about 2 minutes. Lower heat, cover, and simmer 5 minutes. Move the meat to the side. Add the eggplant quarters (there should be about 1 cup liquid in the pan released from the meat; if not add a little water), and continue cooking, covered, until eggplants are tender, about 20 minutes. Stir meat into the eggplants and sprinkle basil into the dish during the last few minutes.

SERVE warm with rice garnished with fresh basil.    **Serves 4 to 5**

* Thai fish sauce is sometimes called *Nampla* (see page 277).

## GORMEH SABZI
### Persian Meat and Vegetables

A popular dish and favorite of Iranian Shedi Aboutalebi, of NADER'S GROCERY STORE, who suggests *Limoamoni* (dried lemons) available in the family shop (see page 59). A pinch of cinnamon may be added to the *Gormeh Sabzi* when meat is simmering; beans and sauce *(Khoresche)* are cooked separately and then combined with the meat.

*¾ pound kidney beans or substitute black-eyed peas*
*3 to 4 tablespoons vegetable oil or clarified butter*
*2 pounds lean beef or lamb, cubed (about 1¼ inches)*
*1 onion, minced*
*Salt*
*Freshly ground pepper*
*5 Limoamoni, or substitute juice of ½ large lemon*
*4 fresh scallions, minced*
*1 large leek, washed and sliced finely*
*1 cup fresh parsley, chopped*
*¼ cup fresh coriander, chopped*
*1 pound fresh spinach or 1 package frozen spinach, chopped*
   *(optional), or substitute any seasonal vegetable*

Soak kidney beans overnight, if using; next day cook beans or peas until tender, drain over a bowl, and reserve liquid for a soup. Meanwhile, heat 2 tablespoons oil and saute meat and onion until raw color of meat turns to rich color and onion softens. Season meat lightly with salt and pepper. Wash *Limoamoni*, prick each with a fork, and add them to the meat with enough water to almost cover. Cover pan and simmer until meat is almost tender, about 35 minutes. In yet another pan, heat 1 to 2 tablespoons oil and saute the scallions, leek, all but 2 tablespoons of the parsley, coriander, and spinach, if using. Saute until cooked, about 10 minutes, adding a little water only if needed. When meat is tender, stir in the cooked beans or peas and the vegetable sauce. Simmer 15 to 20 minutes until all flavors blend. Taste and adjust seasonings, if necessary. Garnish with remaining fresh parsley. SERVE warm over steamed rice. **Serves 6**

## CLASSIC SAUSAGE AND GREEN PEPPER CASSEROLE

In JOE'S PORK STORE (page 151), owner Joe Livoti and Sicilian customer Florence Alaimo touted their mothers' similar sausage and pepper casserole. Neither could remember the Italian name, which proves the theory that the emigrant tends to forget the language of the fatherland before giving up his native food habits. But they agreed on the casserole, except that Joe's mother whipped it up with fresh peas, without tomatoes! Here's Florence Alaimo's version, which bedazzled our taste buds.

1 pound fresh sweet sausage, cut into 1-inch segments
2 green peppers, seeded and sliced
4 onions, sliced into rings
4 potatoes, quartered
3 fresh tomatoes, chopped, or ¾ cup tomato sauce and
    enough water to fill the cup
Salt (optional)
Freshly ground pepper (optional)

In a 2-quart casserole, brown the sausage lightly. Add the peppers, onions, potatoes, cover and place in a moderately hot oven (400°F) for 15 minutes; stir and reduce heat to 350°F and continue baking 15 minutes, covered. Foods will gradually secrete juices in which the potatoes cook. Add tomatoes, stir, and continue baking 25 minutes, uncovered, until potatoes are fork-tender. Season lightly.

SERVE warm.                                              **Serves 4**

## PASTITSIO, CRETAN STYLE
### Layered Pasta-Meat Casserole

Zoe Livadiotakis, of HELLAS-AMERICAN IMPORTS, INC. (page 131), born in Hania, Crete, enjoys this version of *Pastitsio* from her hometown more than any other dish.

> 1 to 2 tablespoons vegetable oil
> 1 pound ground beef
> 1 onion, chopped
> 2 whole cloves
> Salt
> Freshly ground pepper
> 6 cups milk, scalded and cooled
> 14 tablespoons butter (1 cup minus 2 tablespoons)
> 1 tablespoon cornstarch
> 1 tablespoon semolina
> 7 tablespoons flour
> 4 eggs
> 1 to 1¼ pounds cut ziti *
> 1¼ cups Kefalotyri *cheese, grated (Greek cheese substitute for romano locatelli)*

Three preparations are needed for meat, white sauce, and ziti; the meat may be cooked a day or two in advance for better flavor.

TO PREPARE THE MEAT: heat the oil and mash the meat into the pan with the onion, mashing and stirring until meat releases liquid and loses raw color. Slip the cloves into the meat; cover and simmer 20 minutes. Season lightly with salt and pepper (this much may be done in advance).

TO PREPARE THE WHITE SAUCE TOPPING: heat and cool the milk. In a heavy pan, heat 10 tablespoons (1 stick plus 2 tablespoons) of the butter without browning. Mix the cornstarch, semolina, and flour in a cup and gradually add to the heated butter, stirring constantly; cook 2 minutes. Remove from heat and gradually add

---

* Zoe suggested one pound ziti, which makes a rich *Pastitsio*, good for weight-conscious adults; I often use an extra quarter or half pound ziti for teenagers who need more energy, for a thicker *Pastitsio*.

the milk a little at a time. Return to low heat and bring to the boil, stirring constantly. Cool.

TO PREPARE THE ZITI: While the sauce cools, bring to the boil a large quantity of salted water in a pot; when rapidly boiling, cook the ziti until just tender, not mushy. Drain thoroughly, shaking out all the water. Return ziti to the pot and add all remaining butter (except ½ teaspoon to butter the pan). Separate 2 eggs and add the white to the ziti, mixing well. In a small bowl, lightly whisk the 2 yolks with the 2 whole eggs and stir them into the white sauce, with one cup grated *Kefalotyri*. Butter an 11- by 15-inch pan.

TO ASSEMBLE: spread half the ziti on the bottom; cover with the meat, smoothing with a spatula into the corners. Add the remaining ziti over the meat. Cover with the white sauce; sprinkle top with remaining ¼ cup cheese. Bake 50 to 60 minutes in moderate oven (350°F) until top is golden chestnut.

WAIT 15 minutes before cutting into squares.

**Makes 16 to 20 pieces (depending on how you slice them)**


## PASTELES DE PUERTO RICO
### Holiday Steamed Vegetable and Pork-Stuffed Savory Dish

For Puerto Ricans, *Pasteles* means holiday and vice versa, and their anticipation about eating them equals their enthusiasm for preparing them. Many described their methods and proportions, especially Martha Cordero, who lives in the Bronx, whose *Pasteles* are delectable. Like those of many excellent cooks, her measurements are instinctive. Albert Torres, who easily finds superb ingredients in his own tropical stand at ESSEX STREET MARKET (page 16), can make 40 or 50 *Pasteles* in one hour, "But I must work all by myself without any interruptions," he said, and he gives the same advice to you. "And some cooks like to add pigeon peas, raisins, chick peas," he adds. "I don't." *Muchas gracias*, Señor Torres.

6 pounds lean pork from the thigh
2 tablespoons vegetable oil
1 onion, chopped
2 to 3 cloves garlic, chopped
1 whole bay leaf
Large pinch dried oregano
Pinch curry powder
Salt
Freshly ground pepper
2 to 2½ cups dry wine
15 pounds green bananas, peeled
2 to 3 pounds Yautia (tannions), peeled
3 to 4 pounds Calabaza pumpkin ("very yellow")
2 to 3 tablespoons Annatto oil or Achiotina (see note below)
1 cup pitted green olives (preferably pimiento-stuffed), sliced
   or chopped
Papel de Pasteles * (50 sheets) or aluminum foil and string

There are three stages: preparing meat, grating vegetables, stuffing and wrapping in *Papel de Pasteles* or aluminum foil.

TO PREPARE THE MEAT: dice meat into ½-inch cubes. Heat the vegetable oil and saute the onion and garlic until softened. Stir in the pork and saute until raw color disappears. Add the bay leaf, oregano, curry powder, and a light sprinkling of salt and pepper, and drizzle the wine over the meat. Cover and cook 1 hour until pork is tender, adding more wine if necessary. (This much may be done in advance.)

TO PREPARE THE VEGETABLES: grate the green bananas, *Yautia*, and *Calabaza* (a food processor is excellent for this, but the old-fashioned way is by hand). Combine throughly in a large bowl.

TO STUFF: Lay the *Papel de Pasteles* or foil flat; brush with *Annatto* oil or *Achiotina*. Scoop a large serving spoonful of the vegetables and drop into the center of the *Papel*. Slightly flatten

---

* Traditionally, *Pasteles* are encased and cooked in banana leaves, which impart a distinctive flavor. Aluminum foil, however, is increasingly preferred because it retains the heat after cooking until the unwrapping and eating begin and banana leaves are expensive. *Papel de Pasteles*, used by most Puerto Ricans, is available at Albert Torres's stall (page 17), and other tropical stalls.

with your palm and top with 2 to 3 pieces of cooked pork and olives. Stuff in the vegetables by folding over the meat and olives. Encase thoroughly into a small package: lift *Papel* edges lengthwise and fold all across one-half inch to seal. Fold *Papel* again so that the sealed edges are in the center of the stuffed vegetables, and gently flatten. Lift unfolded edges together and fold twice to make a package about 4 × 5 inches. Tie tightly with string. Continue until all *Pasteles* are stuffed and packaged. (These may be frozen at this point, wrapped in freezer wrap.)

TO COOK: place all *Pasteles* in a large pot and cover with salted water. Invert a plate over the *Pasteles*, cover pot, and bring to the boil gently. Simmer 1 to 1½ hours, depending on the size of the *Pasteles*. (If *Pasteles* are frozen, simmer 1½ to 2 hours.) SERVE warm.                                                    **Makes 45 to 50**

NOTE: To make *Annatto* oil, gently heat 1 teaspoon *Annatto* (also called *Achiote Annatto*) in ½ cup vegetable oil, until oil turns red; discard seeds. Cool and use as needed; it is prized for its color. *Achiotina* is a prepared oil, available at Puerto Rican and other Caribbean specialty shops including Albert Torres's stall in ESSEX STREET MARKET (page 16) and tropical stalls at LA MARQUETA (page 106).

### PATLIJAN KARNI YAREK
#### Armenian Stuffed Eggplant

Eggplant is a favorite of Middle Easterners and Orientals. For this Armenian recipe, which I've revised from one given me many years ago by a kind Armenian friend, it saves time to prepare the meat sauce a day in advance, if you can; or you can (frenetically) make the sauce as the eggplant bakes before stuffing.

*1 pound ground lamb or beef*
*2 onions, finely sliced*
*1 small green pepper, chopped (seeds discarded)*
*Salt*
*Freshly ground pepper*
*½ teaspoon ground allspice*
*1 clove garlic, minced or crushed*
*½ cup plum tomatoes with juice*
*3 to 4 sprigs parsley, chopped*
*1 large eggplant or 2 medium eggplants (1¼ to 1½ pounds)*
*4 tablespoons unsalted butter, melted*
*1 tablespoon tomato paste diluted in ½ cup water*
*1 fresh tomato or 2 canned plum tomatoes, sliced*

Heat a heavy frying pan and mash the meat into the pan, stirring and mashing until the color begins to change. Stir in the onions and green pepper and stir until well mixed. Sprinkle in a little salt, pepper, the allspice, garlic, the ½ cup plum tomatoes and juice, and half the parsley. Stir and cook 20 minutes. Cool. (This much may be done a day in advance.) When ready to cook eggplants, using a sharp knife, cut in half lengthwise, again in half and again to make 8 pieces (if using smaller eggplants, cut into fourths). Sprinkle lightly with salt and invert over a rack; let stand 40 to 50 minutes to eliminate bitter taste. Rinse and dry eggplants. Set in a baking dish and brush with the butter. Bake in hot oven (450°F) until light brown, about 10 minutes. Remove and cool slightly.

TO STUFF: Slash eggplant slices across the center to make a cavity for the filling. Divide the filling among the eggplant slices. Set on the baking pan, pour the diluted tomato paste into the pan and dot each eggplant section with sliced tomato rings. Bake in moderate oven (350°F) for 35 minutes.

SERVE hot garnished with the remaining parsley.          **Serves 4**

NOTE: Athina Tembelis of SMILING FRUIT (page 149) enjoys making a Hellenic favorite called *Papoutsakia* (Stuffed Eggplant "Booties") using baby eggplants. The eggplants are cut lengthwise and scooped out; the eggplant is chopped and sautéed with garlic and onions in olive oil, stuffed into the shells and topped with white sauce (see *Pastitsio*, page 290 for the method) and either baked or cooked on the top of the stove.

## HUNGARIAN STUFFED CABBAGE, MEATS, and SAUERKRAUT

Barbara Vajda, of TIBOR MEAT SPECIALTIES (page 98) offers this wholesome meal for anyone wanting to try a new Hungarian dish. "Better made one, two, three days before eating," she suggests.

*1 medium cabbage*
*1 pound lean ground pork*
*½ cup white long-grain rice*
*2 small onions, one grated and one sliced*
*Freshly ground pepper*
*Salt (optional)*
*2 pounds sauerkraut, washed and drained*
*1 pound fresh spareribs or other fresh pork*
*1 pound smoked knuckles or other smoked pork*
*2 to 3 bay leaves*
*4 to 5 peppercorns*
*2 tablespoons oil*
*1 tablespoon flour*
*Ground paprika*
*Sour cream*

To prepare cabbage for stuffing, wash and cut off core; separate leaves and blanch in boiling water for five minutes with the heat off. Drain thoroughly. In a bowl, combine ground pork, rice, the grated onion, a few grindings of pepper, and pinch of salt (you may not need the salt since sauerkraut and smoked meats are highly seasoned); knead thoroughly. Stuff by spooning a heaping tablespoon of the filling into a cabbage leaf and rolling up tightly; continue until all are stuffed and ready to cook. To layer: spread one-third of the sauerkraut in the bottom of the casserole and cover with the fresh pork. Spread another third of the sauerkraut, then the smoked pork; top with the remaining sauerkraut. Set all the stuffed cabbages on the sauerkraut. Sprinkle with the remaining onion, bay leaves, and 4 to 5 peppercorns. Add enough water to come halfway up the casserole; cover tightly. Simmer over low heat for 2½ hours without removing cover. Taste a cabbage for tenderness and continue cooking 15 or 25 minutes, if necessary. To thicken gravy, carefully pour remaining liquid into a bowl (this is done better by two people, one holding an inverted dish over the food to keep intact, the other tilting the casserole). In a small pan, heat the oil and stir in the flour. Stirring constantly, cook until golden but not brown and sprinkle in a generous amount of paprika; cook one minute. Stir in 1 cup of the liquid remaining with the sauerkraut in the casserole (or water) and simmer until thickened, then pour gravy over the food. Simmer 10 minutes, blending the flavors by shaking pan.

SERVE warm with sour cream in a separate bowl.    **Serves 4 to 6**

NOTE: SARMA, Stuffed Sour Cabbage Rolls with Smoked Spareribs, is a Yugoslavian favorite described by Natasha Grgas (pronounced Gur-gas), a Yugoslavian woman living in New York since 1971. She buys ingredients at MUNCAN FOOD CORP in Astoria (page 154). Yugoslavian paprika is sprinkled liberally between cabbage roll and sauerkraut layers in her version (and ground beef and ground pork are combined with rice for the filling in the rolls).

## MOMO
### Tibetan Steamed Beef Dumplings

Gentle and succulent are the *Momo*—dimpled 2-inch dumplings, Tibet's most popular dish—stuffed with tender, seasoned beef and curved into dainty "bonnet" shapes. My first taste of them at

TIBETAN KITCHEN (444 Third Avenue, Manhattan, 684-9209) captivated me into trying them at home. Pema (pronounced Pama) Thondon, a slender, Tibetan woman with black hair, explained that most of the Tibetan ingredients can be purchased at Chinese and Indian shops. *Toh Che Che!*

*½ pound lean ground beef*
*1 large clove garlic, minced*
*2 Gau Tsoi (Chinese chives) or shallots, finely minced*
*1 small leek, finely chopped (about 2 tablespoons)*
*1 inch fresh ginger, minced*
*Salt*
*40 Gyoza wrappers \**
*Oil for steamer*

In a bowl, knead the beef, garlic, *Gau Tsoi* or shallots, leek, ginger, and pinches of salt to make a smooth mixture that is highly aromatic. Marinate a few hours in the refrigerator.

TO STUFF: Divide the meat into 36 or 40 equal parts (depending on how large you like the dumplings). Roll each part into a ball between your palms, then into small ovals. Place each oval in the center of a *Gyoza* wrapper. Wet the edges with cold water and seal into a half moon. Tuck the edges under, bonnet-style.

TO STEAM: Oil the steamer (preferably bamboo) and set the *Momo* on the steamer *without* touching each other (this may be done in shifts). Steam 10 minutes.

SERVE warm with small saucers for dipping sauces. \* \* **Serves 5 to 6**

NOTE: *Momo* are also fabulous fried in hot oil (350°F), turned to brown on both sides and drained, served piping hot.

---

\* *Momo* wrappers are white and similer in size to *Gyoza* wrappers, available in Japanese and Korean shops. I have also used Chinese *Suey Koy* wrappers (which contain egg and are yellow and larger).
\* \* Japanese soy sauce and *Sephan* (Hot Pepper Sauce, page 187), are the traditional dipping sauces for *Momo.*

## VIETNAMESE BANH CUON
### Steamed Pork Rolls

Delicious for appetizers or a side dish to serve when you can buy the *Hofon* * wrapper (fresh, delicate Chinese rice wrapper used by Vietnamese in Chinatown) in the morning. Tasted in the SAIGON RESTAURANT (60 Mulberry St.) where the Vietnamese Dao family runs a friendly, flavorful center for Vietnamese food lovers. Special thanks to Wa Dao for her help. *Com Ung* (pronounced with nasal accent)!

½ *pound cooked ground pork or lean pork, minced*
4 *to 5 black mushrooms, soaked in warm water, drained and*
   *chopped (use liquid for a soup)*
1 *cup cooked rice*
1 *water chestnut, minced*
3 *scallions, sliced into very slender rings*
2 *tablespoons fresh coriander, minced*
*Pinch sugar*
*Salt*
*Freshly ground pepper*
1 Hofon *wrapper (about 25 inches in diameter)*

TO MAKE THE STUFFING: Combine the pork, mushrooms, rice, water chestnut, all but 1 tablespoon scallions and 1 teaspoon coriander, sugar, salt and pepper. Mix well.

TO STUFF: lay the *Hofon* skin on a cutting surface; cut into 5- by 5½-inch rectangles. Spoon ½ tablespoon filling into the middle of each rectangle and spread flat. Fold wrapper into thirds over the filling; turn and fold again in thirds to make 2- by 2½-inch rectangular rolls that are flat. Continue until all are stuffed. Keep covered until ready to serve. Place rolls seam sides down in steamer over boiling water, not touching the steamer. Steam 5 to 7 minutes until hot. Lift onto warm plates, serving four rolls in a row

* *Hofon* wrappers are available four doors from the SAIGON RESTAURANT; the shop has no English identification but can be recognized by the large cauldron opposite the door where the *Hofon* are stored in oil. The kind expert speaks no English, but is very helpful. Usually sold out in the afternoon. Cannot be stored long, even in plastic, except to cut up and simmer a minute or so in broth for a soup.

per person. Garnish with remaining scallions and coriander.
SERVE warm with *Nuoc Mam* sauce (page 188) poured onto the
side of the plate.                                    **Serves 4 to 6**

## GYOZA
### Japanese Spicy Pork Dumplings

Although available frozen, ready-to-cook, this recipe is delicious
to cook from scratch, and all you need are the ingredients and less
than an hour. Although they can be fried, I use the method suggested on the wrapper package—a form of braising, Japanese
style. First set them in hot sesame oil and then, after browning,
add water and steam. For a main dish, you can figure on 6 to 8 per
person. (By adding a rich broth, these make a terrific and filling
soup.) Ingredients are available in Japanese and Korean food
shops.

*½ pound lean ground pork*
*¼ cup Chinese cabbage, very finely minced, squeezed to*
   *eliminate liquid*
*1 small leek, very finely minced (about 4 tablespoons),*
   *squeezed to eliminate liquid*
*1 knob fresh ginger, minced (about 2 teaspoons)*
*3 large cloves garlic, minced*
*½ teaspoon sesame seeds, pounded (optional)*
*Pinch salt*
*Freshly ground pepper*
*1 to 2 tablespoons sesame chili oil (Chima Rayu)* *
*48 to 50* Gyoza No Kawa *wrappers (round noodle-like*
   *wrappers, usually available frozen, 30 per package)*

On a working board, mix the pork, well-squeezed cabbage and
leek, ginger, garlic, sesame seeds, if using, a little salt and pepper.
Knead thoroughly to make a very smooth paste. Divide the meat
mixture into 48 to 50 balls, about 1 teaspoon each. Wetting fingertips occasionally, roll into ovals.

---

* There are many kinds of sesame oil and there are also the sesame chili oils. The
latter, flavored with chili, add a decided *punch* to the dish that you'll enjoy. If you
don't have any, use plain sesame oil.

TO STUFF *Gyoza:* work with 2 or 3 wrappers at a time at first, keeping the remaining wrappers inside a plastic bag (to avoid drying). Half fill a cup with cold water and keep near you. Set a meat oval in the center of each wrapper. Wet all around the perimeter of the wrappers with the cold water. Bring ends up to form a half circle and squeeze to seal. Pinch about 3 pleats in the center top and gently press the *Gyoza* to make it stand on the base, with the pleated section up. Set on a plate and cover with plastic. Continue until all are wrapped.

TO COOK: heat the sesame oil on the bottom of a heavy skillet (just enough to coat the bottom of the skillet). Pleated side up, set *Gyoza* in the skillet. Lower heat and cover for 2 minutes to brown the *Gyoza.* Drizzle enough water in the skillet to cover bottom. Cover skillet and steam over low heat for 10 minutes until cooked and liquid has evaporated.

SERVE warm with pleated side up. Delicious with Japanese *Shoyu* (soy sauce). **Serves 6 to 8**

NOTE: If planning to freeze, steam 10 minutes; cool, and freeze. Brown in sesame chili oil and steam when ready to serve.

## CHA GIO
### Vietnamese Spring Rolls

Once tasted, *Cha Gio* are unforgettable and for me the first taste was in a Vietnamese Restaurant in San Francisco. Tried again in New York, I had fun making them at home. They are not difficult, but frying is tricky because the oil should not be too hot, just hot enough. This version, one of many, is shared by Meng Hua, a Chinese woman born in Vietnam who runs the SONICO TRADING CO., INC. in Chinatown (page 30). Unlike Chinese egg and spring rolls (which are stuffed with sautéed meat and other ingredients), *Cha Gio* are stuffed with *raw* pork or a mixture of pork and shellfish, then fried. Heat *does* permeate the delicate rice paper wrappers as it must before eating pork. *Cha Gio* are delicious served as appetizers or for a main course. Plan on 6 to 8 per person for starters.

¼ *pound (50-gram package) bean threads*
¼ *cup black fungus*
1 *pound ground lean pork or* ½ *pound ground pork and* ½
 *pound shrimp or crabmeat, finely chopped*
½ *onion, finely minced*
2 *to 3 scallions, finely minced*
1 *carrot, slivered into pieces about 1¼ inches long*
2 *eggs, lightly beaten with a fork*
*Salt*
*White pepper*
*Pinch sugar*
1 *pound rice-paper wrappers (sometimes called rice noodle)* \*
2 *to 3 tablespoons flat beer or 1 teaspoon brown sugar*
 *dissolved in* ½ *cup water*
*Lettuce or delicate cabbage leaves to wrap each roll*
*Fresh mint or coriander, chopped for garnish*
*Nuoc Mam Sauce (page 188), poured into individual saucers*
 *for each guest for dipping*

Gather bean threads into a bowl (clumsy when stiff); cover with water and soak until softened, about 15 minutes. Drain and discard water; chop (about 2 cups). In a small bowl, cover the black fungus with warm water and soak 10 minutes (it will swell to about 1 cup); chop finely. Combine the bean threads, fungus, pork, shrimp, or crabmeat, if using, onion, scallions, carrot, eggs, salt, pepper, and sugar. Knead thoroughly. Prepare the rice-paper wrappers: If using whole wrappers, cut in half with scissors; trim edges if rough. Work with 3 or 4 at a time. Dip your fingertips in the beer or sugar-water very lightly and slightly dampen the wrappers (don't drown them) to provide a rich color when fried. Allow wrappers to soften, about 5 minutes. Stack 2 quarters or fold a half wrapper in half for each roll. Spread 1 teaspoon filling along the rounded side of the rice-paper wrapper, about ½ inch from the

* Rice-paper wrappers (white and brittle-textured) are available in most Thai and Chinese shops carrying Vietnamese ingredients and last indefinitely in a dry cupboard. You can buy them in rounds, halves, or quarter circles. Unless you need huge quantities, it is simpler to buy halves or quarters. You can make 16 rolls (16 halves or 32 quarters) with ¼ pound rice paper wrappers.

edge. Fold each pointed side over the filling. Roll up tightly to make 3½- to 4-inch rolls. Set seam side down and continue until all rolls are filled (there may be rice-paper wrappers left over; store for another time).

TO FRY: heat oil in wok, preferably, or deep fryer to height of 1½ to 2 inches to 350°F (the temperature needs to be regulated—not too hot or the wrappers will brown before the filling is cooked). Fry the first roll to test the temperature, turning with tongs to brown evenly. Drain on rack or paper towels. Combine until all are fried and keep warm in heated oven.

SERVE hot, half wrapped in lettuce or cabbage leaf, sprinkled with mint or coriander. Dip in sauce as you eat.

**Makes about 50 Cha Gio**

## CHINESE EGG ROLLS

Superb served immediately after frying. Reheated, frozen, and day-old are never the same. If you cannot use all, better to freeze them *unfried*, thaw out partially, and fry just before serving.

½ pound ground beef or pork (or lean meat sliced into fine,
  ½-inch slices)
2 tablespoons soy sauce (more if you like)
1 teaspoon sesame oil (optional)
3 to 4 grindings freshly ground pepper
1 tablespoon fresh ginger root, minced
Peanut or vegetable oil
1 tablespoon cornstarch
½ pound shrimp, cleaned and minced
½ cup scallions or Chinese chives, minced
2 eggs, lightly beaten
1 cup Chinese white cabbage or flowering white cabbage
  (Tsoi Sum) or Chinese kale (Kai Lan Tsoi), shredded
1 cup celery, thinly sliced
1 cup fresh mung bean sprouts
½ cup onion, minced

½ cup dried Chinese mushrooms, soaked and finely sliced, or
   fresh mushrooms
1 tablespoon fresh coriander, chopped
24 egg roll wrappers
Plum sauce (optional)
Soy sauce

In small bowl, combine the beef or pork, soy sauce, sesame oil, if using, pepper, and ginger root. Marinate 30 minutes, turning once or twice. Heat 2 tablespoons oil in the wok and plop in the marinated meat, sprinkle with 2 teaspoons of the cornstarch, and stir-fry over high heat until cooked, about 5 minutes. Scrape into a strainer set over a bowl. Add 1 tablespoon oil to the wok and drop in the shrimp, remaining teaspoon cornstarch, and scallions or chives; stir-fry until shrimp turns pink. Stirring constantly, add the eggs and cook quickly until scrambled with the shrimp. Add the meat mixture and stir to mix for 1 minute; scrape shrimp and meat mixture into the strainer over the bowl. Now stir-fry the vegetables one at a time, pushing to the side as you stir-fry: heat 1 to 2 tablespoons oil in the wok and toss in the cabbage, celery, bean sprouts, onion, mushrooms, and coriander, and stir-fry for 5 minutes mixing together. Add to the meat and shrimp and mix thoroughly; drain (save drippings for a soup; you don't want liquids in the egg rolls). Taste the filling and season with more soy sauce and pepper if you like.

TO STUFF: spread a wrapper with a point near you. Drop a tablespoonful of the filling near the edge. Turn point back over the filling; turn 2 side points inward toward the filling, then roll back snugly until the last point remains flat. Dampen inside edges with cold water or beaten egg and roll up tightly. Cover with wrap or dampened towel. Continue stuffing egg rolls.

TO FRY: add 3 cups oil to the clean wok and heat to 375°F. Slip 3 or 4 rolls into the hot oil and turn with tongs. Keep oil at a steady temperature and fry about 4 minutes until golden and crisp. Remove to platter and keep warm in oven; continue until all are fried.

SERVE plain or with plum sauce and pass the soy sauce.

**Makes 24 rolls**

# DESSERTS

*For sweetness, honey; for love, a wife.*

BENGALI PROVERB

## ONTBIJTKOED
### Dutch Breakfast Cake

Ludi Kerman, a New York resident born in Breda, the Nether-
lands, reveals that this type of honey cake is also called *Groninger
Koek* and is popular at breakfast on a buttered slice of bread or for
a mid-morning snack with coffee, without the bread and butter.
Dry-textured like European cakes, the flavor is gentle, a cake
you'll like to keep on hand for snacks.

*1 egg*
*½ cup dark brown sugar, packed*
*Pinch of salt*
*½ cup honey*
*3 tablespoons dark molasses*
*¾ teaspoon baking soda*
*½ teaspoon baking powder*
*⅓ teaspoon each of ground pepper, allspice, nutmeg, and*
  *cinnamon*
*¼ teaspoon ground ginger*
*2 tablespoons butter, melted*
*1½ cups flour, sifted*

In a large bowl, beat the egg until lemon-colored; gradually add
the sugar, salt, honey, molasses, baking soda, and baking powder,
spices, and butter. Continue beating on low speed and add the
flour, alternating with ⅓ cup cold water to make a smooth batter.
Turn into a buttered 7-inch loaf pan. Bake in moderate oven
(350°F) about 30 minutes or until an inserted toothpick comes out
clean. Cool in pan for 5 minutes before removing cake from pan
onto a rack.                                              **Serves 8**

NOTE: If you adore the *zwiebach* (German), *biscotti* (Italian), and
*koulourakia* (Greek) family of "dunkers," slice this cake, toast,
and let sit to dry in the oven with heat turned off until really
crisp. Delicious!

## RICOTTA CAKE

Josephine (Jo) Longarino, of CALANDRA CHEESE SHOP (page 116) shares her favorite (and quick) Ricotta Cake—with a warning about the baking: "Keep the door closed; look at it after one hour," then follow directions below.

*3 pounds fresh ricotta*
*1 cup sugar*
*8 eggs, lightly beaten*
*3 tablespoons flour*
*2 teaspoons vanilla*
*½ cup orange marmalade*

In bowl of electric mixer, combine all the ingredients and beat until "nice and smooth." Turn into buttered spring pan. Bake 60 minutes in 350°F oven without opening the door. Open door to look at the cake. Turn off the heat. Allow cake to rest in the oven another hour. Cool. Remove from pan.          **Serves 8 to 10**

## VIENNESE APPLE-SPICE SQUARES

Inspired by a delicious treat at the Ninth Avenue Festival. Quick and not too sweet. Make the applesauce a day in advance.

*¼ cup butter or margarine (more for pan)*
*⅔ cup sugar (more for sprinkling)*
*2 cups fine bread crumbs*
*2 teaspoons ground cinnamon (more for sprinkling)*
*½ teaspoon ground cloves*
*1 teaspoon grated lemon rind*
*3½ cups applesauce (recipe below)*
*1 cup raisins soaked in 2 tablespoons brandy or rum for 5*
   *minutes*
*1½ cups cooked chestnuts,\* chopped, or substitute other nuts*
   *for more texture*

Melt butter in large saucepan and stir in sugar, bread crumbs, cinnamon, cloves, and lemon rind. In another small bowl, combine the applesauce and raisins.

TO ASSEMBLE: Butter an 8-inch square pan and spread ⅓ of the butter-sugar-crumb mixture on the bottom. Spread with ½ the applesauce and raisins, and top with half the nuts. Repeat and top with the remaining ⅓ crumb mixture. Bake in 350°F oven for 30 minutes or until bubbly.

SERVE warm or cold.　　　**Cut into 9 large or 12 smaller squares**

---

\* If lucky, there should be about 32 large chestnuts per pound and they should yield enough for this recipe; if unlucky and many turn out moldy when cut open, let the shopowner know! Dried, peeled chestnuts, available at Italian and some Chinese groceries, are very handy; there are about 32 in ¼ pound or ¾ cup, unsoaked. Soak in advance overnight; half pound should be enough for this recipe. TO COOK *fresh* CHESTNUTS: slash across either end, cover with cold water, and boil 20 minutes. Peel; mash with potato masher or fork.

## BLENDED APPLESAUCE MEDLEY

Wash 10 apples of different varieties (tart, sweet, etc.). Drop apples into boiling water to cover until soft, about 7 minutes. Drain and quickly douse them with cold water. Quarter apples and push through food mill (discard peels and cores inside the mill). Add a generous pinch of ground cinnamon; sweeten to your own taste, if necessary. Thickens the second day.　　　**About 3½ cups**

## SWEET POTATO PIE, SOUL STYLE

Sweet potato and yam desserts are so popular, each version tastes better than the next. This pie may also be made without the crust (with less calories), carefully cut into wedges or scooped with a dessert spoon.

> Pastry dough (recipe below)
> 2 pounds sweet potatoes or yams, cooked in jackets
> ¾ to 1 cup brown sugar
> 2 eggs, separated, at room temperature
> 4 to 6 tablespoons butter
> Pinch salt
> ½ cup milk
> Spices: ½ teaspoon nutmeg or mace, ¼ teaspoon cloves,
>     1 teaspoon cinnamon (all ground or grated)
> 2 tablespoons sugar

When pastry is made, cook the potatoes. Cool and peel them when fork tender and mash or put through food mill. In a bowl, mix the sieved potatoes with brown sugar, egg yolks, butter, salt, and milk; beat in the spices and taste to adjust spices. In another bowl, beat the egg whites with the 2 tablespoons sugar until they form peaks; fold into the sweet potato mixture. Turn filling into the unbaked pie shell. Bake 30 to 40 minutes in 350°F oven until pastry is tender and pie has set. Cool.          **Serves 6 to 8**

NOTE: Make pumpkin or calabaza pie using pumpkin instead of sweet potatoes.

## PASTRY FOR 8-INCH PIE

> 1 cup plus 2 tablespoons flour
> Pinch salt
> 8 tablespoons vegetable shortening or butter
> 2 tablespoons ice water

In a bowl combine the flour and salt. Using pastry blender or 2 forks, cut in the shortening or butter until mixture resembles cornmeal. Quickly stir in the water with a fork; gather dough into a bowl and refrigerate one hour. Roll out on a floured board and press into the pie plate, fluting around the edges with fingertips, or press with tines of the fork. Cover until ready to fill.

## SARAïLI
### Rolled Nut and Filo Pastry, Romanian Style

Gina Hilhoveanu, a helper at SARKIS APROZAR (page 156), enjoys making a pastry popular in her native village of Ployest, Romania. *Saraïli* is known as *Saragli* in Macedonia and Balkan countries, and is rolled into coils and baked, not cut as in the method below.

2⅓ cups sugar
2 tablespoons rum
1 pound filo pastry leaves
¾ pound butter, melted and warm
1 pound walnuts, finely ground

PREPARE THE SYRUP FIRST: combine 2 cups of the sugar with 3 cups water in a pan and bring to the boil, stirring constantly. Boil 10 minutes. Stir in the rum. Cool. Reserve until pastry is baked. In a small bowl, mix the walnuts and remaining ⅓ cup sugar.

TO ROLL THE PASTRY: unwrap the filo and keep covered until ready to use. On a working surface, lay a filo leaf and brush with warm butter. Continue to make a stack of 6 or 7 buttered filo leaves. Sprinkle evenly with the nut mixture. Keeping long end near you, roll up the pastry away from you into a tight roll. Using a sharp knife, cut across diagonally to make ¾-inch wide slices. Set *Saraïli* half an inch apart, cut side down, on a baking sheet. Cover with moistened towel or aluminum wrap to keep from drying. Continue buttering filo, rolling, sprinkling nuts, and cutting until all are rolled and cut. Bake in moderate oven (350°F) for 15 to 18 minutes until golden. Remove from oven and spoon cool syrup on hot pastries. Cool on rack. **Makes 30 to 35 pastries**

## KRUMKAKE
### Norwegian Holiday Crispy "Flutes"

If you're lucky enough to have a *Krumkake* decorative iron (available at MIKE'S DELICATESSENs (page 130) and FREDER-ICKSEN & JOHANNESEN (page 130), on which to griddle these crispy delicacies (or, like me, are lucky enough to have a friend who has one you can borrow), try them. Making them is fun when you are preparing for a holiday with your family. Joyce Kildahl is the expert who taught me how (her other recipe, page 268).

> *1 cup (½ pound) unsalted butter, preferably at room*
> *temperature*
> *1 cup sugar*
> *3 eggs, lightly beaten*
> *6 tablespoons light cream*
> *2 cups all purpose flour*
> *Brown paper*

Using electric beater or by hand, beat the butter until creamy. Gradually add the sugar, eggs, cream, and flour to make a thick batter-dough that stands in soft peaks that flop over (you can adjust the thickness by adding more cream and you don't want it too watery or it will run out of the iron. Meanwhile, heat the *Krumkake* iron* and when hot, place a tablespoon of the dough (not too heaping) in the center toward the hinge. Close the iron and quickly rotate it to the other side; let *Krumkake* bake about a minute (try not to peek until the minute passes by; you'll soon develop a feel for timing). Spread brown paper flat on a table near the iron. When lightly golden, open iron, remove *Krumkake* and set on the brown paper. Quickly but deftly roll up *Krumkake* while hot to make a "flute" roll.** Let cool on the brown paper; it will be delightfully crisp. Continue having fun and avoid eating them all as you grill them! Store in covered containers when completely cool.          **Makes 28 to 30 5-inch "flute" rolls**

* Joyce highly recommends a gas burner to avoid the drippings burning in the electric coils.
** While still hot, *Krumkake* may be shaped into cones like the Scandinavian specialty *Fyllda Strutar* which, when cool, are filled with whipped cream and

## DRIE-IN-DE-PAN
### Three-in-the-Pan Dutch Pancakes

Early Dutch settlers brought to New York their love of pancakes, doughnuts, and cake *(Koek,* pronounced cook—the word from which cookie is probably derived). Many ethnic groups in addition to the Dutch love pancakes. Here is a contemporary version:

*1 egg*
*1 cup milk, lukewarm*
*2 cups flour*
*½ teaspoon salt*
*½ teaspoon baking powder*
*1½ cups currants, raisins, candied fruit, chopped*
*4 tablespoons butter, melted, more for greasing the griddle*
*Brown sugar, maple syrup, honey, or molasses topping*

To make a batter, beat the egg with the milk. Mix the flour, salt, and baking powder and stir into the batter quickly until smooth. Stir in the dried and candied fruits. Heat a large griddle and spread with 1 tablespoon butter. Spoon one tablespoon batter onto the griddle and repeat twice to grill three pancakes at once. Turn to brown on both sides. Top with melted butter and your favorite sweetener. Continue until all pancakes are made.
SERVE hot. **Serves 4 to 5**

## PALACHINTA
### Hungarian Stuffed Crêpes

Bobby Roth shares her favorite dessert, learned at her mother's knee, who learned it from *her* mother, founder of LEKVAR BY THE BARREL (H. ROTH & SON) (page 100). Stuffings can be made from scratch (like this version) or from prepared mixes. *Gassanam Saypan!*

---

berries before serving (youngsters are good at shaping the warm dough); other people have been known to shape *Krumkake* around a paper cup to make "cups." Try whichever you like.

1 cup flour
1 egg, lightly beaten
1¼ to 1½ cups milk
1 spritz seltzer (soda water)
½ cup poppy seeds, ground
½ cup sugar
½ cup golden raisins
Vegetable oil or butter to fry crêpes
Melted chocolate or confectioner's sugar and ground walnuts
  for garnish

In a bowl, stir the flour, egg, ¼ cup milk, and seltzer to make a thin batter. Cover bowl and prepare the filling. In small saucepan, combine the ground poppy seeds, sugar, raisins, and only enough milk to bind the mixture. Cook over low heat until sugar dissolves. Cool.

TO MAKE THE *Palachinta:* heat oil or butter in a griddle or crêpe pan; pour in enough batter to make an 8-inch crêpe. Turn to cook on other side. Keep warm until all *Palachinta* are grilled.

TO STUFF: spoon 1 good teaspoonful stuffing on center of each crêpe, roll up, and garnish with chocolate or the more traditional confectioner's sugar and walnuts. **Serves 4**

## PISANG GORENG
### Indonesian Batter-Fried Yellow Plantains

Thanks to Hari Martini Soedarmasto for this fun recipe! *Trimakasi!*

3 cups flour
Pinch salt
1 egg, lightly beaten
3 to 4 yellow plantains
Oil for frying
Whipped cream (optional)

TO MAKE THE BATTER: combine the flour and salt in a bowl. Make a well in the center and add the egg and ⅔ to ¾ cup water, or enough to make a thick batter. Peel the plantains and if very large, cut across into flour; cut smaller ones into three pieces; cut again lengthwise.

TO FRY: heat the oil in deep fryer to 375°F. Using tongs, dip each plantain in the batter and drop into the oil; fry on both sides, turning to make a flat fritter.

SERVE hot with or without whipped cream.

NOTE: Thai cooks who have adapted this recipe using bananas, drizzle honey on the hot banana balls.

## PLANTAIN DESSERT

Bake or boil the plantains as described for Green Bananas on page 209, or try this for a simple tasty dessert enjoyed by Jamaicans and other Caribbean people.

*2 plantains*
*2 to 3 tablespoons butter or margarine*
*Sugar for sprinkling*
*Ground cinnamon*
*Grated nutmeg*

Peel, slice thinly, and fry the plantains in butter or margarine. Place fried plantains on a warm platter. Sprinkle with sugar, cinnamon, and nutmeg.

SERVE warm.                                          **Serves 2 to 4**

## JAMAICAN STUFFED BANANA-COCONUT PUFFS

Great to make with guests helping and watching and waiting. . . .

*1 ripe banana, peeled and mashed*
*1 cup fresh coconut, shredded*
*1½ cups flour, more if necessary*
*¼ teaspoon baking powder*
*Pinch salt*
*3 tablespoons butter or margarine*
*⅔ to ¾ cups milk*
*Vegetable oil for frying*

Mix the banana and coconut in a small bowl. In a larger bowl, combine the flour, baking powder, and salt. Using pastry blender or two forks, cut the butter or margarine into the flour mixture until it resembles cornmeal. Make a well in the center and add ⅔ cup milk, stirring to make a dough that can be formed into balls in your fingers, adding more milk or flour if necessary. Pick off dough pieces, roll in palms to make balls larger than walnuts. Push a hole into each ball with your thumb; stuff the banana-coconut mixture into the hole and cover the hole with dough. Continue until all are stuffed. In a deep fryer or wok, heat 3 to 4 inches of oil to 375°F; fry 4 to 5 balls at a time.
SERVE hot or cold, better hot.                    **Serves 2 to 3**

## ANOUSABOUR
### Armenian New Year Wheat-Fruit Dessert

Middle Eastern people enjoy the intriguing and chewy mix of whole wheat grains and dried fruits and nuts. Very similar are Jewish *Assoureh* and the Hellenes' *Kolyva* (which are made as a memorial on All Souls Day and for individual memorial services). *Anousabour* is as tasty and nutritious as a dessert can be. (Begin soaking the evening before.) *Happy New Year!*

*1 cup whole wheat kernels, preferably peeled*
*¾ to 1 cup dried apricots, quartered*
*¼ cup honey*
*¾ cup sugar, more or less to your taste*
*1 cup golden raisins or currants*
*1½ cups walnuts, filberts, pistachios, almonds\**
*½ cup pomegranate seeds (optional)*
*Ground cinnamon for sprinkling*

Wash whole wheat kernels in a soup pot (they triple in volume during cooking), cover with cold water; bring water to the boil, turn off heat, cover, and soak kernels overnight. Next day, add more water \*\* and boil the kernels until almost tender—a short time for the peeled and about 1½ hours for unpeeled—stirring frequently and adding water to avoid sticking and burning. When kernels are almost done, stir in the apricots and honey, enough sugar to sweeten (not too much because the raisins will also sweeten the dessert). Continue simmering, so that the liquid remaining will be absorbed to a thick, non-watery texture. Stir in the raisins (save a few tablespoons for garnish) and cook another 5 minutes until they swell up. Add nuts but save some for garnish. Stir in the pomegranate seeds, if you have some. Turn off the heat and turn *Anousabour* into a serving bowl. Sprinkle with cinnamon. Mound the dessert and decorate the top in a raisin-and-nut flower, star, cross, or your own design. Cool.

KEEP refrigerated and serve within 2 days. **Serves 6 to 8**

---

\* Nuts may be toasted in slow oven for 10 minutes, shaking frequently; cool.
\*\* Wheat can be cooked in a very large amount of water and drained, then sweetened and joined by the nuts and fruits; this method needs more watching to be sure the water is totally absorbed—challenging but worth it!

## PLUM PUDDING, OLD ENGLISH STYLE

If it's worth making an old English dessert that the settlers brought to New York, it's worth making it the old-fashioned way even if it takes days to marinate and hours to steam!* And if youngsters ask, "Where are the plums?" just tell them the whole pudding is a delicious plum.

> 10 cups pitted dried prunes, dates, raisins, and currants,
>     mixed and washed
> ¾ cup fine-flavored brandy (more for serving time)
> 1½ teaspoons ground cinnamon
> 1 teaspoon ground mace
> 1½ teaspoons grated nutmeg
> ½ teaspoon ground cloves
> 1 teaspoon ground allspice
> 2 cups sugar
> 1½ pounds beef suet, ground in meat grinder or minced finely
> 1 cup candied orange peel
> ½ cup candied lemon peel
> ½ cup citron
> 1 cup flour or finely ground bread crumbs
> 6 eggs, lightly beaten
> Whipped cream or vanilla ice cream (optional)

In a large pan combine the dried fruits with 1 cup water. Cover and simmer 15 minutes; cool in a bowl. Stir in the brandy, cover, and let marinate one day. Stir in the spices and marinate one more day. When ready to cook, stir in the sugar using a wooden spoon, drain out the excess liquid from the fruits**, then add the suet and stir well. Chop the candied orange and lemon peels and citron and stir them in with the flour or bread crumbs and eggs. Turn into a buttered glazed earthenware pudding bowl. Cover tightly (aluminum foil will do). Place bowl in a larger pan or bain-marie and fill up to the rim with boiling water. Steam for six hours, adding boiling water when needed. Unmold.

* Try to use an English plum pudding bowl of glazed earthenware.
** Save liquid for the pudding, if too thick; or save for mulled wine (1 tablespoon per wine glass heated just to boiling point).

WHEN ready to serve, you may like to drizzle with more brandy and ignite when serving. Serve when flames subside plain or with whipped or ice cream. **Serves 10 to 12**

## ASIAN-INDIAN RICE PUDDING

A universal dessertlike rice pudding takes on a new life with the addition of a characteristic ethnic ingredient: for Hellenes it may be vanilla and cinnamon; for Puerto Ricans and other Caribbean people, a showering of fresh grated coconut; for Asian-Indians, it may be rose water (as it is for Middle Easterners) or the following delicate flavor of cashews and cardamom.

*8 cups milk*
*1 cup plus 1 tablespoon white long-grain rice*
*⅔ cup sugar*
*½ teaspoon salt*
*2 eggs*
*4 tablespoons cardamom seeds, pounded*
*1 tablespoon butter*
*¾ cup white raisins or currants*

In a large pan combine milk, rice, sugar, and salt. Cook over medium heat until sugar is dissolved. When milk begins to boil, lower heat to minimum and continue simmering 30 minutes until almost thickened. Remove from heat. In a small bowl, slightly beat the eggs with a fork and add one tablespoon hot rice pudding. Continue adding rice pudding and beating the eggs until about 1½ cups have been added. Then stir the egg-rice mixture into the remaining rice pudding. Add the cardamom and taste for flavorings. Grease a large baking dish with the butter. Turn the pudding into the dish and top with raisins. Bake in moderate oven for 15 minutes until thickened. Remove from oven.
SERVE warm or cold. **Serves 6 to 8**

NOTE: Fabulous rice puddings are so universally popular, I can't resist including Martha Cordero's (a Puerto Rican friend) identical rice pudding but with a large handful of freshly grated coconut with the raisins instead of cardamom.

## LONG GREEN SQUASH DESSERT

An unusual dessert from an Asian-Indian woman shopping in a specialty market. The proportion of milk to long green squash can be adjusted after scraping and measuring the squash (which will release liquid). For every 2 cups squash, 1 part milk or cream.

*1 long green squash, lightly scraped and grated*
*1 to 1¼ cups milk, half and half, or cream*
*Sugar or honey*
*Ground cinnamon*
*Ground cloves*

In a heavy-bottomed pan, bring the milk to a boil and cook, stirring until some liquid evaporates, about 10 minutes. Stir in the squash and cook until tender, about 20 minutes, adding more milk, if needed. Sweeten to your taste and turn into a dessert bowl. Sprinkle with cinnamon and cloves. Cool. Chill. SERVE cold. **Serves 4**

# FRESH FRUITS, PRESERVES, & CANDIES

*Eating pears also cleans one's teeth.*
KOREAN PROVERB

## GUATEMALAN FRUIT PARFAIT

Inspired by the May Ninth Avenue Festival Guatemala stand. Great in summer. For a simpler array try watermelon, orange, and apple served in "old-fashioned" or other deep glasses.

*½ watermelon, pitted and cut up*
*1 fresh pineapple, peeled and diced*
*3 to 4 oranges, segmented*
*1 honeydew melon, pitted and diced*
*2 to 3 apples, cored and sliced with skin on*
*1 bunch grapes*

Prepare fruits with variety of chunks, dice, and half moon, etc., and arrange in tall glasses (parfait or sundae glasses are perfect). Top with a grape or two.                    **Serves 7 to 8**


## BOLIVIAN FRUIT SALAD

Perfect to climax a simple casserole or soup dinner or supper: all you need is the right season to find all the ingredients (summer and early fall). Serve just before Bolivian coffee.

*1 mango, peeled and diced*
*1 papaya, peeled and diced*
*1 banana, peeled and sliced into rounds*
*1 unpeeled apple, cored, diced*
*Juice of half lemon or lime*
*Sugar to taste (optional)*

In a bowl, combine the mango, papaya, banana, and apple. Drizzle with lemon or lime juice and a little sugar, if you like.
SERVE cold.                    **Serves 4**

## NEW YORK FRUIT RAINBOW
### Fruit Salad

Contrasting in colors and fruit flavors, this medley was inspired by the ready-mixed fruit cups available in plastic containers in many Korean fruit shops of various New York neighborhoods. Slender fruit half moons, eighths, and whole circles echo the graceful curves of cup and saucer (with a fresh leaf between if you have any).

*3 navel oranges, peeled and sliced across into circles*
*2 kiwi fruits, peeled and sliced into rings*
*1 cup strawberries, washed, hulled and sliced across*
*1 cup seedless grapes or mixed grapes, picked off the stems*
*1 cup fresh cherries*
*1 lime sliced thinly into rings with skin on*
*2 sprigs fresh parsley (optional)*

If large, cut oranges into halves or quarters and combine all fruit in bowls without mashing fruit. Arrange in crystal cups or wine glasses when ready to serve with an orange section, kiwi slice, strawberry, and grapes on top for maximum contrast. Top off with a parsley tuft, if you wish. **Serves 4 to 5**

NOTE: In New York, the sky's the limit. Choose melons and tropical fruits, stir in dried fruits, diced pears, apples with skins on to perfect your own rainbow.

## GUAVA

Yellowish and pear-shaped, serve raw or delicious as a jelly (available in 8-ounce portions in tropical fruit stalls) with white cheese—*Queso Blanca*. Seedless varieties are preferred eaten raw: peel and slice across. Seeded types are cut lengthwise and seeds scooped out and discarded before serving. Guava, raw with pinkish or yellow flesh, can be scooped out, mixed with sugar and cream, and piled back into the skin "cups." Or scoop out the guava, and drizzle over it some dessert wine, sugar, and spice and refill.

TO MAKE A SWEETER DESSERT: boil a thin syrup of 1 cup water and ½ cup sugar and poach the guava slices 10 minutes; cool and chill before serving. Guava makes a nice dessert sauce diluted with orange and lemon juice and sugar; it can be mixed with other fruits, coconut, and nuts, and made into custard or chutney.

## LICHI

Native of China, the *Lichi (Litchi, Lychee)* is in season from late June until August and its popularity is matched by its superb flavor. The Chinese mainland variety is the most delicious I ever tasted: very thin outer skin of raspberry red, easily peeled to reveal white juicy fruit that tastes both spicy and peppery. The dark seed is no larger than a child's tooth. A bowlful after dinner, to be peeled and eaten, is stimulating and refreshing.

Our Florida *Lichi,* available in Chinatown in early summer, is more like the Taiwanese variety with a translucent flesh and very smooth-textured, but with a much larger seed. The Singapore variety, with curved spiky skin and large seed, is no flavor match.

*Lichi,* often referred to as a nut, is the fruit of an evergreen and can always be found in cans, in Oriental shops. But after tasting the fresh fruit, like the mango, the canned version will not be as satisfying, but is refreshing, chilled, nevertheless.

## MANGO

A mango convert (one who tasted the fruit only in adult life and began a love affair) becomes a fanatic to make up for lost years. The mango lover haunts markets in Chinatown and Spanish Harlem, Ninth Avenue, and fruit stalls East Side and West Side to taste more. Try them all—Puerto Rican (small, about lemon size); Haitian (medium size, flattish, and pear-shaped—usually the preferred choice in New York); Mexican (medium avocado size, sweet when ripe). In the Philippines, the small, orange-fleshed *Pico* and larger yellow *Kalabau* variety are both glorious, unforgettable. What's more, mango is low in calories (66 calories per 100 grams), high in vitamin A and potassium, and a good source of vitamin C.

TO SERVE: To save the "cup" skins, test your skill (skin "cups" can be frozen and will remain flexible). Use a sharp knife and cut across the longest side of the mango a little less than halfway (to avoid cutting into the large pit); repeat on the other side—you will have two rounds and the large pit. Insert a dull knife between skin and flesh all around the curved side and gently pry up the flesh (this will keep mango intact to cut thin slices); or scoop into balls. Mango, served in the "cups" or combined with other fruit, climaxes a perfect meal. As an appetizer, over prawns, mango slices are an exceptional dish. As a dessert, the large pit and all adhering flesh is served pierced with a serrated knife (for easy handling). But try to save it for yourself to enjoy in private and suck on it until every drop is savored. And I hope it's juicy! *Dum Spiro, Spero.*

## FRESH PINEAPPLE SNACK, PHILIPPINE STYLE

Graceful and artistic, and much easier to do after you've seen the pineapple peeled and pruned. So visit the Ninth Avenue Festival (in May), if you haven't already, where this is always a treat on a stick.

*1 ripe, flavorful pineapple with fine aroma, washed and dried*

Using very sharp knife, cut off pineapple top; peel the pineapple to reveal the yellow flesh and remaining brown spots of the scaly skin. The idea is to remove these spots diagonally to make a graceful curving design around the pineapple.

TO CREATE SPIRALS: beginning at the top, cut a shallow groove diagonally to the *left* of the brown spot where you begin and continue moving the knife down diagonally along the brown spots to the bottom; return to the top at the *right* of the brown spots and cut a shallow groove that will remove the brown spot and continue all the way to the bottom; discard or save for a beverage. Continue cutting diagonally until pineapple is all yellow and the grooves curve all around the pineapple.

TO CUT THE SNACKS: stand pineapple on either end and cut in half, cut again and again to make eighths. Cut away the tough center core, pierce each wedge with a cane skewer.

LOOK at the graceful cutting . . . then eat.               **Serves 8**


## QUENNEPAS

At the Haitian stand in LA MARQUETA (page 106), young Dennis, nephew of the stand keeper, plucked a *Quennepa*—fruit that resembles green lollipops on a branch—handed it to me and said, "Taste!" Peeling off the greenish skin, tougher than a tangerine's, I marveled at the orange, pulpy flesh and its taste—like a persimmon, very juicy, non-acidic. *Quennepas* glorify any fruit bowl. To serve: wash and dry; pick off the branches and dot among other fruits in the bowl, or display with the branches. Peel just before serving. Available in fall and winter in tropical markets.


## PAN DAN
### Asian-Indian Spice and Fruit Offering

Asian-Indians have a delightful after-dinner habit and beautiful containers called *Pan Dan* with compartments for aniseed, rock sugar candy, betel nuts, coriander seeds, freshly grated coconut, whole cloves, and other spices and fruits. Often these spices are served wrapped in a betel leaf and sealed with a whole clove. Guests chew on these spices and relax after a long meal. You may enjoy improvising with small oriental teacups full of various nuts, spices, and fruits to pass around your table on a tray.

## DRIED FRUITS and NUTS

Many ethnic groups enjoy dried fruits, toasted chick peas, and nuts after dinner. When conviviality is high and the party does not want to break up, bring out any of the following in small cups or dishes on an attractive tray for nibbling fun:

*Dried pineapple, papaya, apricots, peaches, prunes, raisins, currants, apples, figs, dates, cherries*
*Walnuts, pistachios, almonds, hazelnuts, pecans, macadamia nuts*
*Toasted chick peas (salted and unsalted versions available in Greek, Italian, and Middle Eastern shops)*

## PALUDEH
### Persian "Water Ice" Fruit

Delightful and refreshing, save this one for summer and use your old-fashioned ice shaver if you have one or your trusty blender to crush the ice cubes.

*1 apple or pear*
*1 orange or peach*
*1 cup grapes or melon*
*2 cups shaved or crushed ice*
*4 tablespoons fruit syrup (recipe below)*

Peel and sliver or grate the apple or pear, orange or peach, and sliver the grapes or melon. Mix them together, then divide them into two deep wine goblets or dessert dishes (preferably glass). Scoop ice into a custard cup or small wine glass and invert over the fruit. Spoon syrup over the ice.

SERVE immediately                                                    **Serves 2**

## FRUIT SYRUP

Fruit syrups are popular among many ethnic groups and unusual berries, sour cherries, raspberry, or pomegranate are nice to keep on hand.

FOR A QUICK SYRUP: combine ⅓ cup honey or ½ cup sugar with ½ cup water and 1 cup semi-sweet wine. You could use 1½ cups semi-sweet wine rather than the water for a richer syrup. Stir in 2 cups fruit juice (orange, grape, berry), a bit of grated orange rind, and boil 10 minutes. Cool and refrigerate. Also delicious spooned on warm sponge cake and let cool with cake.  **Makes 3 cups**

## COCONUT CANDY

Many groups living in tropical climes use coconut so imaginatively it is often difficult to persuade them that coconuts originated in Old World India (as did bananas, mangos, lemons, cucumbers, citron, and eggplants, to name a few). When used in cooking, the coconut milk is extracted (page 184) and stirred into the dish. But for candy, the shredded or chunks of coconut are cooked with sugar and water. It is difficult to choose from the many Caribbean and Brazilian recipes.

*1 fresh coconut, grated and liquid reserved*
*1 to 2 cups sugar (depending on taste and sweetness of coconut)*

In a pan with a heavy bottom, combine the coconut, liquid, and additional water to make 2 cups, and the sugar. Stir over low heat until dissolved. Continue cooking and stirring frequently over medium* to low heat until thickened and candy reaches the hard-ball stage (260°F) or until a drop hardens when dropped into cold water. With cold water, wet brown paper (a shopping bag will do), aluminum foil, or a marble surface and turn the candy onto the wet surface. Spread it with a wet spoon or knife. Cut candy into slices (squares, diamonds, or triangles); cool. Store in covered container. Lasts indefinitely.

---

* Medium heat may caramelize the sugar which is preferred by fewer people than the white candy, so patience in boiling keeps the candy white. Another method is to cook the sugar and water and coconut liquid 10 minutes, then add the coconut, grated or shredded, and boil 30 minutes or until thick enough to spoon onto the surface. Some cooks press the coconut with a spoon while still warm, sprinkle sweetened cocoa on it, and press another dab of coconut candy on top for a candy sandwich.

## LOUKOUM
### Date Candy, Middle Eastern Style

*Loukoum* means delicious candy throughout the Middle East. In Greece, where the idea was adapted during the Byzantine period, *Loukoumi* describes the sugar-powdered rectangular jellies flavored aromatically with mastic or rosewater, sometimes with pistachios. This *Loukoum* is inspired by a rich coil made by John Bas of KALUSTYAN'S (page 57) where it is sliced and sold by the pound.

*1 pound pitted dates
1 to 2 teaspoons rose water (available at Middle Eastern, Greek, and Asian-Indian shops)
½ pound unshelled, unsalted pistachios or ¼ pound shelled, unsalted pistachios
Confectioner's sugar for dusting*

Combine dates with one cup water and bring to the boil. Boil over moderate heat, stirring frequently, until dates melt and reach the soft-ball stage (250°F). Sprinkle in the rose water and shelled pistachios; mix well. Dust marble or other smooth counter with confectioner's sugar and when cool enough to handle, roll dates into a thick coil (1 to 1½ inches in diameter depending on how thick you want the candy). Beginning from one end, make a coil by winding it round and round around itself. Stores indefinitely in covered container.

TO SERVE: Just slice off pieces.                    **Serves 30 to 35.**


## HALO HALO
### Philippine Preserved Fruit "Mix Mix"

Philippine fruits are fabulous, and even beans, green bananas, yams, taro, and sweet potatoes are cooked in coconut milk and cream to make this refreshing dessert. There are many variations and the homemade fruit preserves are impressive. But a hasty *Halo Halo* can be made using ready-made preserves available at Filipino shops (page 77). Lovely served in glass dish or cup. Forget the waistline and enjoy! *Mabuhay!*

*1 cup Coconut Sport (preserved fruit available in jars)*
*11 pieces sweet jackfruit (sweet Langka)\* (preserved fruit)*
*1 cup red mongo or kidney bean preserves or 1 green banana*
   *cooked in 1 cup water with 5 tablespoons sugar*
*3 cups shaved ice*
*1 cup coconut cream (page 184) or evaporated milk*

Using ice cream scoop or rounded spoon, arrange Coconut Sport, jackfruit, or other fruit preserves (3 or 4 kinds) in small rounded mounds in the bottom of the dessert dish. Add a scoop of shaved ice over the fruit and drizzle with coconut cream.
SERVE immediately.                                          **Serves 4**

\* Unless you have seen the larger-than-watermelon jackfruit requiring two men to lift, you won't believe how large the fruit is; the pineapple-colored fruit pieces in jars have been cut into 2-inch segments. Incidentally, these preserved fruits should be stored in the refrigerator and eaten within a few weeks.

## CHOCOLATE-DIPPED FRUIT

John Rath of LI-LAC CHOCOLATES, (page 43) suggests his method of serving chocolates with fresh seasonal fruit. For coffee accompaniment, he selects the house blend from MCNULTY'S (across the street, page 43).

*Bulk chocolate (dark or white depending on fruit)*
*Seasonal fruit (bananas, strawberries, blueberries, pineapple,*
   *apricots, figs, peaches, etc.)*
*Brown paper*
*Wax paper*

Wash and dry the fruit you plan to use. Cut larger fruit into bite-sized pieces for dainty portions; keep handy while you melt chocolate. Over double boiler, gradually melt chocolate. Cool to "baby formula" temperature, "not too hot, not too cold." Pour chocolate on brown paper. Handle the chocolate with one hand and keep your other hand clean to handle the fruits. To coat fruit, pick up a fruit, toss it into the chocolate and quickly cover the fruit with the chocolate and set on wax paper to cool. Continue until all pieces are coated. Leftover chocolate may be stored and reused. Arrange chocolate-covered fruits decoratively on serving platter. Keep in refrigerator until ready to serve.

# BEVERAGES

*A coconut shell full of liquid
is a sea to an ant.*

AFRICAN PROVERB

*Thirst sees rivers.*

GREEK PROVERB

## NEW YORK EGG CREAM

For this refreshing drink you need tall, slim glasses and tastes that
have *not* been nourished by thick milkshakes. Famed as a New
York beverage, its name—containing ingredients not present in
the beverage—is as mysterious as its origins. Try it (you may
decide to add a scoop of ice cream and call it an ice cream soda!).

> *8 tablespoons chocolate or vanilla syrup (of very fine flavor)*
> *1½ cups milk*
> *1 bottle chilled seltzer or soda water (1 pint, 12 ounces)*

In a blender, whip the syrup and milk until foamy. Gradually add
the seltzer water, beating steadily. Pour into glasses.

**Serves 4 to 5**

## MASALA LASSI

India's greatest beverage. Ginger, cumin, pepper, and coriander
are the usual spices. Try this version: it's hot and spicy, with a
taste of Old India. Or make your own *Masala* *

> *1 cup yogurt*
> *½ teaspoon* Mangal Chat Masala * * *(packaged masala)*

Combine yogurt, *Chat Masala* and one glass ice water in blender;
whip for 30 seconds.
SERVE cold.

**Serves 1**

NOTE: *Lassi* is also popular without the spices, sweetened with
sugar (Sweet *Lassi*) or with salt (Salt *Lassi*).

---

* Should you prefer to try your own *Masala* for *Masala Lassi*, I tasted a superb one
with fresh ginger, cumin seeds, black pepper, and fresh minced coriander all
whipped together; you'll have to use your own taste for amount of each spice.
* * This contains: dry mango, black salt, cumin, black pepper, chili, pomegranate
seeds, coriander, mint leaves, ginger, cloves, asafoetida and salt. Available at
SPICE AND SWEET MAHAL (page 58).

## THE NEW YORK TROPICS: TROPICAL BEVERAGES

New York ethnics from tropical climes whip up voluptuous drinks with no more effort than peeling the fruit—pineapples, coconuts, bananas, mangos, papayas, berries, melons, plus the wonderful mainstays—oranges, lemons, limes. Combinations of flavorful fruit are healthful, invigorating, and seem more exciting on the tongue. Pineapple and papaya are among the popular beverages; pineapple and coconut make the popular *Piña Colada*.

### PAPAYA, BANANA, and BERRY DRINK

*1 papaya, seeds removed*
*2 bananas, peeled*
*1 cup strawberries, hulled (or substitute ½ cup raspberries or*
  *1 cup blueberries)*
*Pinch of ground cinnamon (optional)*
*2 to 4 ice cubes*
*Fresh mint for garnish*

In blender whip the papaya, bananas, and berries with cinnamon, if using, until blended. Drop in the ice cubes and whip until ice crushes.

SERVE cold with mint garnish. **Serves 2**

NOTE: Fresh strawberries, orange juice, and bananas, blended with ice cubes and flavored with lime juice is also delicious. For another day, try blending fresh pineapple, coconut cream, and bananas with ice cubes and sprinkle with ground mace.

### JAMAICAN 1, 2, 3, 4 PUNCH

A Jamaican student told us this was "Jamaica's most popular drink." Here's to its flavor and popularity!

*1 of sour (1 part of freshly squeezed lime juice)*
*2 of sweet (2 parts of sugar or syrup\*)*

*3 of strong (3 parts of dark rum)*
*4 of weak (4 parts of water and crushed ice)*
*Angostura bitters*
*Cherries for garnish (optional)*
*Lime slivers, including rind*

In a shaker, combine lime juice, sugar or syrup, rum, water and crushed ice, and a dash of bitters. Shake until mixed. Pour into punch glasses and garnish with a cherry, if you like, and lime slivers.

* Sugar syrup is handy to keep in the refrigerator to sweeten beverages or to poach fresh fruits (flavorings can be added when using). Syrup concentration depends on the proportion of sugar to water: ½ cup sugar per 2 cups water yields syrup with 20 percent concentration; 2½ cups sugar to 2 cups water yields 50 percent concentration. Choose any proportion in between these two extremes depending on how sweet you like it (1 cup sugar to 2 cups water is fine for a punch).

## FRUIT BEVERAGE, FILIPINO STYLE

A tasty drink that can be served with a spoon!

*1 cup fresh lemon juice*
*3 cups pineapple juice (preferably fresh)*
*4 to 5 tablespoons brown sugar or honey*
*6 ice cubes*
*¼ cup rum (optional)*
*1 navel orange, peeled and segmented*
*1 banana, peeled and sliced into circles*
*1 cup fresh cherries or strawberries, stems removed and*
 *cherries pitted*

In a blender, combine the lemon and pineapple juices, sugar or honey, ice cubes, and rum, if using, and whip until well blended, about 2 minutes. In tall glasses or large wine glasses, divide the orange slices, banana, and cherries or strawberries. Pour fruit liquid over solid fruits.

SERVE immediately. **Serves 4 to 5**

## SUGAR CANE

A popular drink in India, China, Hong Kong, South and Central America, and the Caribbean, sugar cane is a tall grass. Its thick stalks can be found in tropical stalls, Hispanic stands and markets, and Chinatown. It is marvelous to suck on and has been a favorite "chewed" food in India since ancient times (the fibrous tissues exercise the gums). The Vietnamese people use sugar cane imaginatively, wrapping shrimp around small pieces and broiling it. But it is very difficult to cut—I cannot describe how difficult. So if you buy some, ask the vendor to cut it to your specifications. You'll enjoy chewing it and might be able to press it for its delicious juice.

## TAMARINDO
### Tamarind

A tropical evergreen, native to Africa and probably Asia, tamarind grows abundantly in the West Indies, the Dominican Republic, and Florida. The reddish-brown pods are stocked in New York markets catering to Caribbean Islanders, Central and South Americans and are usually sold in sealed plastic. Suck on a generous pinch of tamarind if you like tart flavors. A minute or two of this glorious chewing and, suddenly, the smooth seed feels satiny on your tongue. Rinse off the gemstone pits to revel in their ruddy lights, black touches, and their clink in your palm, like exuberant pearls—beautiful for mosaics.

Also available concentrated, in 8-ounce jars, from Asian-Indian shops. A teaspoonful of the concentrate can be stirred into any dish or chutney serving 8 guests.

## JUGO DE TAMARINDO
### Tamarind Beverage

Fresh tamarind beverage—a delicious drink made by Caribbean Islanders—comforts the tongue following a hot and peppery dish.

½ pound (1 cup) tamarind
1 cup water
Brown sugar (optional)
Rum (optional)

Combine tamarind and water in pan and boil 20 minutes. Cool. Using fingers, loosen seeds, and place them in a cup or bowl. Rinse them with cold water to remove all fibers and add to the liquid. Add enough water to make 4 cups. Whirl in blender. Add about 1 teaspoon sugar per cup if too sour.

SERVE cold, with or without a touch of rum.      **Makes 4 cups**


## SPICED TEAS

Spicy teas are aromatic and soothing following some rich meals or exotic meals when you need a climax that maintains the drama. By substituting your favorite ethnic spices, these styles become *yours.*


## AFGHAN TEA

Among the spice teas of the New York world, a superbly fragrant one. For each cup of tea in a pot add 2 crushed (lightly pounded in a mortar) cardamom seeds. Or slip crushed cardamom seeds into the cup before pouring tea.


## SPICED INDIAN TEA

*1½ tablespoons Darjeeling tea*
*1 teaspoon anise seeds*
*3 whole cardamom seeds, crushed lightly*
*6 teaspoons sugar (optional)*

Combine tea, spices, and sugar, if using, with 5 cups water in a saucepan. Bring to the boiling point (do not boil) three times. Strain into a hot teapot.

SERVE immediately.      **Serves 4 to 5**

NOTE: Hot Russian Spiced Tea is fabulous on a wintry day: Heat 3 cups mixed orange and pineapple juice with a little lemon juice, cinnamon stick, and whole cloves, season with sugar or honey; add a strong tea infusion (1 teaspoon *fine* tea leaves to 1 cup boiling water, steeped five minutes, strained), add 2 cups water, bring just to boiling point and serve.

# STREET SNACKS

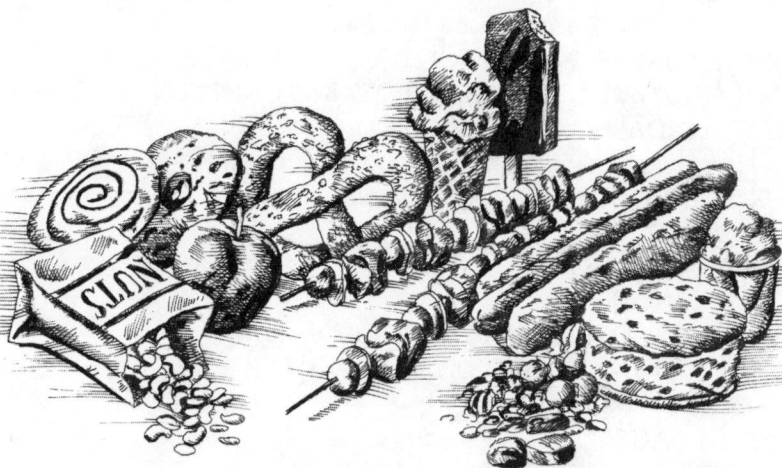

He that never eats too much will never be lazy.
POOR RICHARD'S ALMANAC

## HOT DOGS OR FRANKFURTERS

Though everyone knows how to cook them, I have included them for sentimental reasons because they are tops on the street snack list. Enjoyed since the early appearance of "gobble, gulp and go" snacks (page xxv) they will probably continue to be enjoyed forever! They are aptly described, with other street snacks, by Jenny Young Chandler in "New York's Merchandise Awheel" (Metropolitan Magazine, March, 1900):

> . . . One of the most stirring sights in the city is to view the surging crowds of office boys and clerks that surround the throngs of lunch carts to be found in the region of the Produce Exchange from twelve to one o'clock each day. Tea, coffee, cocoa, rolls, frankfurters, cakes, sandwiches, doughnuts, pie, soup, apples, bananas, and, in short, anything that will pass muster for a quick lunch, may be bought at these wayside lunch counters, while cider, milk, and soft drinks, in their respective seasons, are kept on tap for the thirsty wayfarer. . . .

*Hot dogs or frankfurters, heated in boiling water or grilled*
*Rolls, slit in half, heated on the grill, cut side down, for a few*
  *seconds*
*Mustard, relish, pickles, ketchup, sauerkraut (optional*
  *choices)*

Heat the hot dogs and insert in the heated roll. Season with favorite condiments.
SERVE warm.


## ARGENTINIAN SAUSAGE SNACK SANDWICH

Move over a little, frankfurters. . . . Cesar Gonzalez, born in Puerto Rico, makes his own Argentinian sausage (beef, wine, onion, garlic), impossible to resist as the sausage grills. He runs five midtown street stands (one at 41st and Lexington Ave., and another at 51st and Park Ave.). Cesar calls the sausages *Chorizos*, but said his specialties are not sold in stores. So substitute Spanish, Portuguese, Italian, or other fine-flavored sausages, using his recipe, which he shared.

  6 Chorizos *(each 7 to 8 inches long)*
  *2 large onions, chopped*
  *1 to 2 green peppers, chopped*
  *Spanish paprika (available in Hispanic shops)*
  *6 hero Italian rolls*

On a large grill, brown the *Chorizos,* turning steadily on all sides. When half done, toss the onions and peppers on the grill and saute vegetables without browning; shower them with Spanish paprika, mixing slightly.

TO SERVE: slice rolls lengthwise and place them, cut side down, on grill to heat them, if you like. Fill roll with a *Chorizo,* onions, and peppers. Wrap in aluminum foil (to keep it hot) and fold down the foil from one end as you eat.                              **Serves 6**

## AFGHAN KOFTA on CHAPATI
### Grilled Spiced Beef and Vegetables

Move over, hamburgers, there's a new wave of beef patties. Tantalizing aromas from Afghanistani *Kofta,* grilled by a vendor on the corner of "Swing Street" (52nd) and Avenue of the Americas, pull the lunchtime hungry into a queue (outside Lindy's). Taste them at home.

  *1½ pounds ground beef*
  *4 to 5 scallions or 2 onions, finely chopped*
  *½ cup (large handful) fresh parsley, chopped*
  *¼ cup (small handful) fresh mint, chopped or substitute 2*
    *tablespoons dried mint*
  *Salt*
  *Freshly ground pepper*

*Oil*
*3 or 6* Chapati *rounds*
*Garnishes: ½ head lettuce, shredded*
  *2 fresh tomatoes, thinly sliced, cut into half circles*
  *1 large red onion, thinly sliced*
  *1 green pepper, seeded and thinly sliced*
  *6 tablespoons* Chaka *(page 000) or thinned mayonnaise* \*

In a bowl, knead the beef, scallions or onions, parsley, mint, and light seasoning of salt and pepper. Divide into 6 balls. Roll meat ball in palms and flatten in palms to make 4- to 5-inch patties. Lightly oil a heated griddle. Grill *Kofta,* turning frequently until sizzling. To serve, cover one side of the *Chapati* round with 1 or 2 patties (depending on your appetite), some lettuce, tomatoes, onions, pepper, and a drizzling of *Chaka* or mayonnaise. Enclose with the other half of the *Chapati.* Wrap with aluminum foil or heavy paper to keep warm.
SERVE hot.                                              **Serves 3 to 6**

\* The street vendor serves *Kofta* with mayonnaise. The *Chaka* lends a distinctively Afghanistani flavor.

## GYRO

Hungry, bustling New Yorkers on the run fill Lexington Avenue, especially between 46th and 58th every day but Sunday. A favorite snack spot is the GYRO AND PIZZA shop (599 Lexington, between 52nd and 53rd), run for five years by Nick Evangelinos, a Chios-born man. About 100 pounds of lamb, barbecued on the vertical rotisserie *(Gyro* means round-and-round in Greek) are stuffed into *Gyro* pita sandwiches. Mike, an expert chef, born in Keffalinia, describes his style and I adapted it for a home barbecue for about thirty college-aged students who devoured the sandwiches.

346 · STREET SNACKS

*Ground lamb (Adjust the recipe to your needs, planning at
least ¼ pound meat per person)*
*Spices: Salt and pepper, oregano, ground allspice, paprika,
dried or fresh basil, chopped*
*Lamb fat (from the breast), sliced thinly*
*Pita bread (½ or 1 per person)*
*Garnishes: Tzatziki (yogurt seasoned with cucumbers,
parsley, dill, garlic, vinegar) or plain yogurt, sliced
tomatoes, slivered onions, shredded lettuce, vinegar
(optional), dried oregano*

Knead lamb with spices and be liberal; this should be very spicy.
Cover and rest in refrigerator overnight or for several hours at
least. When ready to broil, shape into hamburger-sized, thick patties. Thread on skewers, alternating with small pieces of fat
(which will baste the meat as it cooks). Press meat and fat tightly
together to resemble a loaf. Grill over charcoal, turning constantly to cook evenly as far from coals as possible. Lay on warm
platter, remove skewer without disturbing the loaf. Slice thinly.
Have pita bread in basket and garnishes arranged in bowls with
seasonings for guests to help themselves.
SERVE warm.                    **1½ pounds ground lamb serves 5 to 6**

## SOUVLAKIA
### Skewered Grilled Meat, Greek Style

In recent years, *Souvlakia* have been selling by the hundreds
(many people can't stop after the first one) very much as they do
in Greece (where cheese pies, chestnuts, pistachios, sesame bread
rings have been popular street snacks for eons). *Souvlakia* are
cousins of Middle Eastern *Shish Kebab* and other skewered meats
elsewhere, only cut bite-size and easy to eat on the run. In New
York, the meat used may be beef or pork; veal may be substituted
as it is seasonally in Greece. Whichever meat is grilling, the
scents are among the street's most appetizing.

*1 pound beef, lamb, or pork, cut into ¾-inch cubes*
*Olive or vegetable oil for brushing (optional)*
*Salt*
*Freshly ground pepper*
*Lemon juice from 2 lemons*
*Dried oregano*
*Crusty bread, sliced*

Skewer the meat on cane or metal skewers and brush lightly with oil if very lean. Grill over charcoal, turning on all sides and, if using pork, cooking thoroughly. Season with salt and pepper; sprinkle or dip into lemon juice, and crush oregano over meat. SERVE each skewer pierced with a slice of bread.　**Serves 4 to 6**

## BARBECUED PORK, PHILIPPINE STYLE

Sizzling and zesty, these snacks are a Ninth Avenue hit at the Filipino shops and at the Ninth Avenue Festival. This recipe is from Maria Cristina Manaloto, BULAKLAK MARKETING INC. (page 77).

*1 fresh pork butt, sliced ⅜ inch thick (not thicker)*
*Chinese Barbecue Sauce or Hoisin Sauce*
*Vinegar*
*2 to 3 cloves garlic, crushed*
*Juice of lemon or lime*
*Salt*
*Freshly ground pepper*

Slice the meat into 1½-inch squares about ⅜ inch thick. Make a marinade using Chinese Barbecue Sauce or Hoisin Sauce, vinegar, garlic, lemon or lime, and salt and pepper. Skewer the meat and marinate overnight in the sauce (this can be done in a tall pan; Maria uses a plastic bucket for her quantities). Grill over charcoal. SERVE immediately.　**Serves 6**

## LAHAM AJIN
### Syrian Pizza

Selling briskly in the DAMASCUS BAKERY (page 127), these spicy snacks may be made at home, thanks to the kindness of Dennis Halaby, a very courteous young man enthusiastic about his work. The dough, like a pizza's, is rolled, then sprinkled with the meat sauce and baked. *Laham Ajin* will be a big hit in your home, too. *Chukran!*

*1 dough recipe (page 349)*
*1 pound ground lamb*
*1 to 2 tablespoons oil*
*1 onion, minced*
*2 cloves garlic, crushed or minced*
*¼ green pepper, chopped finely*
*¾ cup to 1 cup tomato sauce*
*2 teaspoons ground allspice (more if necessary)*
*Salt*
*Freshly ground pepper*

You may prepare the dough and cook the sauce while the dough rises, or make the sauce a day in advance and make the dough 1½ or 2 hours before serving.

TO MAKE THE SAUCE: in a pan, mash the lamb over medium heat only long enough to make it grainy and lose its raw color (½ cup water will hasten this procedure); do not cook any longer. In another pan, heat oil and saute the onion, garlic, and green pepper until softened. Stir in the meat, enough tomato sauce for a medium thick mixture, allspice, and season with salt and pepper, adding more allspice to make it spicy. Heat to boiling point. Cool. Shape the dough circles as described on page 349.

TO BAKE: spread a few heaping tablespoonsful of the meat sauce on the dough circle, not to the very edge. Bake in 400°F oven for 15 minutes or until browned on the edges.

SERVE hot.                    **Makes 8, 5-inch or 9, 4-inch Laham Ajin**

## MINIATURE PIZZAS

No doubt, pizza is among the most popular of all street snacks for all age groups (my college class chose it as one of the ten most "American" dishes). These are hand-sized and much easier (maybe not as much fun) as those huge wedges everyone slurps over on the streets. Use the same dough recipe used for *Laham Ajin* (page 348) and your originality for toppings.

   *1 dough recipe (follows)*
   *2½ to 3 cups spicy tomato sauce*
   *1 cup mozzarella cheese, grated*
   *Mushrooms or hot sausage, sliced*
   *½ cup Parmesan or other grated cheese*

Shape dough into circles about 5 inches in diameter. Spoon ½ cup sauce on each circle; sprinkle with mozzarella, mushrooms, or sausage (or both), and grated cheese. Flute the sides to keep sauce from running over the edge. Bake in 400°F oven until browned around the edges and cheese melts, about 15 minutes.

## DOUGH FOR LAHAM AJIN OR MINIATURE PIZZAS *

Begin 1½ to 2 hours before serving.

   *1 package (¼ ounce) dry yeast*
   *3 cups flour (more for board)*
   *½ teaspoon sugar*
   *1 teaspoon salt*
   *1 teaspoon vegetable oil*

In a small bowl sprinkle the yeast over ¼ cup water; stir and cover. Let rest until doubled, about 15 minutes. Meanwhile, in a large bowl, combine the flour, sugar, and salt. Make a well in the center and add the swollen yeast and ½ cup warm water. Mix by

* This dough will also cover one 16-inch pizza pan if dough is rolled into one circle. You can use the pizza expert's trick: Over your fists, turning the dough quickly, move your fists under the dough.

mixer or hand to make a soft dough, adding more water, if necessary. Turn onto a floured board and knead 5 minutes. Brush with oil and set in warm bowl; cover with plate and blanket and let rise until doubled, about 45 minutes. When ready to assemble *Laham Ajin* or Miniature Pizzas, punch dough down and knead on a floured board. Divide into 7 or 8 balls; roll each dough section into a circle about ⅛-inch thick. Keep covered as you work; now they are ready to sprinkle with filling and bake.

## EMPANADAS and EMPANADITAS
### Spanish Turnovers

A new snack on 49th Street and Avenue of the Americas, introduced in 1983 by Argentinians and other South Americans. Miniatures are *Empanaditas* and the 4- to 6-inch versions, *Empanadas*, all appetizing, fried or baked.

> *Dough:* 2 cups all-purpose flour
> 1 teaspoon baking powder
> Pinch salt
> Pinch sugar (optional)
> 8 tablespoons mixed butter and oil or vegetable shortening
> 2 eggs (one separated, one lightly beaten)
> 6 tablespoons dry wine, sherry, or flat beer and water
> (mixed ⁵⁰/₅₀)
> Fillings (recipe follows)
> Shortening for frying

TO MAKE THE DOUGH: In a bowl, mix the flour, baking powder, salt, and sugar. Work in the butter and oil or shortening using your fingers or pastry blender. Pour the egg yolk and mixed liquids into the well; mix quickly to form a dough. Cover; refrigerate at least 3 hours. Bring to room temperature an hour before rolling dough. When ready to roll, have the remaining egg white and fillings handy. Divide dough in half and roll out as thin as you can; then roll it even thinner. Cut into 2½-inch circles for *Empanaditas* (an empty baking powder can is perfect for this size) or any size larger you prefer. Brush egg white on the dough circles. Place filling in center (a scant teaspoon for the small or up to a tablespoon for the larger turnovers). Fold dough in half to enclose filling; decorate edge with tines of a fork. Brush turnover with beaten egg (save half of this egg for the filling). Fry in deep, hot shortening (360°F) until brightly golden and crisp; or bake in moderately hot oven (375°F) for 18 minutes until golden brown. SERVE hot.

**Makes 40, 2½-inch or 22, 4½-inch turnovers to serve 3 or 4**

FILLINGS: Cheese, chicken, ground meat, seafood, vegetables, and fruit are popular. Use zucchini, celery, carrots, spinach, and other vegetables to chop into the filling for textural variety. The clue: season with your favorite spicy seasonings. Use the following as a guide. (The following amount should be plenty for the above amount of dough.)

*½ pound cheese (cottage, farmer's, ricotta, queso blanca, etc.),*
*    or lean ground beef or chicken, shrimp, rinsed sardines, etc.*
*2 to 3 cloves garlic, minced*
*2 to 3 scallions, minced*
*1 Jalapeno pepper or 2 chilies, seeded and chopped*
*Small handful fresh parsley, chopped*
*Dried oregano or fresh coriander, chopped, or grated nutmeg*
*    or other herb or spice*
*2 to 3 tablespoons grated fresh zucchini or chopped celery*
*Salt*
*Freshly ground pepper*
*½ beaten egg (saved from dough recipe above)*

Mix all the filling ingredients in a bowl well in advance so that flavors can permeate each other. Add the ½ beaten egg (the remaining half is for glazing the turnovers). Mixture should be spicy. If planning to freeze the turnovers, lightly saute raw meats and seafood before stuffing; otherwise, they may be stuffed raw and cooked immediately. Bon Appétit!

## UKOY or OKOY
### Fried Shrimp and Vegetables, Filipino Style

Mixing and frying in hot oil in a 20-inch wok, you see untiring and smiling women making these snacks (often called *Lumien* without the shrimps). The same batter may be used to fry large shrimps for appetizers. *Annatto* provides the reddish color.

> 2 cups or ½ pound tiny shrimp (dried may be substituted, soaked)
> ½ pound bean sprouts, washed and drained
> 1 cake tofu, sliced into strips
> 2 cups combined slivered carrots, celery, scallions, and Chinese cabbage (more if needed)
> 1½ cups flour
> ½ cup cornstarch
> 2 teaspoons baking powder
> 1 teaspoon salt
> White pepper (optional)
> ¼ cup **Annatto** water made by soaking 2 tablespoons **Annatto** (note, page 000) in ¼ cup warm water 15 minutes; drain
> 1 egg, lightly beaten
> Vegetable oil for frying

Wash and clean the shrimps, pound slightly and soak in ⅔ cup water; after 30 minutes drain over a bowl and reserve the liquid. If using dried shrimp, reserve the liquid for the batter. Have the sprouts, tofu, and vegetables in separate bowls.

TO MAKE THE BATTER: in a bowl, mix or sift together the flour, cornstarch, baking powder, salt, and pepper if using. Make a well in the center and add the *Annatto* water, egg, and enough of the reserved shrimp liquid to make a thick batter; beat until smooth.

TO FRY: In a deep fryer or wok, heat a large quantity oil to 360°F and maintain at that temperature. Spread about ½ cup bean sprouts in a dish, sprinkle with some shrimps and vegetables; add enough batter on the top to cover and lift with a spatula into the hot oil. Fry on both sides.

SERVE hot.                                                    **Serves 6**

## FALAFEL
### Pita Snack

Very popular among Jews and Arabs, and all the patrons of the *Falafel* snack bars.

Hot Pita bread
Falafel (recipe below)
Fried eggplant slices
Fried zucchini slices
Chopped cucumber salad
Sliced tomatoes
Creamed Tahini Salad *
Seasonings: salt, pepper, vinegar, olive oil, dried oregano or
   savory

* Make Creamed Tahini Salad by whisking ½ cup *Tahini* (a sesame seed emulsion available in Middle Eastern, Greek, and Arabic shops) with ⅓ cup lemon juice, 1 to 3 cloves crushed garlic and a dash of ground cumin and chopped fresh parsley.

## FALAFEL

4 tablespoons cracked wheat or wheat germ
3 cups cooked chick peas (canned may be used, drained),
   mashed
1 large egg, lightly beaten
2 to 3 tablespoons bread crumbs (more if necessary)
2 teaspoons each dried thyme and marjoram, crushed
Small pinches of white pepper and cayenne pepper (more if
   necessary)
Salad oil for frying

Place cracked wheat or wheat germ in a bowl and pour boiling water over it to cover; allow to stand 50 minutes, if using cracked wheat, or 10 minutes if you use wheat germ. Add to the wheat the mashed chick peas, egg, 2 tablespoons bread crumbs, herbs, and peppers, kneading well to make a thick and spicy mixture that can be rolled in your palms. Add more bread crumbs if necessary and taste for seasoning. Form into balls smaller than walnuts. Heat the oil to a level of ½ inch in heavy frying pan. Slip the *Falafel* into the oil, turning to cook until golden on all sides. SERVE hot stuffed in the pita bread with suggested condiments listed above.                                    **Serves 4 to 6**

## TEMPURA, KOREAN STYLE
### Vegetable Fritters

Gil Soo Kim, has operated a unique street wagon at 42nd and Third Avenue since 1979. He specializes in Oriental snacks—egg rolls, *Gyoza* (Japanese dumplings) * and *Tempura*, a Japanese fried batter fritter. Preparing his *Tempura* fritters at home, he reheats them in his 12-inch deep fryer and sells them to hungry New Yorkers. Wearing a printed apron with matching sleeve protectors, he can be seen after the busy lunchtime is over, polishing his stainless steel wagon. Gil Soo Kim graciously shares his great idea and adds, "Use any vegetables you like and make it hot."

> 2 medium potatoes, peeled
> 4 scallions or 1 large onion
> 1 green pepper, stem and seeds discarded
> 1 large carrot
> 1 large stalk celery (optional)
> Vegetable oil
> 2 cloves garlic, crushed or minced
> 1 to 2 chilies, diced, or 1 teaspoon chili powder (more to
>     taste)
> 1⅔ to 1¾ cups flour
> Salt
> Freshly ground pepper
> 1⅔ to 1¾ cups water

Sliver potatoes, scallions or onion, pepper, carrot, and celery, if using, to about 1¼-inch lengths (there should be about 4 cups of mixed vegetables). Heat 2 teaspoons of the oil in a small pan and

---

* *Gyoza* dumplings are available frozen, ready to cook, at Korean and Japanese shops; or make at home, recipe, page 299. Called *Mandu* in Korean, *Gyoza* are increasingly identified with Koreans who enjoy (and sell) them so much. They are delicious!

saute the garlic and chilies about 2 minutes without browning; remove from heat. In a large bowl, mix the flour, salt, and several grindings of pepper. Stir in 1⅔ cups water to make a fairly thick batter, stirring as little as possible. Add the sauteed garlic and chili and more chili powder and pepper to make it tasty. Add the vegetables; if too thick add a few tablespoons water. Heat oil to a 2-inch level in a heavy frying pan or wok. When very hot, but not smoking, drop serving spoonsful of the batter into the hot oil and flatten to make 4-inch rounds; fry 3 or 4 at a time. Turn over when chestnut-colored and fry a total of 5 minutes until potatoes are tender (taste the first one to adjust time and oil temperature). Continue until all are fried; drain on paper towels.

SERVE hot. **Serves 4 to 5**

NOTE: Gil Soo Kim forms his fritters into cakes, working on an oiled surface, and uses a deep fryer. The above method, adapted for home frying, is simpler without a deep fryer. Use whichever method is more convenient for you. These fritters vary every time I make them, depending on the amount of liquid in the vegetables. The two tricks: flavor the batter to make it tasty; avoid making fritters thick so that they will be crisp.


## TACOS, SHINNECOCK STYLE

Not Mexican, these are New York Indian *Tacos*, a traditional dish of the Shinnecock Indians as made by Sandra Lacy who learned from her mother and grandmother. Not sold on New York streets (yet), they seem to belong, in spirit, among Street Snacks.

*Indian Fried Bread (page 236)*
*1 pound kidney beans\* or pinto beans, cooked*
*½ pound sharp New York cheese, grated*
*½ pound ground beef, cooked, seasoned with onion and chili*
    *powder*
*1 to 2 onions, finely shredded*
*½ to 1 head Iceberg lettuce, shredded*
*2 to 3 tomatoes, slivered*
*Chili powder*

When ready to serve, sprinkle on each fried bread circle: Hot kidney or pinto beans, cheese (it will melt), ground hot beef, onions, lettuce, tomatoes, with another dollop of beans on top. SERVE hot and pass the chili powder.           **Serves 12**

NOTE: Who can resist the Mexican *Tacos*, increasingly popular as sandwich snacks, easily assembled by youngsters: Heat tortillas on an oiled griddle and bend in half; add sauteed ground beef (seasoned with grated onion, salt, pepper and fresh, chopped coriander), shredded Monterey Jack cheese, shredded lettuce, slivered tomatoes; and shower with any favorite hot sauce before indulging your appetite.

\* If you use kidney beans, prepare them as suggested in the Succotash recipe (page 286), and continue cooking until tender.

## "HOLY BAGEL"
### Sesame Seed Bread Ring

Don't be fooled by the name; this hunger appeaser is a favored street snack from Egypt eastward through the Middle East. Called "Bagel" in Jerusalem and in Greece called *Kouloura* ("ring"), it is, without doubt, the most popular and least expensive street snack. In New York, emerging in 1982 on violet-colored street wagons, the "Holy Bagel" is made by a firm in Sunnyside. This recipe is *not* the same version (the street snack in New York is promoted as "saltless") but is a wonderfully hearty snack, nevertheless, inspired by the "New York" ethnic bread ring. These are 5 inches across with 2½-inch "hole." Should you like a larger "hole," read note below.

*1 package dried yeast*
*1 tablespoon sugar*
*4 cups flour (more for sprinkling)*
*¾ teaspoon salt*
*2 tablespoons soy or vegetable oil (optional)*
*1 tablespoon olive oil or substitute vegetable oil*
*½ pound sesame seeds*

In a small bowl combine the yeast and 1 teaspoon sugar with ½ cup warm water; dissolve and let rise until doubled, about 15 minutes. Meanwhile, heat a large bowl (in hot-water bath) and dry the inside; put flour, remaining sugar, and salt in the warm bowl. Add the soy or vegetable oil, if using, and rub until absorbed. (Adding oil prolongs the bread rings' shelf life and adds to the flavor.) Make a well in the center and turn in the swollen yeast and one more cup warm water. Mix quickly and knead to form a soft ball, adding flour to your fingers if needed. Knead on a floured board until smooth and elastic. Cover and keep warm until doubled, about 1 hour. To make the rings: Divide dough into 10 equal parts. Knead each part slightly one at a time and roll into 15-inch ropes about ¾-inch diameter. Pinch ends together to make a ring; smooth to hide the seam. Set on baking sheets that have been rubbed with the olive oil; turn over to coat with oil on both sides. Have sesame seeds in a shallow bowl and dip oiled ring in sesame seeds to cover thoroughly; set rings on baking sheet, two inches apart. Cover the 10 rings until doubled, less than one hour. Just before baking, put a pan with boiling water on the bottom rack of a 425° oven. Place rings on baking sheets in middle of oven and lower to 400°. Bake 15 to 18 minutes until golden color. Cool on racks.     **Makes 10 rings, 5 to 5½ inches in diameter.**

NOTE: To make larger-holed rings, divide the dough into 8 or 9 equal parts, roll into ropes and form rings. Bake as above; about 5 minutes less baking time will be needed. These rings freeze nicely and can be sliced horizontally and toasted for breakfast— with butter and honey. Remaining sesame seeds may be saved for another day.

## SWEET BREAD RING VARIATION WITH MAHLEPI

For a delicate sweet bread variation on the sesame ring: instead of water, substitute warm milk, add a few extra tablespoons of sugar, 1 egg, and 1 teaspoon ground Mahlepi,* and butter instead of oil. Knead the dough exactly as above. When dipping rings in sesame seed, brush first with melted butter to help cover densely with sesame. Bake as above.

* *Mahlepi (Mahlep)* is a delicate and distinctive spice available in Greek, Middle Eastern, and Arabic shops.

## HOT PRETZELS

One of the oldest fun snacks, suggested in the Pennsylvania Dutch style. Try it!

*4 to 6 large soft pretzels, heated*
*Spicy yellow mustard*

Using a knife, cover the pretzel top with mustard.
SERVE warm or cold. **Serves 4 to 6**

## "SNOWBALL" WATER ICE

Heavenly refreshment on the street to anyone who remembers the joy of a one-cent "Snowball" water ice after school. And you can still get them shaved to order, instantly flavored with syrup from the bottle shaken over the ice—cherry, orange, lime, strawberry . . . at 116th Street in Bay Ridge, Brooklyn, and other New York corners.

*Shaved or crushed ice*
*Fruit syrup*

Mound the shaved ice in a Dixie cup and shower with your favorite fruit syrup.
SERVE immediately.

*The end is the thickest of the porridge.*
IRISH PROVERB

# INDEX

Falafel, 353-354
Feijoada, black beans with meats, 239-240
Fettucine a la carbonara, 235
Filipino (Philippines) recipes:
  Fruit beverage, 337
  Halo Halo, 330
  Lapu-Lapu, 255
  Pork, barbecued, 347
  Sinegang soup, 203
  Ukoy, 352
Filo:
  in Aushak, 173
  in Saraïli, 311
Fish. See Seafood and fresh water fish
Food habits, ethnic:
  Changes and demographics, xx
  Cross-cultural, xxviii
  Early New York, xv-xviii
  See Ethnicity and ethnic food markets. Fairs and festivals. Holiday dishes
  Settlements, xix-xxi
French recipes:
  Cassolette, 260
  Haricots verts, 210
  Mussels, Brittany, 175
  Rillettes, 178-179
Fruits. See Desserts. Fruits, preserves and candies
  Dipped in chocolate, 331
Fruit and ice:
  Filipino, 330
  Persian, 328
Fruits and nuts, 328
  Anousabour, 316
  Pan Dan, 327
Fruit syrup, 328-329
  with "Snowball," 358

Gefilte fish, 253-254
German foods:
  Early foods, xvi
  Sweet and sour red cabbage, 211-212
Ghanaian hot shrimp sauce, 258
Goat, curried, 275
Goulasch soup, 198
Grains (including pasta) and legumes (pulses), recipes, 228
  in Anousabour, 316-317
  See Bread. Rice. Soups. Wheat
  Couscous, 282-283
  in Succotash, 286-287

Gravlax (salmon), 176
Greek recipes:
  Artichokes and fava beans, 209
  Gyro, 345-346
  Pastitsio, 290-291
  Souvlakia, 346-347
  Stuffed quails, 276
Green beans, 210
Guatamelan fruit parfait, 323
Guava, 324

Haitian recipes:
  Cassava "bread," 214
  Fish and green bananas, 249
  Hot sauce, 186
  Pois et Riz (Pois ac Diri), 238
Herring appetizer, 175
Holiday recipes:
  Armenian pudding, 316-317
  Chinese festival cake, 229-230
  Christmas mixed greens, 225-226
  Norwegian Krumkake, 312
  New Year's Day soul food soup, 191
  Pasteles de Puerto Rico, 291-293
Hopping John, 193
Hot dogs (frankfurters), 343
Hungarian recipes:
  Cabbage, meats and sauerkraut, 295-296
  Goulasch soup, 198
  Palachinta, 313-314

Indonesian recipes:
  Gado Gado, 230-231
  Peanut sauce, 186
  Rames, 230-233
  Rendang, 233
  Sambal sauce, 187
  Sate Ayem, 231
  Sate Kambing, 232
Irish foods:
  Early foods, xvi
  Stew, 273
Italian recipes:
  Calamari appetizer, 177
  Clams a la marinara, 177-178
  Fettucine a la carbonara, 235
  Foglia Mista di Natale, 225-226
  Meat sauce, 271-272
  Ricotta cake, 308
  Sausage and pepper casserole, 289
  Shrimp with Pizzaiola Sauce, 259

# MARKET INDEX